# Spirits
## of
# Globalization

# Spirits of Globalization

*The Growth of Pentecostalism
and Experiential Spiritualities
in a Global Age*

*Edited by*

Sturla J. Stålsett

scm press

British Library Cataloguing in Publication data

A catalogue record for this book is available
from the British Library

Published with support from the Research Council of Norway

0 334 04054 X
978 0 334 04054 5

First published in 2006 by SCM Press
9–17 St Albans Place, London N1 0NX

www.scm-canterburypress.co.uk

SCM Press is a division of
SCM-Canterbury Press Ltd

Printed and bound in Great Britain by
William Clowes Ltd, Beccles, Suffolk

# Contents

*The Contributors*                                                    ix

**Introduction: Pentecostal Growth and Global
Transformations**
   *Sturla J. Stålsett*                                               1
Religion in a Globalized Age – Looking for Connections –
Neo-Pentecostal Expansion – Critical Potential? – Voices
and Violence – Diplomacy and Dialogue – Pentecostal
Resistance to Domination? – Spirit Transcending Spaces
and Moments

1 **Spirits of Globalization: Pentecostalism and Experiential
   Spiritualities in a Global Era**
   *Harvey Cox*                                                      11
Two Global Waves – Globalization and Pentecostalization:
An Intricate Relationship – A Continuum of Contending
Forces – Mainstream Mystics, Not Fundamentalists –
Cultus and Culture: Pentecostalism as Market Spirituality?
– Counter-Cultural Values

2 **Pentecostalism, Shamanism and Capitalism within
   Contemporary Korean Society**
   *Sung-Gun Kim*                                                    23
Pentecostal Growth in Korea – Religion in Contemporary
Society: Some Theoretical Considerations – The Nexus
between Shamanism and Pentecostalism – The Affinity
between Pentecostalism and Capitalism – Looking Ahead

3  Crossing Boundaries: The 'Universal Church' and the
   Spirit of Globalization
        *Berge Furre*                                              39
   The 'Universal Church': A Case of Neo-Pentecostal
   Growth in a Globalized World – Studying IURD: Main
   Characteristics – Different from Traditional Pentecostalism
   – A Religious Transnational Corporation? – Addressing the
   Needs: Day by Day – Faith as an Instrument – Struggling
   against Evil – Religious Experience – IURD as a Neoliberal
   Religiosity? – Survival in a Merciless Society – Political
   Influence?

4  Globalization and Subjectivity: A Reflection on the
   'Universal Church of the Kingdom of God' in a
   Perspective Drawn from Psychology of Religion
        *Mary Rute Gomes Esperandio*                              52
   Experiencing IURD Worship – IURD as a Response to the
   Needs of People Affected by Globalization – IURD and the
   Spirit of Globalized Capitalism – Final Considerations

5  Indentured Theology: White Souls/Black Skins?
   Decolonizing Pentecostals within the Indian Diaspora
        *Sarojini Nadar and Gary S. D. Leonard*                   65
   'Indian' Pentecostals in KwazuluNatal – South African
   Pentecostalism's 'Classical' Proto-history – The Origins of
   the South African Indian Diaspora – The Operational
   Historical and Theological Rationale – Black Pentecostal
   and Black Consciousness? – Colonization and Indian
   Mission Work – The Faith Movement and American
   Imperialism – A Search for Meaning – Group Dynamics
   and Process – Forging a Theoretical Basis for Analysing the
   Bible Studies – Bible Study 1: HIV/Aids – Bible Study 2:
   Gender Justice and Children's Rights – Bible Study 3:
   Ethnicity and Culture – Of Responses and Reactions –
   Hegemonic Entrapment or Black Liberation? – Towards a
   Conclusion: Triple-Indentured Pentecostals at the
   Crossroads? – Case Study 1 – Case Study 2

6 Global Warfare and Charismatic Resistance: The Case
of George Khambule (1884–1949) and the Book of
Revelation
*Jonathan A. Draper* 90

'I am Greater Than Him' – George Khambule (1884–1949)
– The South African Native Labour Corps (1916–1918) –
The Effects of the First World War on the Soldiers – The
Effect of this on George Khambule – The Ritualization of
Memory – Conclusion

7 The Dark Side of Pentecostal Enthusiasm: Abraham's
and Sara's Sacrifice in Knutby, Sweden
*Jone Salomonsen* 107

Faith with a Licence to Kill? – Case Study 1: California.
'How Can You Say No to God?' – Case Study 2: England.
'She Would Not Cry at All' – Case Study 3: Knutby,
Sweden. Lethal Text Messages from God – Theological
Underpinnings of the Crimes – Theological Hermeneutics –
Ethics – Leadership – The Constructive Challenges of
Pentecostalism

8 Charismatic Mission, Miracles and Faith-Based
Diplomacy: The Case of Aril Edvardsen
*Oddbjørn Leirvik* 131

Conservatives in Dialogue – Faith-Based Diplomacy – Aril
Edvardsen in Pakistan and Sudan: Faith- and Prayer-Based
Diplomacy? – Inclusive Jesus-Mission and Faith-Based
Diplomacy – Conclusion: Pentecostal Mission and
Interreligious Dialogue

9 Embracing Life: An Interfaith Dialogue between
Confucian Self-Cultivation and Charismatic Christian
Self-Transformation
*Wai Man Yuen* 145

Confucian Understandings of Self-Transformation – *Jen*
and Self-Cultivation – Different Theories of Mind in
Confucianism – The Relationship Between *Jen* and *Li* –
Charismatics' Understanding of Self-Transformation –

# Contents

William James's Definition of Religion – Applying James's
Religious Theory to an Explanation of Pentecostalism – A
Comparison between Confucian Self-Cultivation and
Charismatic Self-Transformation – A Critique of
Charismatic Christianity from a Confucian perspective

10 **Pentecostalism and Normalization**
   *Andrew Thomas*                                           160

   Liberation from Normalization? – Liberation from
   Language? – Private Languages and Solitude

11 **Resistance to Domination as a Charism of the
   Holy Spirit**
   *Harold Wells*                                            170

   Experience: Pentecostalist and Liberationist – The *Ruah* of
   Prophecy: A Spirit of Resistance – Spirit-Filled Jesus –
   Anti-Imperial Church – Charisms of the Spirit in the
   Pauline Church – Convergence?

12 **Revisioning Pneumatology in Transcultural Spaces**
   *Sigurd Bergmann*                                         183

   'The Spirit Dwells Among Us' – Fire from Heaven, Bushfires
   on Earth: Why Revision Pneumatology? – Translocal and
   Transcultural Passages – The Spirit-in-between:
   Atmospheres of Inhabitation

13 **Offering On-Time Deliverance: The Pathos of Neo-
   Pentecostalism and the Spirits of Globalization**
   *Sturla J. Stålsett*                                      198

   '*Agora!*' – Neo-Pentecostal Pathos and Neoliberal Spirit –
   Immediate Satisfaction of Desire – Victory through
   Sacrifice – Justifying Victimization and Supporting the
   Victims? – The Theological Challenge: Towards a Non-
   Sacrificial Pneumatology of the Cross

*Further Reading*                                            213
*Index of Names and Subjects*                                225

# The Contributors

**Sigurd Bergmann** is Professor of Religious Studies in the Department of Archaeology and Religious Studies at the Norwegian University of Science and Technology.

**Harvey Cox** is the Hollis Professor of Divinity, Harvard University, USA, where he has taught since 1965. He has also been visiting professor at Brandeis University, USA, Seminario Bautista de Mexico, and the University of Michigan, USA.

**Jonathan Draper** is Professor of New Testament at the School of Religion and Theology, University of KwazuluNatal in South Africa.

**Mary Rute Gomes Esperandio** is a psychologist and doctoral researcher in practical theology at the Ecumenical Postgraduate Institute, São Leopoldo, Brazil.

**Berge Furre** is Professor of Church History at the Faculty of Theology, University of Oslo, Norway, and has been Guest Researcher at Escola Superior de Telogia, São Leopoldo, Brazil.

**Sung-Gun Kim** is Professor of Sociology at Seowon University, Korea. From 1995 to 1996 he was visiting professor in Korean Studies at the University of Toronto.

**Oddbjørn Leirvik** is Associate Professor in Interreligious Studies at the Faculty of Theology, University of Oslo.

**Gary S. D. Leonard** served as an ordained pastor with the Apostolic Faith Mission of South Africa until 1994 and lectured for ten years at its Indian section Bible College in Durban.

**Sarojini Nadar** is Lecturer in Biblical Studies (Old Testament) at the School of Religion and Theology and Lecturer in Ethics Studies at the School of Philosophy and Ethics at the University of KwazuluNatal. She is also the International Co-ordinator of the International Network of Advanced Theological Education (INATE).

**Jone Salomonsen** is Professor in Theology and Gender Studies at the Faculty of Theology, University of Oslo.

**Sturla J Stålsett** is General Secretary in the Church City Mission in Oslo. Between 2001 and 2005 he led the research programme 'Religion in a Globalized Age' (RIGA) at the Faculty of Theology, University of Oslo. He has been Associate Professor of Systematic Theology at the same faculty, and guest researcher at the Departamento Ecuménico de Investigaciones (DEI) in San José, Costa Rica (2002); Escola Superior de Teologia in São Leopoldo, Brazil (2004); and the Centre for Development and Environment, University of Oslo (2005–6).

**Andrew Thomas** is a doctoral researcher in Philosophical Theology at the University of Nottingham.

**Harold Wells** is professor of Systematic Theology at Emmanuel College, Toronto School of Theology, Canada.

**Wai Man Yuen** is Associate Professor and Reichelt Chair at the Lutheran Theological Seminary in Hong Kong, China.

*

The editor wishes to express his gratitude to all the contributors to this volume; to Andy Thomas for excellent secretarial and editorial assistance; to the Faculty of Theology, University of Oslo; to the Research Council of Norway for financial support; and to the editors of SCM Press.

SJS, Oslo, February 2006

# Introduction: Pentecostal Growth and Global Transformations

## STURLA J. STÅLSETT

The rapid growth of Pentecostal churches throughout the world has caught the interest of theologians, historians of religion and social scientists for several years.[1] Their growth has been fast and strong. Meanwhile, Pentecostal churches and charismatic spirituality resist easy categorization in both theological and socio-political terms. As new trends and patterns have emerged, many speak of neo- or even post-Pentecostal churches. A common trait, though, is religious experience; there is a strong emphasis on the centrality of emotions in religious worship and truth. Hence these are 'experiential spiritualities' in the felicitous phrase of Harvey Cox (Cox, 1995: 18).

Before this recent interest, however, Pentecostalism had been a rather marginalized phenomenon within the field of academic theology and religious studies, as well as in the social sciences. The reasons for this neglect would in themselves provide interesting and probably revealing material for more than one book. But now Pentecostal religion is simply not that easy to ignore. The growth in Pentecostal and experiential or charismatic spirituality has been extraordinary in recent decades. Figures vary, but according to conservative estimates suggested by David Martin, one in eight Christians today are Pentecostal, amounting to at least 250 million (Martin, 2001: 1). Some suggest much higher figures, 400–500 million, thus claiming that Pentecostalism represents one quarter of Christianity.[2]

This overwhelming and, for many, unexpected growth in Pentecostalism coincides with what has been called the age of globalization.[3] Many see an affinity between globalizing forces and the spiritual worldview and practice of (neo-) Pentecostal religiosity. Are these phenomena interconnected? What would be the connection? Is it causal or coincidental? Do the processes of neoliberal, Western globalization and the growth of Pentecostalism mutually reinforce each other? If so, why should this be the case? Is there perhaps something inherent in this version of global structuring of social, economic and political affairs that calls for a particular kind of 'experiential religiosity' like Pentecostalism? What kind of political effect could (neo-) Pentecostal movements have? What drives their internationalizing missionary effort, and what effect does it have on the processes of globalization happening around and within it?

One hundred years ago, Max Weber wrote his famous essay – published as two articles in 1904–05 – on the Protestant Ethic and the Spirit of Capitalism (1976). Weber's hypothesis was that capitalism was a product of the particular Protestant ethic that developed in Western Europe in the centuries following the Reformation. With a clear awareness of limitations and complexities, the aim of this volume is to raise a similar question in our own time regarding the growth of charismatic, 'experiential' religion, and globalization.


## Religion in a Globalized Age

This study is undertaken in the context of a larger research programme at the Faculty of Theology, University of Oslo, entitled 'Religion in a Globalized Age: Transfers and Transformations, Integration and Resistance' (RIGA). This programme is a result of the Research Council of Norway's effort to promote research on globalization and internationalization within the humanities and social sciences. Within the broad thematic of how religion influences global transformations, and vice versa, we have chosen two axes of particular interest. The first one is between transfers and transformations. Whatever else globalization may or may not be, it is most certainly characterized by transfers, travel, transport, flows and communication of an unprecedented magnitude and speed. This is also true of religion. It travels faster and more often than before, from different origins and to different destinations. How does this affect the content and forms of the living faiths of today?

The second axis is the one between resistance and integration. In what ways do religions represent sources for opposing the globalizing forces? And in what ways do they rather further the integration into or adaptation to globalization? Obviously it is not simply a question of either/or, and we are interested in looking into the multifaceted and often paradoxical ways in which different religious expressions and practices, particularly on the margins of global society, affect and are affected by globalization. We believe that understanding the role of religion is crucial for analysing and proposing solutions to the most urgent challenges of humanity in our globalized era. Hence, in 2004 we published a book on religion and politics – between integration and resistance: *The Power of Faiths in Global Politics* (Stålsett and Leirvik, 2004). Now we turn our attention to the remarkable religious development related to the growth of Pentecostalism and experiential spiritualities around the globe. In doing so, we will work with cross-cultural and interdisciplinary approaches. The very object of study itself demands such an approach.

## Looking for Connections

Within the significant range of literature on this phenomenon,[4] our book particularly takes its cue from Harvey Cox's influential *Fire from Heaven: The Rise of Pentecostal Spirituality and the Reshaping of Religion in the Twenty-First Century* of 1995. In his introductory chapter to this present volume, then, Professor Cox, of Harvard University, sets out the search for connections between globalization and Pentecostalism. He does so first by discarding some common theories. In Cox's view, we are not here facing a capitalist ideological conspiracy. Pentecostals are not 'crypto-entrepreneurs in clerical garb', as he puts it. We must look for a subtler link between the market revolution and the Pentecostal upsurge. Like Weber in his time, we should rather seek something like a 'selective affinity' between Pentecostalism and globalization, Cox believes, not forgetting that charismatic, experiential religiosity is also generating currents counter to market globalization. In a splintered postmodern world, Pente-costalism invites people to 'plunge into the chaos in order to overcome it', by the power of the Holy Spirit. In doing so, Cox points out, it provides a bridge back to primal, pre-modern belief and ritual prac-tices, such as exorcism: 'Unlike enlightened Protestants and Catholics, Pentecostals never claim that spirits of the folk religion are illusory. Rather, they proclaim that God can defeat and vanquish them. This theology provides, ironically, both a *bridge* from the spiritual world of the old religion and a *dam* against its powers' (see below, page 17).

This point about the remarkable interface between pre-modern spiritual beliefs and practices and the postmodern era of globalization is further developed in a Korean context by Sung-Gun Kim (Seowon University, Korea) in his chapter 'Pentecostalism, Shamanism and

Capitalism within Contemporary Korean Society'. Seeing the advent and unprecedented expansion of the modern Pentecostal movement as one of the most important events within twentieth-century Christianity, Kim claims that the Korean Pentecostal phenomenon, which began in the 1950s following the Korean War, has succeeded on two fronts: first, it can demonstrate phenomenal church growth; and second, there has been a generalization of Pentecostal beliefs within the country. Among the main reasons for this, Kim finds the fact that evangelical Protestant Christianity in Korea, especially Pentecostalism, successfully draws upon ancient Korean forms of shamanism as well as introducing modern capitalistic American materialism. As a result, Kim sees this as a religion 'of success' rather than one 'of suffering'.

## Neo-Pentecostal Expansion

One could ask whether it is not particularly in this acute tension between contemporary suffering and expectation of success related to globalization that the new wave of Pentecostalism prospers. The next two chapters focus on the recent 'Universal Church of the Kingdom of God' (Igreja Universal do Reino de Deus – IURD), which originated in Brazil around 1977 and is now a major player on the global religious arena. Berge Furre (University of Oslo) presents a case study of this church which provides a felicitous point from which to look at some basic sociological, political and theological aspects of the present Pentecostalization of religion in the global age. Furre sees the phenomenal growth and worldwide expansion of this church as an indication that it has succeeded in presenting itself as a strategy of survival in a society 'without mercy'. According to Furre, it is thus closely related to the impact of economic globalizing processes, albeit it in contradictory ways.

Berge Furre distinguishes IURD from other Pentecostals. Along with one of the leading Brazilian scholars on the subject, Leonildo Silveira de Campos (1997), he prefers to speak of IURD as 'Neo-Pentecostal'. Neo-Pentecostalism, as the term is used in this volume, is a new form of Pentecostal religion in which spiritual warfare, exorcisms, immediate healings and personal prosperity in this world have replaced traditional Pentecostalism's emphasis on speaking in tongues; on strict, pietistic morals; and on Jesus' second coming and eternal salvation.[5] It should be noted, then, that this usage differs from the way the term was understood by sociologists of religion in North America in the 1970s, a usage that Harvey Cox also notes (1995: 152ff.), namely as referring to charismatic renewal in mainline churches, both Protestant and Catholic.[6]

Continuing to focus on the case of the IURD, Mary Rute Gomes Esperandio (Escola Superior de Teologia, Brazil) looks particularly at its role in the 'production of subjectivity' under the pressure of globalization. Applying a perspective from the psychology of religion, Esperandio argues that the central focus on sacrifice (in the form of tithing and money-offering in particular) in IURD preaching and practice, actually may result in a strengthened sense of self-confidence and survival capacity in the believer. In the act of sacrificing, the believer must let go of a passive attitude towards sufferings and make a 'self-investment'. The experience of being able and 'worthy' to present an offering to the Almighty God (and thus gain a legitimate 'right' to receive blessings in return), sets off a process of individual empowerment, Esperandio argues. The person may thus gain strength to face the concrete sufferings of everyday life: diseases, unemployment, drug addiction, family disruption, and so on. Esperandio, herself a Brazilian psychologist, suggests that there is in this sense a significant interconnection between the practice of sacrifice and narcissistic structures of the human mind.

## Critical Potential?

Does this potentially empowering side of (neo-)Pentecostal spirituality also entail critical and counter-cultural thinking and praxis? Cox clearly sees such a potential, whereas both Furre and Esperandio do not see in the IURD any force for real protest against the dominating and marginalizing mechanisms of globalized society. They rather see the IURD as helping people to cope by adjusting to prevalent capitalist values. Moving to another context, that of South Africa, the quest for a critical awareness of the cultural and political entrapments often hidden behind a religious veil, remains crucial. In their original and creative study of Pentecostalism among the Indian migrant population in the Durban area of South Africa, Sarojini Nadar and Gary Leonard (University of KwazuluNatal, South Africa) claim that this group historically suffers from a triple entrapment: first, as 'indentured'[7] labourers under British colonial rule in the Province of Natal, and the later Christian Nationalist apartheid regime; second, under Afrikaner civil religion in its supposed a-political Pentecostal and unapologetic racist guise; and third, through the imported North American 'faith gospel'. Using the method of contextual Bible study together with Pentecostal leaders in this region, Nadar and Leonard seek to bring out a critical self-reflection on this situation of the Indian Pentecostal community in South Africa, to see whether it would be possible for the group to forge a language of resistance to this political and spiritual (neo-)colonization under Westernized globalization. Their conclusion is negative: they find that Indian Pentecostals through their uncritical adoption of right-wing American faith-gospel teaching continue to exist as indentured labourers for what is a 'white' kingdom.

## Voices and Violence

Remaining in the same region but moving a hundred years back in time, Jonathan Draper (University of KwazuluNatal) sheds new light on an intriguing case in which charismatic, experiential spirituality did in fact seem to empower a kind of ethnic and cultural resistance to global dominance. The Zulu prophet George Khambule founded an indigenous Christian movement in the early 1920s in the aftermath of the military defeat of the Zulu kingdom, in which he and his family were positioned on the colonial side, after his own service in the First World War in France. His prophecies were written down in diaries and hymnbooks and continued to be performed orally, but they were also rewritten and adapted within the community long after his own death. The key inspiration for the prophecies came from Khambule's interpretation of the book of Revelation. What led Khambule to make the transition from being a rural Zulu collaborator with the colonial regime to becoming a 'prophet' and 'vicegerent' of the kingdom of God on earth who would rule over all nations, the black and the white? Draper finds a plausible answer to this in Khambule's traumatic experience of global warfare. He thus indicates an interesting link to the contemporary question of how charismatic and experiential spiritualities today may be interpreted against the background of often conflictive and violent globalizing processes.

In Khambule's case, charismatic experience leads in the direction of overcoming violence and war. However, the relationship between prophetic voices and acts of violence is ambiguous indeed. The recent horrific and tragic murder case in a small Pentecostal congregation in Knutby, Sweden, is a contemporary case in point. In 2004, a young woman was condemned for murdering the wife of the congregation's pastor. During the legal process, it became clear that she had been under strong pressure to commit this crime from the pastor himself. The girl was made to believe that she was following orders from God. Text messages on her mobile phone, apparently sent by the pastor, were received by her as words from Godself. Comparing this tragic case with two other cases in which charismatic religion played a prominent part, Jone Salomonsen (University of Oslo) critically explores what she calls the 'dark side' of Pentecostal spirituality, particularly as it relates to sacrificial theological modes of thinking. In cases such as these one often finds among Pentecostal groups a failure to take responsibility for one's own – or others' – violent acts by maintaining a profoundly magical and dualist worldview according to which evil has external causes, she claims. In this sacrificial and Manichaean worldview, war and violence are inevitable and hence justified for the sake of the good, God or salvation.

## Diplomacy and Dialogue

But can charismatic religion also prevent violence, and reduce conflicts? At a global level, it is clear that religion has regained political importance during the last decades (see Stålsett and Leirvik, 2004). Religion is a source of conflict as well as a resource for peace. Hence the role of religious communities and religious leaders in conflict resolution has become a focus of interest for academics and politicians alike. How does the global wave of Pentecostal religiosity with its traditionally otherworldly and apolitical focus fit into this picture? In his chapter 'Charismatic Mission, Miracles and Faith-Based Diplomacy: The Case of Aril Edvardsen', Oddbjørn Leirvik (University of Oslo) points to a shift in the traditional roles in this regard. Inter-religious dialogue and efforts for peace are not any longer the lone task of the so-called liberal wing of Christianity. Recent developments in the global ministry of the Norwegian charismatic leader Aril Edvardsen point in a direction similar to the largely evangelical initiative in the USA that Douglas Johnston (2003) labels 'faith-based diplomacy'. In creative and at times bold ways Edvardsen is carrying out diplomatic efforts, partly in understanding with the Norwegian Government, that seem to be more open-minded in terms of the possibility for interreligious dialogue and more tolerant to differences than is usual in religious leaders of his type. Simultaneously, he continues to perform a charismatic type of evangelization focused on miraculous healing.

From her vantage-point in Hong Kong, China, Wai Man Yuen (Lutheran Theological Seminary) takes another approach to inter-religious dialogue in relation to charismatic Christianity. In what ways could charismatic Christianity engage in and learn from a dialogue with another cultural tradition and living faith? In particular, Wai Man Yuen stages such a dialogue with regard to the Confucian concept of self-cultivation on the one hand and the understanding of self-transformation that she finds to be central in Chinese charismatic faith on the other. The purpose of making a comparison between these two distinct religions is not only to forge common understanding between them, but also to challenge them to change their presupposition of validity and to adopt a new paradigm of interpreting their significance and meaning to the world today.

## Pentecostal Resistance to Domination?

The rise of experiential spirituality or primal religion in different contexts poses the challenge to Christian theology to revive and reformulate its own reflection on God the Spirit, her transcending presence and transformative power. If this particular spirituality is attached to present-day global transformations, such a reconstruction of pneumatology and Christian spirituality will have a huge transcultural and interreligious potential. In what ways could the Holy Spirit be seen as inspiring and empowering human life and global community under present conditions?

Due to both the aforementioned academic neglect of Pentecostal spirituality and theology, and the presumed otherworldly and a-political stance of Pentecostalism, it is tempting to see these churches as merely promoting passive adaptation or even resignation when faced with domination and oppression. But one should probably look again. In these traditions, beliefs and practices – as Draper also shows in the case of the prophet George Khambule – there may be hidden strategies of resistance. Inspired by a Foucaultian analysis of power and domination, Andrew Thomas takes as his point of departure the oppressive side of 'normalization'. Looking back on his own experiences in a Pentecostal community in England, with its speaking in tongues (glossolalia) and its 'strange behaviour' ('manifestations of the Spirit'), Thomas asks whether these can be interpreted as liberation from this 'normalizing' pressure? Do such practices represent attempts to break out of the control of abnormality that is at work in Western culture? While paying attention to this potentially liberative side of charismatic practices, Thomas also asks to what extent they may merely represent a transference of the strategies of normalization to new spheres: the 'abnormal' behaviour is seen as 'normal', and thus becomes disciplinary again, within the charismatic community.

In a more explicitly theological essay, Harold Wells suggests that resistance to domination should be seen as a charism of the Holy Spirit. Holding together two trends that often have been seen as antithetical, namely liberation theology and Pentecostal spirituality, Wells sketches out fundamental elements of what he calls a broad inclusive pneumatology. In doing so he seeks to establish a continuity, seeing the Spirit of God the Creator as a spirit of resistance vividly and critically present in the prophets, in Jesus and in the early Church, and further on in Pentecostalism, liberationist Christian social activism, and even in secular movements for justice and peace.

### Spirit Transcending Spaces and Moments

In his original and thought-provoking chapter entitled 'Revisioning Pneumatology in Transcultural Spaces' Sigurd Bergmann (Norwegian University of Science and Technology) suggests a related, but nonetheless different approach to the renewal of Christian doctrine on the Holy Spirit. Bergmann wishes to draw attention to the contemporary experience of increased pressure on both humans and non-human creation stemming from globalizing processes. These processes, with their dynamics of de- and respatialization, challenge us to work more profoundly with *spatial* categories, he holds. Anchoring his thought in Gregory of Nazianz's theological insights from the fourth century, Bergmann sketches out elements of a pneumatology that aims at breaking out of violently reduced life space, to transform 'places of captivity into open plains of freedom'. In elaborating such a pneumatology, he suggests that the metaphor 'atmosphere' is helpful. Atmospheres can be seen as *vestigia Dei* (God's traces on earth), with the help of which humans can navigate in God's horizon, and negotiate on the centre and periphery of the globalized world in a new way. In such a way, Bergmann believes, 'we can follow the Spirit into a transfigured creation'.

In my concluding chapter I return to the overall theme of the book, the interrelationship between globalization and (Neo-)Pentecostal or experiential spiritualities. With a twist on Weber's classical title, I argue that there is a relationship between the 'pathos' of Neo-Pentecostalism and the neoliberal version of capitalism that obtained something close to global hegemony in recent decades. This relationship is complex. Nevertheless I propose that the interconnection between these two mega-trends can fruitfully be sought for in two characteristics that Neo-Pentecostalism and present-day neoliberal globalization seem to have in common: immediate satisfaction of desire, and success, or victory, through sacrifice. Having elaborated on how I view these affinities, I end by reviewing some of the theological implications of this. In short, I stress the need for developing a non-sacrificial pneumatology of the cross, that could also make room for the experiences of suffering, and the desire for healing and well-being, of the many people leaving Neo-Pentecostal temples without having received the blessing that they were promised.

## Notes

1 See e.g. Martin, 1993; Alvarez, 1992; Boudewijnse, 1991; Sjørup, 1995; Stoll, 1990; Stålsett, 1995; Willems, 1967; Barrera Rivera, 2001; Campos, 1997; Garrard-Burnett and Stoll, 1993; and Martin, 2001.

2 Probably the highest estimate is to be found in the 2001 edition of the *World Christian Encyclopedia*. Barrett and Johnson, who are charismatic Christians themselves, claim that Pentecostal and charismatic movements within different traditional denominations and in new independent churches now encompass as many as 524 million believers (Barrett, 2001).

3 By 'globalization' we refer to global processes of transformation that broadly since the end of the Cold War (1989) have made a profound impact on all societies around the globe, although in asymmetrical ways and to differing degrees. These processes of transformation are primarily driven by two factors: the digital revolution and the configuration of the world economic system according to neoliberal, i.e. free-market principles. Although these processes are ambiguous and open-ended, in their present dynamics they tend towards increased interdependency as well as a significant polarization of power and privileges, favouring a global (primarily 'Western') elite of nations, corporations and citizens. Cf. e.g. Held and McGrew, 2000, and Stålsett, Sturla J. (ed.), *Religion in a Globalised Age: Transfers and Transformations, Integration and Resistance* (forthcoming 2007).

4 See note 1 above, and the bibliography at the end of this book.

5 See e.g. Mariano, 1995: 28f.

6 David Martin (1990: 177) also uses 'Neo-Pentecostal' about charismatic groups within mainstream Christian churches.

7 Workers brought into Natal from other countries, controlled by immigration authorities, and bound by strict contracts ('indentures').

# 1. Spirits of Globalization:

## Pentecostalism and Experiential Spiritualities in a Global Era

### HARVEY COX

Let us face the uncomfortable truth. The model of development we are accustomed to has been fruitful for the few, but flawed for the many. A path to prosperity that ravages the environment and leaves a majority of humankind behind in squalor will soon prove to be a dead-end road for everyone.

Kofi Annan, UN Secretary General, World Symposium on Sustainable
Development, Johannesburg, September 2002

My research has led me to make this bold statement: In all human history, no other non-political, non-militaristic, voluntary human movement has grown as rapidly as the Pentecostal-Charismatic movement in the last 25 years.

Peter Wagner (quoted in Synan, 1992: ii)

## Two Global Waves

As the new millennium rushes forward, two large-scale trends seem to be converging and overlapping. One is the implacable sweep of what is usually called 'globalization' (what its exponents call 'the market revolution'), now reaching into the most remote and secluded provinces on earth. It is a revolution which – like all previous instances of that genre – carries banners embossed with millennial promises. But few of these have as yet been realized. Instead of the rising tide lifting all the boats, we have seen a steep plunge in the already spare living standards of the impoverished majority of humankind. Today 358 billionaires – some of them the citizens of 'poor' countries – control more wealth than the total national income of countries comprising 45 per cent of the world's population. Paying the interest on their loans has become the largest item in the budgets of some poor countries. In one recent year the government of Uganda, to take only one example, spent $3 per person on health care, but $17 per person repaying its foreign debt. This is a country where one in five children will not reach their fifth birthday, largely as the result of diseases that could be prevented through modest investment in primary health care. But the 'market revolution' also bears many of the marks of a religion. The key phrase in its vocabulary, albeit scratched in fine print on the escutcheon, is 'not yet'. It is a locution highly familiar to those who study the messianic dreams and heavenly visions of the world religions. 'Just have patience [another word religions have long valued] for another development decade – or maybe two or three,' the poor are assured from the lofty Sinai of the International Monetary Fund, 'and *then* you'll see how everyone's cup will run over.'

The second globe-encircling movement is a religious one. Despite solemn assurances of His demise by modernization theorists, God – or more correctly, the gods and goddesses – have staged a remarkable resurrection in the late twentieth century. A renaissance of Islam is under way. Buddhism, once declared an anachronism by Western scholars, now has a firm foothold in the West, including in Hollywood. But of all the newly resurgent religious movements none is exploding faster than a recent hybrid of Christianity – neither Protestant nor Catholic but a 'third force' – that is generally called the 'Pentecostal-charismatic movement'. Having emerged from the Southern white Holiness and the African-American traditions of late nineteenth-century America, it is adding new adherents by the thousands every day, especially in Latin America, Africa, on the Pacific rim, and more recently in the former Soviet republics. In mainland China a recent observer has written that the extraordinary growth of this movement, combined with the widespread fascination with Christianity among intellectuals, could result in as much as 30 per cent of China's population becoming Christian by 2040. Worldwide, the Pentecostal-charismatic explosion already includes as many people as all the other non-Catholic branches of Christianity put together, and if current growth rates persist, will equal Catholics in number by the third decade of this century.

What makes the appearance of these two movements – globalization and the Pentecostal wave – even more fascinating is that they are both spreading in the same areas of the globe, in what used to be called the 'Third World'. While capitalism may be slowing down, some even say stagnating, in the birthplace of the first industrial revolution, it is soaring on what used to be called the periphery, especially in China and India. A market development economist of my acquaintance recently described with considerable enthusiasm what a lift he gets from visiting China, where the construction cranes swivel under flood-lights all night and 'you can almost smell the growth!'

When he said that, I was reminded of a visit I recently made to South Korea where people pray all night by the thousands on the holy mountain and you can almost smell the growth of Pentecostalism. From a minority of 5 per cent just after the Korean War, Korean Christians now claim about 35 per cent of the population. They are still growing rapidly, and almost all the growth is attributable to Pentecostalism. The Yoido Full Gospel (Pentecostal) Church at the centre of Seoul is the largest single Christian congregation in the world. It has 650,000 members. A colossal church building seating 24,000, where a symphony orchestra accompanies the hymns, is filled six times every Sunday. The same amazing proliferation proceeds apace else-where. A million people gather for the Easter service of a Zion church in South Africa. In Brazil on a given Sunday more people worship in Pentecostal churches than in Catholic churches. It is becoming evident as the millennium proceeds that the venerable old term 'Christendom' has become obsolete. The majority of Christians are now black, brown or yellow, and live in the non-Western world.

## Globalization and Pentecostalization: An Intricate Relationship

Globalization and Pentecostalization: it is hard nowadays to find anyone who, whatever opinion they have of these two mega-trends, does not agree that they are surely under way. The great puzzle is why so few ask the question that is staring us in the face: What is the con-nection between the two? The mystery of this strange inattention deepens when one remembers that the great founders of social science like Max Weber and Emile Durkheim could scarcely have conceived of analysing either one of these current socio-cultural tidal waves without probing its relationship to the other. The intention of this book is to overcome this inattention, endeavouring to probe the intricate relationship between these two movements.

As we turn to this task, however, we should avoid some of the superficially plausible theories of the correlation between the two trends that have sometimes been advanced. One such theory of the connection, now almost universally discarded, was that a nefarious conspiracy clearly existed. Multinational corporations were scheming hand-in-glove with evangelical missionaries to uproot hapless natives from their quaint indigenous rites and at the same time immunize them against the virus of liberation theology. The goal of this malicious strategy, it was alleged, was to destroy the two major barriers to capitalist expansion – traditionalism and religion – so that the target populations, like Aids victims, would lack the white corpuscles needed to resist the all-consuming market.

Another theory held that the leaders of the Pentecostal-charismatic movement are really crypto-entrepreneurs in clerical garb: the either knowing or unknowing vanguard of the capitalist juggernaut. Some feared so-called invasion; others welcomed it. One of its supporters, Peter Berger, writes, 'What one may expect is that the new Protestant internationale will produce results similar to those of the preceding one – to wit, the emergence of a solid bourgeoisie, with virtues conducive to the development of capitalism.'[1] But this theory seems increasingly implausible. There are critical differences, not only between the current global industrialization and the previous one, but also between the kind of religion that seems fused to today's market revolution and the previous spurt of sectarian-Calvinist pietism. Further, the more one ponders Singapore and mainland China, the clearer it becomes that despite the hopeful rhetoric about and the allegedly self-evident correlation of democracy with capitalism ('free markets and free elections'), the two seem all too easily separable in many places. A one-party China continues to consign dissidents to prison even as the GNP soars.

Instead of opting for one of these shaky theories of the critical link between market globalization and third-stream Christianity, I think we need to look for what scholars sometimes call 'selective affinity', or even for something still more subtle. What differentiates the present economic mega-trend from the first industrial revolution is that it is happening much faster, it is not being generated by national but by multinational elites, and the present hi-tech industrial/information wave does not require workers with a Puritan worldview.

But why, one might ask, does a market economy require any kind of religious worldview at all? Why not just count on those sturdy old-fashioned virtues of greed and self-aggrandizement? Once again Peter Berger's work on 'economic culture' moves us toward an answer, but it does not move us far enough. Capitalism, Berger points out, just does not generate enough 'mythopoetic' energy. It has never, one might say, inspired the songs it needs to celebrate its own qualities. And despite the valiant efforts of advocates like Michael Novak to crank up a theology of capitalism, nothing very convincing has ever come of the effort. In contrast to the songs that hymn the glories of egalitarianism, socialism or liberation, capitalism seems tone deaf. Admittedly, televangelism (with flamboyant personalities such as Tammy Faye Bakker) sometimes comes close to providing this cheering section. It often appears to be the quintessential religio-capitalist achievement. The line between programme and commercial, always thin at best throughout the TV industry, disappears almost completely.

But this theory also fails to persuade. The vast majority of the people who are drawn into Pentecostalism come not because of a televangelist but because a neighbour or relative has invited them. Having once visited, they obviously find something they have been looking for. Furthermore, it is difficult to believe that nearly half a billion people have become Pentecostals because they are all push-overs. There is something else happening here.

A third and far more sophisticated view of the link between the market revolution and the Pentecostal upsurge holds that it is a kind of late twentieth-century reprise of the role earnest Methodists and Baptists played in the first industrial revolution. This theory suggests that the Pentecostals are providing the same kind of work ethic of thrift, punctuality and sobriety that supplied the reliable workforce for the Satanic mills of the UK and the industrial expansion of the United States. According to this view the ethos of the new Pentecostal-charismatic movement supplies just the cultural values the market revolution needs and without which it would falter. But I am not persuaded by this theory either, because the movement, as I will show, is also generating counter-currents to market globalization, currents which will need to be considered in any comprehensive understanding.

## A Continuum of Contending Forces

Clearly a truly comprehensive assessment of the interconnection between globalization and Pentecostalism would have to include a region-by-region analysis. To a certain degree, this is what the present volume does. In this introductory chapter, I will rely on some selective sampling. First, however, I would like to call attention to a common mistake. Although many observers continue to confuse Pentecostalism with 'fundamentalism', the two are not the same. To the unpractised eye Pentecostalism often resembles fundamentalism. But the similarities are superficial, while the differences between the two are more important than the surface similarities. The centrality of ecstatic utterance is a case in point. Fundamentalists simply do not stand for it. To this day, the moment any Southern Baptist congregation permits 'tongue speaking' it is immediately excluded from the Convention, whose leaders recognize that Pentecostalism is not a mere extension of fundamentalism. It is something quite different, which, were its inner logic to play itself out, could completely subvert text-mediated religion. Pentecostals have more in common with Saint Catherine of Siena than with John Calvin.

In considering some sample case studies, let us look first at Guatemala. This is an obvious choice since it may have the largest percentage of Pentecostals of any country in Latin America, a continent on which the movement is growing perhaps faster than anywhere else. Furthermore, as one scholar writes, the groups that appeared there 'had little or no affiliation with churches, groups or monies from the United States'. To understand this it is important to remember that although Guatemala has had a series of secular, anti-clerical *governments*, the vast majority of the *population*, especially the Indians, was always deeply religious. In fact, it is precisely this indigenous religiosity, not just in Latin America but also everywhere in the world, which sometimes provides the richest soil for Pentecostal expansion. In Central America and the Andean region one can find men and women who a few years ago were *curanderos*, practising one or another form of folk healing rooted in traditional religion. Today many of these folk healers are Pentecostal preachers and healers, still practising a healing art that stands both in continuity and in conflict with what they previously did.

In Korea, as well as in China, the folk religion is shamanism, and significant elements of shamanic lore such as trance, exorcism, healing and mystical flight have been swept up into Pentecostal worship. The same assimilation is going on in sub-Saharan Africa, where dancing, drumming and ancestor veneration, generally discouraged or forbidden by Protestants and Catholics, are welcomed into Pentecostal services. In many of these places it is 'speaking in tongues' which opens the way for this back-door assimilation (usually labelled as 'syncretism' by its critics). After all, from a psychological perspective, tongue-speaking itself is an example of ecstatic utterance, possibly also a form of mystical trance.

It is understandable that many observers can be misled about the uncanny assimilative powers of Pentecostalism, which contribute to its rapid growth. Pentecostal preachers often passionately inveigh *against* local indigenous religious practices at the very moment those same practices are re-emerging, often in only slightly modified form, within Pentecostal worship itself. Try as these energetic preachers will to urge their people to turn their backs on the Satanic forces around them – whether in Umbanda or shamanism or Vodun – these same preachers of these forces also affirm their reality by recognizing the power. The people in the congregation may be grateful for the high wall their strict moral codes erect between them and the dangerous and fallen world around them, but at the same time they see that spiritual world as *a continuum of contending forces and clashing powers*.

Here is a vital, if too often missed link between globalization and Pentecostalism. The market revolution results in massive uprooting, displacement and the destruction of traditions. The result, for millions of people, is a sense of bewilderment and disarray. Chaos is one of the principal ways in which the poor experience the globalizing landscape. But Pentecostal worship with its ear-splitting noise and tumultuous prayer is something of a homeopathic cure. It invites people to plunge into the chaos in order to overcome it, by the power of the Holy Spirit. Unlike enlightened Protestants and Catholics, Pentecostals never claim that spirits of the folk religion are illusory. Rather, they proclaim that God can defeat and vanquish them. This theology provides, ironically, both a *bridge* from the spiritual world of the old religion and a *dam* against its powers.

But traffic on the bridge travels both ways, and the question of whether Pentecostalism is taming and assimilating the local shades or being assimilated by them is never fully decided. For example, there are Pentecostals in America and Europe who have their doubts about whether the Yoido Full Gospel Church represents Christianized shamanism or shamanized Christianity. In any case, for millions of uprooted people around the world, Pentecostalism clearly provides a symbolic safe place that enables them to survive the ravages of the new industrialization without completely abandoning their traditional symbolic world. This is one secret of its extraordinary growth. But we are still left with a serious question: why has this same movement grown so quickly in other regions of the world where the conditions were different from those of either Guatemala or Korea?

Here we come upon yet another theory. It suggests that Pentecostalism grows fastest not among the most downtrodden but among those lowly ones who aspire to move higher, a logical target audience for the marketers. The health and wealth gospel preached by some Pentecostals seems to confirm this. But explaining the power of Pentecostalism both as a comfort to the afflicted (as the old compensation theories of religion once did) and also as a helpful staging area for transition into the world of the shopping mall also leaves a lot to be desired. If Pentecostalism thrives *both* when things are getting better *and* when they are getting worse, its appeal must come from a deeper source.

## Mainstream Mystics, Not Fundamentalists

My own work on global Pentecostalism has convinced me that each of these theories of its astonishing growth helps, but not very much. The reason I baulk at seeing Pentecostalism as a new edition of fundamentalism is that the power of Pentecostalism can be understood most clearly precisely at the point where it *differs* from classical fundamentalism. Indeed, when Pentecostalism first emerged in its present form during the famous Azusa Street revival that began in Los Angeles in 1906, at first among black custodians and domestic servants, soon attracting lower-class whites as well, the fundamentalists were among its most vociferous critics. One of these antagonists, using a phrase Pentecostals have not forgotten over the century, called them 'the last vomit of Satan'. Spurned and ridiculed by the downtown churches as 'holy-rollers', they were also attacked even more vehemently by fundamentalists, who were afraid that the Pentecostal belief in a direct, unmediated experience of God would undercut the authority of scripture and doctrine.

This fundamentalist attack on Pentecostalism should not come as a surprise to students of the history of religion. Pentecostals are, after all, what Margaret Paloma calls 'main street mystics'. But text-oriented religions have had a problem with mystics for millennia. Fundamentalists and conservative Christians also stridently disagreed with the Pentecostals' claim that miracles still take place in the present age. This explains in part the struggle between the Pentecostals and such fundamentalists as Jerry Falwell (a battle which came to a head in Falwell's takeover of Jimmy and Tammy Bakker's Christian theme park, 'Heritage USA'). The current Pentecostal-charismatic movement is not, as some writers claim, a layer on top of the old fundamentalism. It is a departure from it (albeit still using some of its terminology). As I have said, this tension was there from the beginning. Not long after the Pentecostals appeared on the scene one stern Princeton Presbyterian naysayer declared that, because they believed in contemporary miracles, they were just as bad as Catholics. In this judgement, incidentally, he foreshadowed some more recent sociological analyses which suggest that Latin American Pentecostalism might better be understood as a mutation not of evangelical Protestantism but of popular folk Catholicism. For countless disorientated people, pouring into the huge, intimidating cities of the continent from the impoverished countryside, they reconstitute fragments of their previous lives, including its popular Catholicism, as best they can. In the midst of the jarring urban bedlam they can still find – in one of the Pentecostal congregations – the same miracles, healing, and a welcoming company of new brothers and sisters to replace the *compadres* left behind in the village. The pastor becomes the surrogate *patron*, and they can even reclaim some of the exhilaration of the fiesta in the dancing and singing of the nightly prayer meetings. The Mexican religious historian Jean-Pierre Bastian demonstrates considerable insight when he calls the Pentecostals 'Catholics without priests'.

Why do I insist that Pentecostals are not to be understood as a subspecies of fundamentalism? The dispute may sound esoteric to modern secular ears, but it is utterly crucial to grasping the astonishing appeal of Pentecostalism today. It is *because* they are experiential and not as text-oriented, and *because* they believe that the age of miracles did not end with the apostles, that they are making such headway. It is easy to make mistakes in this slippery area. I know full well that Pentecostal preachers love to prowl the stage – and often the aisles as well – with a large Bible in their hand. But one should notice how rarely they actually open it. The Bible is a *symbol* of authority, not a text to be exegeted. Also, having now attended perhaps 150 Pentecostal services on four different continents, I know that the testimonies and prophecies are heavily laced with biblical allusions. But this is just the point. Pentecostalism represents a massive 're-oralization' of a tradition that has become fixated on texts (cf. Draper below, pp. 90–106). Its style is narrational, not disquisitional. Sermons are not lectures sprinkled with a few anecdotes, but stories, often dramatically re-enacted, with an occasional doctrinal observation interjected.

## Cultus and Culture: Pentecostalism as Market Spirituality?

This raises another critical point about the study of Pentecostalism: the central importance of the orality of the cultus. Obviously this makes worship available to semi-illiterate people, but a whole lot more is also at stake. Pentecostal worshippers not only speak, they speak 'in tongues'. They dance, jump and whirl. They sometimes lie on the floor doing what they cheerfully call 'rug time', or being 'slain in the Lord'. They sometimes run around the church. Although there is not as much of it as their critics once claimed, they sometimes do collapse and roll on the floor (from whence arose the derogatory term 'holy rollers'). This highly physical form of worship often shocks other Christians, but it is hardly new in the history of religion, even in biblical religion. One need not turn to whirling dervishes or Hindu fakirs for precedents. Reading between the lines of the Old Testament prophets will do it. Also, when St Paul warns the Corinthians against too much ecstatic expression in worship, we can be sure that something of the kind was certainly going on at the time in Corinth. Even when warning against excessive speaking in tongues, the Apostle lets it slip that he too speaks in tongues – 'more than you all' – an aside Pentecostals love to quote to Bible-pounding fundamentalists.

The centrality of cultus in Pentecostalism implies that we must avoid making the common error many social scientists do when they scrutinize the influence of a religion on society. Some are so intent on studying the 'social teachings' of churches that they neglect the obvious connection between cultus and culture. But what happens when we do examine the cultus–culture connection in Pentecostalism? One theory suggests that the authoritarian structure of Pentecostal polity habituates its members to accepting the same authoritarian style in the society at large. Since capitalism at this early stage of its development must not be burdened with 'an excess of democracy', it is argued, this religiously imbued deference to those in charge helps it along. This theory also holds that Pentecostalism cultivates a direct and individual relationship with God, and this promotes the kind of individualism the market also requires. Add to this that its highly emotional worship also encourages a kind of immediate gratification, a spiritual disposition whose material equivalent the consumer market can cash in on at the local *supermercado*. According to this description Pentecostalism is almost tailormade for the market-consumer culture just as ascetic Protestantism was suited to an earlier stage of capital accumulation (cf. Stålsett's contribution, pp. 198–212).

This all sounds very plausible, but it leaves many questions unanswered. It does not account for a pivotal aspect of the Pentecostal cultus: 'speaking in tongues', 'praying in the Spirit' or, as it is termed in the bloodless idiom of comparative religion, 'glossolalia'. I suggest that the massive return of ecstasy to contemporary Christianity is not an outgrowth of fundamentalism (which is after all a modern phenomenon) but an eruption of something far older, more basic, more experiential and more universal. I have called it 'primal spirituality' (Cox, 1995). If this proves to be the case, the relationship between the new Christian expansion and the market revolution may be far more complex than it appears to be. How?

The standardization and homogenization of mass capitalist culture famously deprives people of genuine experience. That same mass culture also thins out community and encourages individualism. How is this connected to the massive return of experiential religion? Though Pentecostals are sometimes accused of fomenting individualism, what converts report time and time again is that they have discovered a new and powerful sense of *belonging*. They often describe their congregations in familial language. Through its ceaseless advertising onslaught, market culture relies heavily on pandering images of the life it says we should all aspire to. But part of the power of Pentecostalism is its attack on the perverse values of 'this fallen age'. Although they have more recently compromised on this conviction, the early Pentecostals were determined not to be seduced by the 'wiles of this world'. Recently some Pentecostal leaders have tried to revive this rejection of 'worldliness' as a critique of consumer culture, which they rightly see as hyper-eroticized and deceitful, promising what it is ultimately unable to deliver. This suggests that Pentecostalism cannot be cast merely as the handmaiden of market globalization. There are simply too many elements in the Pentecostal worldview that do not comport well with market capitalism.

But that is, of course, not the whole story. Pentecostalism also has its cadres of Mercedes-driving 'name it and claim it' preachers who tell their people that if they are not rich it is their own fault for not trusting God enough. Much more so than in the earlier wave of Protestantism, Pentecostalism – as the authors of this book show – is dangerously subject to authoritarianism. And when Pentecostals become middle-class, they do often forget that their original mission was to the dispossessed. Although their movement started on the wrong side of the tracks among penurious whites and even poorer blacks, many Pentecostals would prefer to forget that history and climb up the echelons of power and privilege.

## Counter-Cultural Values

In short, just how the Pentecostal-charismatic movement will ultimately relate itself to the new late-capitalist revolution remains an
unfinished story. The movement obviously enables millions of people
to cope with the jarring world of modernity without completely sever-
ing their ties to traditional culture. This may be the most basic reason
for its growth. But, to recall St Paul again, Pentecostalism is somehow
'in but not of this world'. It nourishes important counter-cultural
values. As one who is not completely comfortable with the projected
global triumph of market-consumer civilization, I see it as a hopeful
sign that some Pentecostals now cultivate these values more energeti-
cally. Unlike fundamentalists, Pentecostals have now begun to produce a critical and self-reflective tradition.[2] Young Pentecostal pastors
and theologians are studying social ethics and liberation theology. In
sharp contradistinction to fundamentalists, they are attending what
their forebears in the faith would have condemned as modernist semi-
naries and divinity schools. Many are co-operating in ecumenical
organizations and working with other churches in social action programmes. The Pentecostals who do so are often criticized for their
efforts by their more conservative co-religionists, but they in turn
warn those colleagues against aligning themselves with the Christian
right. In short, the Pentecostal-charismatic movement today is not a
phalanx but a battlefield. Further, it is a battlefield on which much will
be decided that will go far beyond the movement itself.

*Notes*

1 In his foreword to Martin, 1993.
2 Cf. Salomonsen's call for this, and Wells' appropriation of Pentecostal terminology in a theological project (below, pp. 107–30, 170–82).

# 2. Pentecostalism, Shamanism and Capitalism within Contemporary Korean Society

## SUNG-GUN KIM

### Pentecostal Growth in Korea

It is important to acknowledge that any understanding of the characteristics of contemporary Korean society would not be complete without some knowledge of its religious culture as a representative cultural phenomenon.

> Korea has one of the most dynamic and creative Christian traditions in the world today, which is deserving of study in its own right. Korean Christians have begun to play a major role in world Christianity, including leading active ministries on virtually every continent, serving in leadership roles on many church governing bodies, and spearheading charitable activities around the world.[1]

This worldwide presence needs to be better recognized and understood by non-Koreans as well as Koreans themselves. Hence to understand modern Korea, the importance of Christianity within the broader culture cannot be overestimated. Just as Buddhism and Confucianism made important cultural contributions within traditional Korea, Christianity has become exceedingly influential in modern Korea, particularly in its Pentecostal guise.

It is true that since the 1960s modern Korea has experienced a so-called 'compressed modernization', affecting a multi-religious situation under rapid urbanization. Indeed, in spite of the secularization thesis promulgated within the 1980s, religion not only has survived, but has flourished, especially within the non-Western world. Hence, as Peter Berger has recently admitted, the assumption that we live in a

secularized world is false (Berger, 1999: 2). From this, we could raise
the conceptual question of the validity of the secularization thesis itself
within the Asia context. The dynamics of religious change in Asia are
too complex to be slotted with ease into the Western conception of
secularization. Within Asian cities (Singapore, Hong Kong, Seoul,
etc.) modernization and urbanization do not appear to contradict the
presence of a high level of religious consciousness and practice. What
might be called 'religious urbanization' (Clammer, 1984: 53) is an
important aspect of the history and social life of Asia, especially
modern Korea.

In this context, the purpose of this study is to clarify and evaluate
the cultural and social implications of the remarkable growth of
evangelical Protestant Christianity, especially in its Pentecostal guise
within Korea since the 1960s. The advent and unprecedented expansion of the modern Pentecostal movement, which began at the turn of
the century, can be considered one of the most important events within twentieth-century Christianity. In the midst of the constant debate
upon the heretical nature of the movement, the Korean Pentecostal
phenomenon, which began in the 1950s following the Korean War,
has succeeded on two fronts: first, phenomenal church growth; and
second, the generalization of Pentecostal beliefs within the country
(Ma, 2000). So the Korean mega-churches – numbering among the
world's twenty largest congregations – are mostly Pentecostal, either
in affiliation or in nature, by virtue of their style of worship and
preaching, regardless of any denominational ties (Ma, 2000: 2).

## Religion in Contemporary Society: Some Theoretical Considerations

For the German system-theorist Niklas Luhmann, the central structural feature of modern and global society is 'differentiation' on the
basis of function (Luhmann, 1982: 238–42). In his view, there is a
difference between how a subsystem (for example, polity, law, economy, science, religion, education, art, health, and the family) relates to
society as a whole and how it relates to other social systems, especially
other subsystems. Luhmann analyses the former in terms of *function*
and the latter in terms of *performance*. Among several subsystems in
contemporary society, it is religion that has been seriously undermined
by 'privatization' – the process by which certain institutional spheres
become removed from effective roles in the public sphere (especially in

the arena of economic production and power) (McGuire, 1997: 58). As a result, some theorists point to differentiation as evidence of the declining influence of religion (McGuire, 1997: 276).

This said, there are two important implications of extensive institutional differentiation: one for the situation of the individual, and the other for society at large (McGuire, 1997: 277f.). With respect to the individual, differentiation appears to go hand in hand with the discovery of self – the unique individual within society. For society at large, the process of differentiation makes it harder to mobilize the commitment and efforts of its members. Values from one separate sphere do not readily motivate behaviour in another. As a result, regarding the location of religion in contemporary society, religion is relegated to the private sphere. The individual's desire for meaning and belonging must therefore be pursued within the private sphere.

Within the sphere of religion, function thus refers to 'pure' religious communication, variously described as the aspect of devotion and worship, the cure of souls, the search for enlightenment or salvation. Function is the pure, 'sacred' communication involving the transcendent and the aspect that religious institutions claim for themselves: the basis of their autonomy in modern society. Religious performance, by contrast, occurs when religion is 'applied' to problems (such as economic poverty, political oppression) generated in other systems but not solved there. Through performance relations, religion establishes its importance for the 'profane' aspects of life; but in the process, non-religious concerns impinge upon pure religious consciousness, demonstrating the fact that other societal concerns condition the autonomy of religious action (Beyer, 1994: 80).

Among the many ideological effects or impacts of religion that have been suggested, the following summary contains the most notable (Thompson, 1986: 78): (1) the opiate of the people (Karl Marx)[2]; (2) a compensation for those who suffer in this life through the promise of a higher status in the spiritual realm (Weber, 1963[1922]: 113); (3) a transitional ideology helping the worker to adjust to the requirements of capitalist industrialization or 'modernization' by inculcating a religiously-sanctioned work-discipline (Weber, 1976[1904–5]: 115); (4) creating a form of community that eases the passage from that of a traditionally based community (*Gemeinschaft*) to a more impersonal, rational and contractually based social order (*Gesellschaft*) (Gilbert, 1976; Semmel, 1973). It has also been suggested that religion resulted in the channelling off of the potentially revolutionary leadership of the working class (Halévy), and the formation of a reformist tendency

among the 'aristocracy of labour' (Thompson, 1986: 78). The nineteenth-century French historian Elie Halévy, in contrasting England
with revolutionary France, stressed the idea that John Wesley's
Methodism helped prevent violent revolution within industrial
England (Halévy, 1949). This shows that most organized religions
(such as Christianity) within capitalist social systems are substantially
pro-capitalist, and are thereby not inclined to support the radical
political organization of the working class. Regarding the ideological
impact of Methodism, the historian A. D. Gilbert suggests that its
most widespread appeal was to groups whose economic and social
positions were improving, and that this echoed the aspirations of the
working class rather than their despair (Gilbert, 1976). Contrary to
Gilbert, who stresses the 'positive' function of the Chapel, E. P.
Thompson in his seminal work, *The Making of the English Working
Class* (1968) saw the Chapel communities as instruments of the
middle class for exercising social control and instilling discipline
within the working class.

In the meantime, there have been some Korean studies on the
reasons for the rapid growth of Korean Protestant churches during
the late 1970s and early 1980s.[3] Most of these studies have been
undertaken by eminent sociologists of religion and scholars of religion
in Korea. As a whole, in explaining the reasons for the remarkable
spread of Protestant Christianity in the country, these studies seem to
display a certain commonality in distinguishing three main factors:
(1) cultural factors, (2) internal factors, and (3) social factors. After
reviewing the main arguments of these studies, I have found that
they are mostly inclined to treat these three factors in too separate a
fashion. As a result, it seems to me that they exhibit similar difficulties
in properly accounting for the Korean evangelical movement's explo-
sive growth exemplified by the case of the Yoido Full Gospel Church
(YFGC) specifically. In my opinion, all three factors have a particular
quality of their own, but they are more closely interrelated and intertwined than these studies would ordinarily assume. In an attempt to
redress this point, this present study examines closely the following
two interrelated and/or intertwined factors in turn: (i) the nexus
between shamanism and Protestantism (especially Pentecostalism)
and (ii) the affinity between evangelical religion/Pentecostal Christianity and capitalism. It is argued here that while the former (i) apparently
seems to be closely linked to both the aforementioned 'cultural'
factors (1) and 'internal' factors (2), the latter (ii) is related to both the
'internal' factors (2) and 'social' factors (3) respectively.

## The Nexus between Shamanism and Pentecostalism

In Korea, behind all the imported religions there existed a pre-Confucian, pre-Buddhist and pre-Taoist indigenous belief. In its most primitive form, shamanism – a faith common to all tribes ranging throughout north-east Asia, Mongolia and Siberia – became the predominant religious ethos of the Korean people (Eliade, 1972: 461f.; Clark, 1961: 174). The core of shamanism is that of a polytheistic and poly-demonic religion based on the animistic worship of spirit beings. In addition, shamanism adopted from Buddhism most of the accretion of magic, charm-making, crystal-gazing and dream interpretation (Clark, 1961: 178). Thus Eliade describes shamanism as 'techniques of ecstasy' (Eliade, 1972: 4). In brief, spiritual exorcism, direct communication with the spirits and healing are the major aspects of shamanism.

In addition to animistic beliefs, within Korea's shamanistic pantheon there developed a concept of a hierarchy of the gods.[4] Above all the spirits stood one supreme ruler named Hananim. Koreans regarded Hananim as the celestial god of the heavenly kingdom (Palmer, 1967: 208). Korean faith in Hananim became an integral part of Korean thought from primitive times. Conviction of the belief in Hananim was strengthened, not reduced, by the introduction of the amorphous Confucian concept of *ch'on* (Chinese: *t'ien*). Furthermore, Korean Neo-Confucianists of the Yi dynasty fell strongly under the influence of their own indigenous beliefs, which in part called for a 'personalized' view of God. Their interpretation of Zhu Xi – long the accepted exponent of Confucian doctrine, which identified God with reason and law – proved to be a Korean deviation. As a result, whereas Zhu Xi tended to rule out a 'personal' God, Korean Confucians tended to affirm one (Chung, 1959: 129).

At the very outset of their proselytizing effort, American Christian missionaries recognized Hananim as a distinctive Korean deity, unusually suited to their own conception of God (Palmer, 1967: 16). It was easy to accept Hananim as the counterpart of the Christian God; hence there was no need for them to discourage or oppose the concept. As Scott has observed,

The Koreans have always *Hananim*, a name which covers the idea of the one supreme mind, one God. This God of the Koreans is similar to the God of the Jewish Old Testament . . . On this deep-seated monotheism the Christian missionary has built the amazing success.[5]

Hananim was a point of contact with Korean culture, the like of which missionaries in China did not have. In *Korea and Christianity* (1967), Spencer J. Palmer could therefore conclude, 'As a personal transcendent God, clearly the supreme deity of the Korean people, *Hananim* was uniquely suited to prepare the Korean people for belief in the Christian God' (Palmer, 1967: 18). Thus being part of its essential Korean religious heritage, the monotheistic concept of God originally developed from Korea's shamanistic pantheon, and its personalized view of God was helpful, rather than harmful, for the expansion of Christianity in the country from the very beginning. Protestantism, as the latecomer in Korea (unlike the early-comer, Roman Catholicism), readily adopted the term *Hananim* as the Supreme God, and thus became fundamentally significant in providing a point of contact between Korean religious culture and the imported faith, thereby allowing for a smooth transition from the native concept of God to that of the Christian image (Kim, 2000: 123). So the Korean theologian Yu Tong-shik draws our attention to the role of shamanism in the process of adopting Christianity in Korea in the following manner:

> First, it helped accept with little reservation the notion of the Christian God and his heavenly world. Second, it helped adopt a religion of pragmatic prayer for blessings and avoidance of disasters in this world. Third, it has become dependent faith. And finally, it has promoted the conservatism of Korean society.[6]

In short, we could stress once again that traditional shamanism meets the Protestant religion through its 'personalized' view of God.

In line with this, given that most modern Koreans in the 1970s and 1980s were still shamanically-inclined in mindset, and spirit-worshippers in calamity, we could contend that the shamanic 'personalized' view of God as the supreme God presiding over the affairs of heaven and earth, and controlling the fate of human beings, was fundamentally important in the rapid progress of Christian evangelicalism. This was especially true in its Pentecostal guise which stressed spiritualism or spiritism, described as,

> the philosophical doctrine that nothing is real but soul or spirit: the doctrine that spirit has a real existence apart from matter: the inter-

pretation of a varied series of abnormal phenomena as for the most part caused by spiritual beings acting upon specially sensitive persons or mediums. (Kirkpatrick and Schwarz, 1983: 1248)

In this context, it is noteworthy that among the liberal wing of Christianity, various religious scholars such as Cox (1995: 222), Elliott (1989: 30–9), and Reynalds (2000) cite Paul Yonggi Cho of the YFGC as being a particularly vivid example of Christian shamanism. Hence, Cox in his important *Fire From Heaven* (1995) can state,

Korean Pentecostalism's unerring ability to absorb huge chunks of indigenous Korean shamanism and demon possession into its worship . . . What troubles people everywhere about the Korean case is that the degree of importation is so extensive that some wonder out loud what has absorbed what . . . To a visitor schooled in shamanism, the worship at the Yoido Full Gospel Church bears a striking resemblance to what is ordinarily known as 'shamanism' . . . (Cox, 1995: 222–4)

Earlier, and in similar manner, the Anglican scholar, Charles Elliott could maintain,

As we talked, I began to realize that comfort – that refusal to be embarrassed by material success – is the essence of this religion. And Cho himself is quite clear about that. 'We meet needs that people have,' he said. 'We give them what they want, what they are looking for . . .' What they are looking for is shaped and influenced by their experience and by their expectations. The former is their daily life. The latter is their consciousness and unconscious memory of the ancient role of the shaman. Life is harsh, alien and threatening, full of *han*. The shaman offered catharsis, *jung*, play and blessings. Cho and his many imitators offer an emotional release, sympathy – and blessings. (Elliott, 1989: 32)

Finally, in the same context, Jeremy Reynalds, after presenting some severe criticisms against Pentecostal Christianity among non-Pentecostal scholars, could conclude,

Korean Christians tend to see Christianity as a path to material prosperity. That trait is a residue of shamanism, the native folk religion for centuries in Korea and other Northeast Asian countries. In

shamanism the shaman (a quasi medicine man or woman) is asking
to intercede with the spirits to ensure one's health or business success. Many professing Christians (in Korea) contend that the gods
of shamanism and the God of Christianity are kindred spirits. In this
research I will contend that there is a relationship between the gods
of shamanism and Korean mega-church pastor Paul Yonggi-Cho. I
will propose that the relationship existing between shamanism and
Cho is that they both seek to resolve a common human propensity
(the desire to be well off) and that in so doing Cho makes his faith
utilitarian, and that with the long history of shamanistic influence
on the Korean culture there is thus a favorable environment created
for the receiving of his message. (Reynalds, 2000: 1)

If we accept these aforementioned statements at face value, then Paul
Yonggi Cho appears to meet the qualification of being a Christian
shaman to a greater or lesser degree. Perhaps it is not surprising that the
biblical concept of God's spiritual blessing of humankind eventually
became distorted within the Korean (Pentecostal) church. However, it
is interesting to point out here that Korean Pentecostals disclaim
similarities between Korean Pentecostalism and shamanism (Reynalds,
2000: 13–16). For example, Wonsuk Ma, the Academic Dean at the
Asia Pacific Theological Seminary in Baguio, Philippines, contends
that Cho's message

is not to bring the Christian message to the animistic motif of blessing, but with social changes (after the liberation and much poverty)
the other-worldly outlook had to change and the Lord used Cho to
bring this long-neglected part of God's message to the Korean
churches. (Ma, email to Reynalds, in Reynalds, 2000: 13)

In Ma's opinion, perhaps Asian churches such as the YFGC may
provide some timely advice towards the numerically declining
Western-based liberal churches.
    In this context, I would agree with the insight of Robeck on the issue
of shamanism when he states,

What it has enabled him (Paul Yonggi Cho) to do is to speak to a
broader constituency and in a sense reel them in . . . What he is
doing is connecting with these people and helping them to move
from that conjuring in which divination takes place apart from God
and brings them into a charismatic experience which is very directly

in relation to God. (Robeck, email to Reynalds, in Reynalds, 2000: 15f.)

Commenting on the allegations of Christian shamanism raised in his book *Fire from Heaven*, Cox following his Korean visit (including the YFGC) could later write: 'The paradox is that the Korean churches do preach against Shamanism, but at the same time they incorporate and Christianize elements of the Shamanistic world view and practice' (Cox, email to Reynalds, in Reynalds, 2000: 16). Indeed Cox repeatedly emphasizes that one of Pentecostalism's great strengths is its capacity to integrate pre-Christian cultural expressions into Christian practice. For him, the incorporation is not problematic. Put simply, Cox thinks that shamanized Christianity is entirely acceptable. This stance seems to be congruent with James Grayson's theory of emplantation (Grayson, 1995), which placed the remarkable growth of Korean Christianity heavily on minimizing the contradiction between the new faith and Korean values and on reducing the conflict between the new faith and Korean traditional religions (Kim, 2000: 130).

In the meantime, David Martin, a leading sociologist of religion specializing in the evangelical revival (especially Pentecostalism) experienced within the 'Third World', has provided excellent suggestions as to the rapid expansion of Protestant Christianity including Pentecostalism in Korea (Martin, 1993: 138–41). According to Martin, there are two separate tracks (Martin, 1993: 140). One track has already led to the combination of the aura of modernity with that of Christianity, especially Protestant Christianity. This, in his view, appealed more to the 'lower upper' groups. The other track leads to the combination of Christianity with the aura of the most archaic layer of Korean religiosity: shamanism. This, in Martin's opinion, appeals more to the 'upper lower' groups.

This relationship between conservative Protestantism (Presbyterian or Pentecostal) and shamanism is perfectly natural, even though it perhaps comes as a surprise. Hence Martin can state,

The world of New Testament Christianity contains 'demons' and it announces victory over 'the powers'. The world is, in fact, a common substrate all over the five continents . . . Shamanism and spiritism are nearly everywhere, just below the surface or actually on the surface of contemporary life. Certainly it is on the surface in the Yucatan, in the Sertao and in Seoul. (Martin, 1993: 140)

In a similar vein, on the early spread of Christianity Peter Meinhold can aver,

> This intense expansion is to be explained neither by the occasional help which the church was able to offer the lower classes, nor by the stricter moral code which the Christians opposed to the heathens. The strongest motive force in the spreading of the faith was the awareness that belief in the uniqueness of Jesus' person and works also meant victory over the powers of this world . . . It (Christianity) acquired a tremendous force of expansion – a force which cannot be accounted for by reference to social or sociological impulses – namely belief in the conquering force of faith. (Meinhold, 1972: 411)

It is to be noted that in the New Testament the words 'Satan', 'devil' and 'demon' appear 48, 24 and 88 times respectively. So believing as they do in the universal presence of spirits, it neither was nor is difficult for Korean converts to Christianity to accept the doctrines of the spiritual nature of God. Unlike the 'option for the poor' exercised in *Minjung* theology, where evil is primarily located within societal structures, the concern for the poor within Pentecostalism locates evil within the spirit world. The Pentecostal emphasis in Korea is really to see 'the Kingdom' both present *and* future, as signs of the Kingdom, especially that of divine healing and the 'baptism of the Spirit' (Martin, 1993: 146). In this context, it should be stressed that besides an emphasis on private prayer, including 'loud prayer' and corporate intercessory prayer all night and in the early morning, exorcisms, healings and miracles prominently and specifically occur within the growing churches of Korea (Martin, 1993: 147). It is said that apart from casting out demons from several thousands of people, a Minister of Sung Rak Baptist Church (well known for his emphasis on exorcism) has raised seven people from the dead, three of them before their funerals. This would be a potent source of growth and popularity. To my surprise, Martin can state, 'Maybe Christianity itself began in a similar manner' (Martin, 1993).

In summary, from the perspective of church history, it is true that Pentecostal Christianity within Latin America, Africa and Asia resembles the primitive Christian Church as recorded in the Acts of the Apostles. Similarities are the urban character of their congregations, exorcism, healings, and the baptism of the Holy Spirit and so forth. Their most distinctive Pentecostal doctrine is the baptism of/in the

Holy Spirit (Ma, 2000: 5). Given the fact that in the twenty-first century, humanity (as in Latin America) has an ever-increasing interest in spiritual matters – that is, spiritism and shamanism – as Cox predicts, the Pentecostal movement, especially in its Korean manifestation, is expected to continue to supply a leading dynamic to the continuing development of Christian (Pentecostal) spirituality in this new century. It is argued here that a positive aspect of the religious function of shamanism, which is closely linked with evangelical/Pentecostal Christianity, should be rediscovered and re-emphasized.

## The Affinity between Pentecostalism and Capitalism

In order to bring into greater relief the main reasons for the large-scale Protestant Church expansion within Korea, the nexus of evangelical religion (especially Pentecostalism) and economic ethos should be closely re-examined. The sociologist Kim Kyong-Dong sees no special connection between the expansion of Protestantism and the Korean economic take-off in the 1960s, even though both occurred with remarkable rapidity at the same time (Kyung-Dong, 1988: 216; Martin, 1993: 154). While Kim Kyong-Dong denied the affinity between Protestant Christianity and capitalism, the Presbyterian, and former sociologist of religion, Revd Noh Chijun recently admitted the connection to a certain degree.[7] In my view however, Noh did not examine this relationship deeply enough.

According to Martin, the dual expansion of the 1960s – Protestantism and economic development – was in itself related to complex influences derived in important measure from America (Martin, 1993: 154). To my understanding, the rapid growth of Protestantism, especially Pentecostalism, was not possible without the 'cultural' radiation which emanated in a general way from the then powerful Protestant religious culture of the United States. In this context, it is noteworthy that, as Martin says, those Koreans who migrated to America were disproportionately Christian, as a consequence of close ties between the US and Korean Christians. During the Korean War (1950–53), the first American Pentecostal denominations established evangelical missions in Korea. In 1952, the American Assemblies of God sent Abner Chesnut as their first missionary to Korea. He first made contact with the Chosun Pentecostal Church. The Korean Assemblies of God was organized in 1953. The next year, the Korean Assemblies of God opened its first Bible School, Paul Yonggi Cho being one of its first students. Following his graduation Cho commenced his ministry in 1958 with a small number of converts in an army tent located in a poverty-stricken slum area in the city of Seoul. In 1961 Cho gained valuable experience when he served as interpreter for Sam Todd, an American Pentecostal healing evangelist. As a result of his involvement in Todd's meetings, Cho's church increased in numbers. An important by-product of Cho's involvement with Todd was his introduction to the so-called 'prosperity gospel', espoused by such American healing evangelists as Oral Roberts (Reynalds, 2000: 8f.). As is well known, the prosperity gospel emphasizes a God who guarantees success. Put differently, the gospel of prosperity has often been criticized for the way that it emphasizes the resurrection to the neglect of the cross (Elliott, 1989: 47).

From this, Cho eventually presented the 'Threefold Blessing' and 'Fivefold Salvation' as an authentic Korean version of Pentecostal theology (Ma, 2000: 4). The 'Threefold Blessing' included salvation for the soul, material prosperity and physical health. It is primarily Cho's theological stance on divine healing, blessing and prosperity that has generated so much controversy. It is to be noted that the 'Threefold Blessing' is a new theological category which classical Pentecostalism with its innate urgency for evangelical mission did not know, it being uniquely Korean. As I have previously intimated, this theology of blessing had its existential roots in the poverty-stricken Korean situation of the 1950s and 1960s. That this element of blessing is the flagship of Korean Pentecostal belief suggests a direct influence from the 1960s charismatic movement in the West rather than from classical Pentecostalism. The charismatic or neo-Pentecostal movement in the 1960s married the Pentecostal message with material and present blessing (Ma, 2000). Classical Pentecostals emphasize the age beyond the present, while charismatic Pentecostals stress the present age. Scholars such as Paul Martin, founder and director of Wellspring Retreat and Resource Center in Albany, Ohio, point out that there are distinct similarities between the prosperity gospel (of which Cho is a practitioner) and the New Age movement (Reynalds, 2000: 19). They contend that both contain elements of magic as well as an innate power to create one's own reality. For me, although both share a common emphasis on the importance of personal experience within religion, the former differs in placing a far stronger social/institutional framework provided by the Church, together with much clearer and stricter moral rules and disciplines.

Like the primitive Christian Church, in offering the gift of the Holy Spirit to all women and men without distinction, charismatic Christianity, including Cho's YFGC, certainly helps engender a new self-confidence in those who had previously been economically marginalized (Woodhead, 2002: 175). By bringing the spiritual realm into such direct contact with the material world, charismatic Christianity shares a similarity of features with many indigenous religions such as shamanism and spiritism, and may take over some functions of the former, including exorcism and healing. Also, as with the evangelical tradition from which it flows, charismatic Christianity affirms the pre-eminent value of the family and 'domesticates' and 'tames' men by affirming the traditionally 'womanly' values of care, love and responsibility. In short, Pentecostals or evangelicals promise to transform individuals and families. The powerful behavioural transformation within Pentecostal families leads to capital formation of all kinds – spiritual, moral, social and economic. This is a con-temporary form of Max Weber's *Protestant Ethic and the Spirit of Capitalism* with Korean (as well as African, or Latin American . . .) families ascending from the margins to respectable lower- and solid middle-class status. In this process, the Pentecostal congregations exert control in these transformations – and create the resources necessary for economic productivity and self-government.

After the Korean War, in Martin's terminology (Martin, 1993: 153), the whole US Protestant package of religion including Pentecostalism, economic dynamism, progress and egalitarianism could be welcomed by many forward-looking Koreans as good for them and good for Korea. As a result, in post-war Korea, Protestantism became an important and indispensable link between the US Government and the authoritarian regimes of Park Chunghee, Chun Duwhan and Noh Taewoo. This is best exemplified by the famous story of Revd Billy Kim, Suwon Central Baptist Church, who in 2000 also served as the President of the Baptist World Alliance (BWA). Interestingly, Revd Kim, whose wife is American, was very close to all three Korean dicta-tors Park, Chun and Noh, and finally received the Moo-Goog-Hwa Medal from the Korean Government under Noh's regime in 1993.[8] As is well known, these regimes placed economic advance before due democratic process. As Martin can state,

Protestant fundamentalism helped prevent the political system from blowing up, thereby illustrating again one of the classic contentions of Halevy with regard to Methodism and revolution in England. It

also joined forces with all those elements in Korea which sought
mobility and rising material standards . . . Most Koreans cared more
for bread than for votes, and many of them found even a rising
gap between rich and poor tolerable provided at least the poor
were somewhat better off . . . What the expanding fundamentalist
churches offered was a hope, a therapy, a community – and a network. They fended off chaos and anomie.

In discussing the relationship of religion, and of Pentecostal
Christianity in particular, to economic advance in Korea, some
final account must be taken of the utilitarian spirit of traditional
shamanism. Some of the churches partook of the utilitarian spirit of
traditional shamanism, which again bears on the economic issue.
(Martin, 1993: 155)

Berger has drawn attention to the utilitarian attitude towards the
gods themselves in 'low' Confucianism (cf. Peter Berger in Berger
and Hsiao, 1988: 9). The Christian 'Spirit' in the eyes of devotees did
deliver in terms of health and wealth, and was therefore not demoted
but promoted. The Korean religious scene, Christian or otherwise,
was and continues to be one of rivalrous syncretism and pragmatic
adaptability, thereby paralleling what is happening in the economic
sphere (Martin, 1993: 155). The Korean case, where many faiths
compete for followers, supports Finke and Stark's interesting argument (1988: 41–9) that competition among religious bodies – rather
than reducing the credibility of each – serves to increase the level of
religious mobilization.

## Looking Ahead

Following Martin, this study has revealed that evangelical Protestant
Christianity, especially the Pentecostalism exemplified by Paul Yonggi
Cho's YGFC, successfully draws upon ancient Korean forms of
shamanism as well as introducing modern capitalistic American materialism. As a result, Protestantism in Korea, especially Cho's YGFC
with its famous 'triple blessings', is the 'religion of success' rather than
'the religion of suffering'. Further, as we have noted, the new Christian
churches create structures which are in some ways parallel to those
found within the economic sphere. So, according to Martin, in the
Korean context, how one evaluates the continuing successful growth
of the Pentecostal churches depends equally on how one evaluates

'consumer capitalism' in an age of globalization (Martin, 1993: 160). In this respect, I would stress the following:

> Evangelicals are particularly susceptible to the idols of materialism, in part because evangelical success and commercial success are so easily intertwined. In an entrepreneurial, media-oriented environment, successful ministries become powerful financial engines. It therefore becomes hard to distinguish between marketing the gospel and commercial success. (Hatch and Hamilton, 1992: 31)

With respect to religion's place within globalization, all contemporary world religions confront a similar structural predicament, related to the globalization of mass societies and the porous pluralism of late modernity. In a nutshell, the main structural predicament or dilemma of world religions is that while their privatized (pure) function is increasing, their public influence is decreasing.[9] In this regard, evangelical Protestantism, and especially Pentecostalism, is no exception. Although Pentecostalism is called to be a leader in the worldwide growth of religion, and as some would contend, the 'pentecostalization of the (entire) church' (Spittler, 1988: 421), this feature can be directly related to the present Korean religious situation, where the issue of its public influence still remains unquestioned. In this regard it is important to note the recent and at times vociferous voices of certain young M.Div. students of the YFGC espousing a 'political theology' or a 'theology of socio-political participation'.[10] It is true that Pentecostal Christianity as a whole lacks a definitive political theology. In the view of these young students, their own church with its emphasis on 'experience' rather than 'doctrine' has naturally succumbed to a pragmatic accommodation towards authoritarian regimes, thereby and ironically achieving such rapid numerical growth. Because of this, Protestant Christianity – and especially Pentecostalism within the turbulence and division in terms of ideology, region, class and generation experienced within contemporary Korean society – is in some real sense viewed as 'controversial'.

## Notes

1 'Why a professorship of Korean Christianity?' (The Center for Korean Studies, UCLA) in www.isop.ucla.edu/korea/christianity.asp (accessed 10/09/04).

2 Karl Marx, 'Contribution to the critique of Hegel's philosophy of right', in Bottomore, 1964: 43f.

3 For important examples in Korean, Noh Kilmyong, 'Religious Growth in the 1970s and Its Prospects' (in Korean), in the Korean Sociological Association, ed., *Hanguksahoe Uodirokagoitna* ('Where is Korean society going?), Seoul: Hyundaesawhoe Yeonguso, 1983, pp. 85–106; Lee Wongyu, *Hanguk Kyowhoeui Sahoehakjok Yihae* ('A sociological understanding of Korean Protestant churches') (in Korean), Seoul: Sungseo Yeongusa, 1992; Suh Woosuk, 'A sociological study on the middle-class mega-churches' (in Korean), *Hanguk Sahoehak* ('Korean Sociological Review'), Korean Sociological Association, 1994, pp, 151–74; Yun Sungyong, *Hyundae Hankuk Chonggyo Munwhaui Yihae* ('Understanding contemporary Korean religious culture') (in Korean), Seoul: Hanwul Academy, 1997; Noh Chijun, *Hanguk Kaeshingyo Sahoehak* ('A sociology of Korean Protestantism: the crisis of Korean Protestant churches and its prospects') (in Korean), Seoul: Hanwul Academy, 1998.

4 Chung Tae-wi (David Chung), 'Hanguk sahoe-ui chonggyo-chok honhapchuui' ('Religious syncretism in Korean society') (in Korean), *Sasanggye* 8: 3, March 1960, p. 208.

5 R. Scott, 'Warring mentalities in the Far East', *Asia* 20: 7, August 1920, p. 699, quoted in Palmer, 1967: 18.

6 Yu Tong-shik, *Hanguk Chonggyo Wa Kidokkyo* ('Korean Religions and Christianity') (in Korean), Seoul: Kidokkyo Sohoe, 1965, pp. 37–8.

7 Kyung-Dong, 1988; Noh, *Hanguk Kaeshingyo Sahoehak*, p. 29.

8 'The story of Revd Billy Kim' (in Korean), *Monthly Chosun*, September 2000.

9 Kim Sung-Gun, 'Globalization and the structural predicament of contemporary world religions' (in Korean), *Hanguk Sahoehak* (Korean Sociological Review), The Korean Sociological Association, 2002, 36: 2, pp. 157–92; 265–6.

10 For example, see Chung Chong-Hyun, 'A study of political participation among Pentecostal Christians in Latin America' (in Korean), M.Div. thesis, Graduate School of Theology, Hansei University, 2003, pp. 85–9.

# 3. Crossing Boundaries:
## The 'Universal Church' and the
## Spirit of Globalization

### BERGE FURRE

A white dove in a red heart. You can hardly avoid seeing this sign-board when visiting the mega-cities in Africa and Latin America and parts of southern Europe. It shines towards you from huge 'cathedrals of faith' in city centres – from Rio de Janeiro to Lisbon, from Buenos Aires to Johannesburg, from Santiago to London, from Paris to Tokyo. You find these signboards most often in the poorest urban areas, in *favelas* and shantytowns and *bidonvilles* – on the walls of old cinemas, closed factories, remodelled shops. Stairs – broad or narrow – lead up and inside: 'We are open! Always.' For this is the church of the street. Here the dove flew in – and found a heart.

## The 'Universal Church': A Case of Neo-Pentecostal Growth in a Globalized World

It all started around 1977 in a *favela* in Rio de Janeiro. Soon it spread all over Brazil. Now you can find the 'Igreja Universal do Reino de Deus' (IURD) – the 'Universal Church of the Kingdom of God' – in perhaps as many as 80 countries. 'Universal': a world to be conquered! The founder of IURD, Edir Macedo, called himself 'bishop' and settled in New York. There – in the urban centre of world capital – the new Rome was to be built, in the neighbourhood of Wall Street.

In the context of our attempt at discerning the 'spirits of globalization', analysing the possible interrelation between the growth of experiential spiritualities and market-driven global transformation, we may ask: Is this event, the foundation and growth of IURD, important? Does it represent the fourth phase of Pentecostalism? Or is it something very different from more traditional, mainstream Pentecostal churches? Feudalism became the cradle of Catholicism, and commercial capitalism gave form and wings to Protestantism. Can IURD now be a signal announcing the coming of a postcolonial religion of globalized capitalism? Could IURD serve as an illustration of the possible connection between neoliberal globalization and experiential religion? In addressing such wide-ranging questions, it should be noted that the success of IURD so far has been most notable in Latin America and Africa, and somewhat modest in other regions.

Christian religion has always crossed borders in waves, in different epochs and forms: through mission and trade, by weapons and economic power. In the beginning of the twentieth century Pentecostalism represented a new wave: from Azusa Street in Los Angeles to St Olav's Street in Oslo. In our day, yet another wave of charismatic and Pentecostal movements is changing the image of Christianity in large parts of the world – in a spirit of globalization. In his introductory chapter, Harvey Cox has already given a broad picture of this 'fire from heaven' (cf. also Cox, 1995). To what extent could this 'fire' be identified as a movement? Or are we rather seeing several, very different movements – emerging at the same time as economic, social and cultural globalization creates new conditions for spreading a religious message?

### Studying IURD: Main Characteristics

Together with Mary Esperandio (see below, pp. 52–64), and in the framework of the research programme on Religion in a Globalized Age (RIGA), I have been studying IURD – beginning in Brazil where its growth has until now been exploding. It is obviously the most rapidly expanding church in this vast country. And now it is spreading to most countries in the world. We are certainly not the only researchers in the field: there is a broad interest in this church – mostly among sociologists and anthropologists in Brazil. It is my impression that most of the research on charismatic movements in Brazil is now focusing on this Igreja Universal. But it is also interesting to observe that most of the research on Pentecostalism in other parts of Latin America hardly mentions IURD. One reason could be that this church falls outside the pattern or established maps of charismatic movements. Another could be that the Brazilian 'markets of research' are different from those in other parts of Latin America.

Is IURD part of the picture Harvey Cox draws in his *Fire from Heaven* and in the introductory chapter to the present volume? Are they Pentecostals? What can the study of this church add to the over-all understanding of Pentecostalism and experiential spiritualities in our age? One could even be tempted to start by asking even more fundamental questions: Is IURD a Pentecostal church; is it Christian at all – or something else?

## Different from Traditional Pentecostalism

Some differences between IURD and mainstream Pentecostalism are striking:

- The 'classic' Pentecostals originated in the USA, in the 'First World'; IURD was born in Brazil, the 'Third World'.
- The Pentecostals built tight communities from below; IURD builds strict hierarchies – from above.
- The Pentecostals built simple assembly houses; IURD now builds shining 'cathedrals of faith'.
- The Pentecostals have councils of elders, and grassroots; IURD has executives, trusts and subsidiary companies.
- The Pentecostals have independent congregations and loose net-works in constant cleavage; IURD has a centralized world organi-zation around a 'pope' and a 'curia' – Edir Macedo and his council of bishops.
- The Pentecostals speak and pray in tongues in the meetings; IURD offers spiritual services and 'help centres'.
- The Pentecostals receive the Holy Spirit as the 'latter rain'; IURD exploits the Holy Spirit for very practical purposes.
- The Pentecostals accepted poverty in this world, waiting for the golden streets in the next; IURD puts its trust in wealth and prosperity in this world – showing little interest in the next world.

## A Religious Transnational Corporation?

To an astonishing extent, IURD has adopted the transnational corpo-ration as a model. On the top there is the Executive Board with the General Director – Edir Macedo. This is where the strategies are developed, and the currents of capital are directed into new offensives and new cathedrals. This is where pastors and bishops are rewarded through being transferred to more promising markets – when they have been found to be effective in building churches and raising money. And this is where the unsuccessful are removed – or sacked. It is also from this top level that orders are issued to every corner of the global corporation: in May 2004, for instance, it was decided that on every altar in every church a great wall of bricks was to be built. It was the wall of Jericho! Every bishop and every pastor was instructed to proclaim that the wall was to be brought down – by faith – in every human being and in every congregation. Behind the wall prosperity was waiting for the faithful.

Every church, regardless of size, has a similar internal design: a rather large podium called 'the Altar'; a pulpit in the middle of the podium; a table with the seven-branch candelabrum; a cross; and above the altar the text: 'Jesus Christ is the Lord'.

Every weekday has a fixed programme of services from early morning to late night. Each church usually offers from five to eight daily services. In these gatherings, the pastor does not beat around the bush in his sermons. He enters directly into the concrete problems of poor people especially.

## Addressing the Needs – Day by Day

*Monday* is for your financial problems. Come with your documents of debt and unpaid bills and lay them on the altar! God will free you from the debt – now or later! By faith!

*Tuesday* is for your illness, headache, pain; for your grief, and your incompetent doctors! Touch the painful place on your body – and God will free you from pain.

*Wednesday* is for your internal strength and spirituality.

*Thursday* is for your family and marriage. Bring along photos and objects from members of the family, lay them on the altar and pray in a loud voice that they shall be saved. Counselling and prayers in IURD will solve the conflicts and reunite your family – in the name of Jesus!

*Friday* is for your liberation – from evil spirits, from sorcery, and witchcraft. This is the day for your liberation from failure, from nightmares, from envy – from all kinds of 'spiritual problems'. Friday is the day to eliminate the Demon who is destroying your life; it is the day to overcome the Devil. In the name of Jesus.

*Saturday* is the day for 'Therapy of love' – for you.

On *Sunday* morning the Holy Spirit comes in the meeting – to you. And Sunday evening is for miracles.

In each one of the meetings, faith is proclaimed as the universal solution. The first breakthrough of the wall of Jericho is faith, the pastor proclaims:

If you are poor – by faith you will be rich.

If you are in debt – by faith you will be free of debts.

If you are sick – by faith you will be healthy.

If you are an alchoholic – by faith you will stop drinking.

If you are addicted to drugs – by faith you will be freed from your addiction.

If your family is in a mess and divorce is threatening – by faith it will be healed.

## Faith as an Instrument

In this way, we can see that IURD preaching of faith is fundamentally instrumental. The superior aim in life is 'prosperity'. The means to obtain this is faith. Faith is a tool to change your life here and now. Contrary to what has often been the case in Christian, and especially Pentecostal preaching, here the aim is not salvation from this world. It is not 'peace with God' or forgiveness of sins or a reign of justice some time in the future. The aim is prosperity here and now, primarily material prosperity. Faith is the remedy. Hence the main motto of IURD, the slogan by which it can be recognized worldwide, is *'pare sofrer'* – stop suffering! Come to IURD with your problems – of debt, of poverty, of pain, of conflict. You will find help. It may take some time to get well, and to reach prosperity. But if you join a 'current' (*corrente*) – a series of meetings over five or seven or ten weeks – a change will certainly occur, IURD promises. A course of 'personal development', in the language of personal counselling, may be the solution. You should be tenacious, not give in. You should come with your problem: if it is a financial problem you should come on Monday – and then the following Mondays. Together with all the others you will pray loudly – all at the same time – like a thunderstorm through the house. And the pastor will pray to deliver you from all your financial worries. Then you can also show your faith through offering. You should pay your tithe – and pay more – to show that you have strong faith. The logic is simple and compelling: the money you pay to the church is the proof of your faith.

And you experience being together with other people with the same problem. The Monday meetings of IURD are sometimes called the 'General Assembly of Employers'. Often in these meetings you will get some kind of object or symbol, as an advance of the prosperity to come. It may be, for instance, a key made of thick paper – to unlock your 'jail of debt'. After a few Mondays you will see that the debt is diminishing. And after ten weeks your finances will be OK. If they are not, the cause could be lack of faith. But then you should only start again – in faith – and pay. Continuously paying money – sacrifice – is presented as the fundamental expression of faith.

Or, say you have a terrible migraine, and can't afford to go to the doctor, or experience that doctors can't help you. Tuesday is your day. You will get a programme. You pay tithe and more every Tuesday. After six Tuesdays the pain will be gone, the pastor promises. And if it is not, you can start on a new 'current'. Investing more money, you show more faith – and then prosperity will come.

Or you get a small bag with salt – to place under your pillow. Or a tiny jar with water from the Sea of Gennesaret. Or a bottle of holy water – useful for many things. Every week you give money to God. And week by week you will see that your problems are being solved.


## Struggling against Evil

What is the ultimate root of all these problems, according to IURD? It is evil, personified in devils, spirits, and the Devil. As we saw, Friday is the day for the decisive confrontation with the Devil. Now is the time to get everything out of your body and soul – all the evil that keeps you down in misery, slavery, poverty and misfortune. The assistants wander around in the huge hall of the church, staring with suspicion at the participants, place one hand on the head and the other hand on the neck, pray and shout that the evil spirit must leave: Out – right now! If evil is seriously resisting, not wanting to leave the body of the possessed, then she or he is taken to the altar. Now there will be a brawl, a fight – a bodily fight – between the pastor and the spirit – or even with the Devil himself – while the assembly supports the pastor by shouting and praying. Everybody is asked to place their hands on their heads, look to the cross in the ceiling, and pray loudly. While the pastor roars: Out! Out! And finally – with loud screams – the Demon lets the person out of his grip. The obsessed is freed. Applause flows towards the altar. Applause for Jesus!

Now everybody is smiling, embracing each other: We have conquered the Devil! In IURD churches in Africa the assembly dances: everybody, a waving ocean of happy people. Afterwards people go home – perhaps to a small room in a filthy street, a tiny hut open to wind and weather, or a shack of wooden pieces and tin and cardboard – knowing within themselves that they have overcome Satan. Now life will change!

### Religious Experience

What is the pull? What brings millions of people to the temples of IURD? Without doubt, the answer must be the religious experience. Interestingly, when compared with traditional Pentecostalism, religious experience in IURD is not primarily that the Holy Spirit touches your tongue. Nor is it, as in mainstream historical churches, that you feel God's forgiveness, or good moments in silent company with God. The religious experience is receiving the pastor's convincing promise of food on the table, money in the purse, a head without drugs, a body without pain, a family without war, a full-time, well-paid job. All this will be yours, perhaps today or tomorrow, certainly tomorrow. That is the pastor's promise. All you need is to show your faith.

In this way the believer may leave burdens behind, feeling uplifted by the music, the pastor and the preaching. He or she may regain faith in himself or herself – because she feels that the faith comes from God, and gives strength and courage. There is a regenerative moment: now it is time to apply for a job, drop the bottle, and convince the husband or wife to be converted. Now is the time to begin a new life. Empowered by the Holy Spirit!

### The Role of Theology

What kind of theology forms the basis of IURD? At first, the Bible was said be the only foundation, sufficiently clear in itself. But related to the missionary outreach, the globalization of IURD, Edir Macedo edited three small books entitled *The Doctrine of the Universal Church*. Their content is not very impressive. Theology is not the strong point of IURD. In general, Edir Macedo and IURD draw on various elements from other charismatic movements – on themes such as exorcism, proclamation of faith, and the role of prosperity. Kenneth Hagin's 'proclaiming of prosperity' is well known. And books from Tuzla and other charismatic centres in the USA are to be found in the shelves of the bookstores of IURD. You don't find many separate original elements in the preaching of IURD, either. The originality of IURD lies more in the composition of the elements – the way it exploits the elements of faith, the entirety of the presentation. This is what, in terms of its numerical growth, obviously 'works'.

## The Role of Money

But IURD is also an enormous money machine. The worldwide apparatus and the huge new temples bear witness to considerable financial success. Where does the money come from? The church is certainly not being sponsored by the CIA as old conspiracy theories would be likely to claim. The money generally comes from poor people. As I have shown, IURD methods of raising money are not particularly sympathetic. Everybody is told that they should pay tithe. If you need certain services, concerning health or economy for example, you have to pay more, in order to prove your faith.

At some meetings in Brazil money collection was the theme three times during the service. Envelopes are always distributed – for money today or the next day – and the participants are reminded of the bank account number. And the pastor proclaims again and again that money is the expression of faith, the proof of faith. Offering money is the individual answer to the collective appeal. People are even told that they should offer more than they can afford. In this way they can 'test God' – that he really is paying back more than he receives (cf. Malachi 3.10).

## Crossing Frontiers

IURD is crossing frontiers. In Johannesburg the minibuses from most parts of the city fill up the Plain Street. At 6 o'clock in the morning every work day, thousands walk up the stairs and enter between the heavy columns into the Cathedral of Faith to attend the first service and shout to God that this day will be better than yesterday, that on this day, the good life will begin. Then they go to their work, their shop, their factory, their sales table on the sidewalk. Or they go to their 'nothing' – to the job that God soon will give them – in faith.

The new temples are magnificent, with their stained-glass pictures in the windows, the enormous cross in the ceiling in stained glass in many colors – the huge pulpit on the altar – and the words 'Jesus

Christ is the Lord', in Johannesburg written in three languages. The pastor is always dressed elegantly – white shirt with tie, black trousers. The assistants too look good. There are perhaps twenty, fifty of them: mostly young people – women in white blouses, blue skirts matching the scarf with IURD sign – the dove in the heart. They look so correct, so clean, so nice, that they could just as easily be working in the reception lobby in a financial firm on Fifth Avenue in New York. This, too, is a sign and a foretaste of a better life to come.

IURD is also present in New York. Not on Fifth Avenue, but just a few miles away from it – in Lower Brooklyn. Here an IURD congregation gathers in a small room for only about fifty persons, a former shop. A pastor and thirty persons, mostly women, are present. They are all black, poorly dressed, with downtrodden shoes. Here too, they shout and scream their pain to God: 'I don't accept this poverty! I don't accept my misery! God, where are you? Why are you hiding?'

## The 'Curia' of *Igreja Universal*

Like a Vatican the 'curia' of '*bispos*' around Edir Macedo guards the universal – that is, global – church. And Macedo's message is communicated worldwide every week in *Folha Universal*, which is the main IURD organ, printed in more than a million copies in Brazil, and reproduced in the smaller Folhas around the world where IURD is operating. His voice is heard from hundreds of radio transmitters – and televisions – on hired time or stations that IURD has bought or built. For the converts of IURD Macedo is close at hand with his message day after day – on radio, TV, Internet – and in the temples. And he issues decrees – without any opposition. As for instance in 2003, when he declared that every member elected to a political assembly in Brazil, the Senate and Deputy Chamber, should renounce their titles as pastor or *bispo*. Even his cousin Crivela had to accept it.

## IURD as a Neoliberal Religiosity?

Are there elements of 'neoliberalism' in IURD? Could we see global capitalism reflected in the profile of this church? There are several ways in which the organization, structure and strategies of IURD seem to be shaped by models from the universe of the globalized economy.

The system is utterly *hierarchical*: from the assistants – who do most of the boring jobs such as cleaning and washing without payment –

through to the pastors and bishops, and up to Macedo himself. The pastors and bishops are moved around – one year here, two years there – some time in Africa, later in Portugal. Tight bonds between pastor and community are not allowed to develop. The pastor is dependent on the bishop above – not the congregation below.

Those who come to IURD are more like *consumers* or *customers* than members of a community. The collective responsibility lies in the hierarchy not at the grassroots. Those who come and are helped are expected to pay. The most important bond to the church is the tithe, and the backbone of the organization is the *dizimistas* – those who pay tithe. It seems that people remain in the church, not because of a warm community, but because they experience that the church gives answers to their quite earthly problems; it offers protection and hope.

The system of IURD works in a way like a market system of *buying and selling services*. And, as we have seen, the aim of life as presented by IURD is largely to *obtain economic success*. In this way, it seems to me that the values of neoliberalism are very close to the values of IURD. As there are economic 'tigers' operating in the globalized economic world, it is tempting to see IURD as a 'tiger' partly in the same jungle. It is adapted to this jungle and proposes an answer to those overthrown by larger beasts in this jungle of globalized market economy – persons isolated in the loneliness of individualism in a global economic culture that is crushing and splitting up the values of solidarity.

## Survival in a Merciless Society

I have followed more than fifty services of IURD on four continents. I have read numerous books, magazines, articles, brochures. I have listened to radio programmes, and had conversations with pastors and ordinary visitors. It struck me one day: There is a word I have never heard. I cannot remember that I have heard the words: 'Love thy neighbour'. I have never heard it from the altar. Nor have I seen it in IURD written material. Salvation for the family? Yes, but apparently not for the neighbour – our co-wanderer on this earth. Not to mention 'Love your enemy'. I cannot remember having heard the words 'grace' or 'mercy' either – except in the final formal blessing of the service.

Perhaps we are at a crucial point here: IURD is a strategy for survival in a society without mercy. The point is to survive – to manage life – in a society where everyone must compete in order to acquire scarce and necessary benefits. This is what it is all about: to survive –

with God's help. The neighbour will have to help himself. IURD thus offers a straw for survival for the individual in the competitive privatized and liberalized society where everybody has to care for themselves. Here there is hardly room for grace and love of neighbour. The priority is to survive – save oneself.

A consequence of the globalized economy is *migration*. IURD seems to follow the emigrants – offering a faith to marginalized immigrants across the globe. Also in this sense, IURD seems to offer a faith adapted to globalized capitalism, increasing its own following (and income) by offering an individual answer to the challenge and damaging effects of global capitalism. And yet, IURD does not offer any visible source of resistance to this global capitalism.

You find IURD in Bergen Street in Brooklyn among the Spanish-speaking immigrants, in the houses where the language earlier was Norwegian. You find IURD in Brixton in London – where the races clashed some years ago. You find IURD in Paris among the immigrants from black, francophone Africa. You find IURD in Tokyo – helping poor Japanese returning to Japan from the misfortune of a generation in Brazil, and discriminated against by the 'traditional' Japanese. And you find IURD almost everywhere where there is immigration from Portugal – marginalized immigrants from the most marginalized country in western Europe. IURD takes root among those who have lost their roots.

The atmosphere, the environment and the setting of IURD is different from country to country, although the weekly programme is the same all over the world. But this programme is a frame: within this frame there is room for differences and variations in accordance with the local culture and tradition. In Brazil and South Africa the evil spirits have names, for instance: names from traditional religions. In New York the evil spirits don't have such a clear anthropomorphic or demonic expression: the pastor speaks more about headache, economic debacle, and sickness – and less about the demons behind.

IURD expresses itself in modernity. *Modern technology* makes its establishment and expansion possible through hundreds of radio and TV transmitters. The programmes of Record, the third largest TV network in Brazil, are transmitted to Angola and Mozambique. The liberalization of the finance markets opens for systematic investment in communications to the best markets. And the internet is important too for drawing people to the nearest church. IURD is crossing borders – by radio, TV, internet, travelling pastors and bishops, and through economic transactions. IURD is a transnational religion.

But just as IURD makes use of the internet it also carries pre-modern traits or elements: spirits and gods in old African religion get a new important role as images of the enemies of Jesus, and enemies of prosperity. As we have seen, magic on a broad scale enters into the practice: objects are distributed in the meetings as amulets. When placed under the pillow they protect against evil spirits. Plastic bags around your feet keep the Devil away during the meeting. The layer of traditional African religion – hidden somewhere below the Christianity imported by the missionaries – wakes up to new life under the exorcisms of IURD.

The church is urban in its social setting, but religious ideas from the countryside are strongly present. In IURD the old and the new, the pre-modern and the modern are mixed together to form a religious postmodernity.

Yet it is more the similarities that strike me, when following IURD across borders, than the differences. When the great church in Johannesburg was brimming over with ecstasy and six obsessed persons were brought to the altar to fight with the assistants and pastors on the altar, it struck me that I had seen this before, exactly this scene. I had seen it in Brazil, somewhat better off economically, but in this scene similar to South Africa. The two strongest countries on each continent, with much common history of slave trafficking and racial conflict. The spirits who wake up in IURD's temples in South Africa had long ago followed the goddess of the ocean, Iemanja, over the South Atlantic. And now they meet in IURD – on both sides of the ocean.

## Political Influence?

Does IURD have any political influence? Space prevents a thorough analysis of the subject here. And it is difficult to present a general picture. We have to deal briefly with curious paradoxes. In Portugal IURD attempted to establish a party – 'Partido da Gente' – which turned out to be a huge fiasco. In Angola it seems that IURD was supporting Unita and their allies in the war against MPLA. In South Africa, IURD was established just at the time apartheid was crumbling and thus avoided the political burden which many Pentecostal churches had to carry due to their weak stand against apartheid.

What about Brazil? In the elections that made the leftist candidate Luis Ignacio Lula da Silva president, leading IURD personalities in fact voted for Lula in the second round – while they had condemned him more or less as a demon four years before. The leaders of the older and even larger Pentecostal church Assembleias de Deus voted for the conservative candidate Jose Serra.

But I was really surprised when I heard about Nova Canaã ('The New Canaan') in Bahia. It is a large *hacienda* which IURD has bought to give land to poor agricultural labourers and a help to poor children – in a dry, almost desert area. The basic idea seems to bear distant parallels with the radical and strong landless movement (MST): Land to the landless! This even turned out to be the best card of IURD's Marcelo Crivella in elections. He was elected senator with no fewer than 3 million votes from the State of Rio de Janeiro. Solidarity and collective support – building a new institution with collective values in the desert: could this be another paradox in IURD?

In London I found a 'help centre' – helping poor people and migrants with work, immigration papers, and so on. The same thing in Johannesburg: those who could not buy a newspaper or who were illiterate could come and get help to read job advertisements, and get clothes presentable for a job interview. One possible explanation could be that as IURD becomes strong in a country, the social problems become so pressing that the question of social and economic reform becomes imminent: IURD cannot stand aloof. During the weeks of the election campaign in Brazil 2003 every service of IURD ended with presentation of 'our candidates' – in big pictures rolling behind the altar. In other words, IURD's members and friends got a very clear message of how to vote. The Folha Universal in fact contains much social critique, although it is rather empty of proposals and political demands in the social area.

In any case, IURD involvement in – or withdrawal from – politics is relevant. Many would maintain that the present government, as indeed any government in Brazil, can only establish a stable rule if they get at least some support from the 'evangelicals' – and especially from IURD.

# 4. Globalization and Subjectivity:
## A Reflection on the 'Universal Church of the Kingdom of God' in a Perspective Drawn from Psychology of Religion

MARY RUTE GOMES ESPERANDIO

Born as one of the youngest daughters of postmodernity, she is only in her late twenties. She is Brazilian, attractive, and has an incredible capacity to adapt to various cultures. Bearer of an overwhelming self-esteem and courage, she disregards boundaries and does not mind being excluded, or contrasted to others. Instead, she prides herself in peculiarity, since it confirms her singularity and power. She is undoubtedly prosperous and successful and defies all obstacles to fulfilling the destination announced by her name: Igreja Universal do Reino de Deus (IURD) – The Universal Church of the Kingdom of God. The global planet is its limit.

Within the context of the theme for this book, IURD is itself a rich subject of study, with numerous possible approaches. Berge Furre has already presented this church, some of its basic characteristics, developments and global outreach. I would like to take a closer look at this phenomenon from a perspective drawn from the psychology of religion. Some of the questions in my mind are the following: Why has this church been so remarkably successful and able to expand to such a great extent? What kinds of subjectivity and religiosity are produced in a church with such characteristics? What consequences can be foreseen as a result of this type of subjectivity production?

This chapter is divided into two parts. IURD clearly represents a case of what Harvey Cox has called 'experiential spirituality'. Experiences and emotions play a central part in its kind of religiosity. In the first part of my chapter, then, I present IURD from a quite personal, experiential perspective, describing one of their meetings in Brazil with a view also to my own feelings when participating in their worship. I will also be adding two small descriptions of meetings in other countries. In the second part, I will present a reflection on the character of this particular church from the perspective of psychology of religion, particularly seeing it in its interrelationship with the prevailing values of present-day globalized capitalism, and with an emphasis on the way in which it contributes to the process of subjectivity production in this particular context.

## Experiencing IURD Worship

We begin in Brazil. This is IURD's place of birth. It is 7.30 p.m., 8 November 2002, an ordinary Friday in Porto Alegre, in the south of Brazil. Today's theme is 'liberation'. Around four thousand people are present in the enormous IURD Cathedral of Faith. The assistants run among the seats handing out some kind of white 'protection' supposed to be worn on our feet. The protection is called the 'circle of deity'. This circle will 'cleanse' and 'protect' us. The evil withdrawn from the body will be concentrated in the circle. The foot protection will be given to the pastors or assistants at the end of the meeting, and, later on, be burned.

Having all put on the 'circle of deity', we form a big circle around the inside of the temple. It takes a while; people, holding hands, struggle for room. Then the pastor starts praying. He names several spirits from Afro-Brazilian cults, and orders these demons to manifest themselves right there, 'in the name of Jesus'. The prayer lasts for a long time. Most of the participants pray together in a loud voice. In the meantime, pastors and assistants walk around the great circle, observing with 'clinical eye', seeking to identify demons that are about to manifest themselves.

The environment is intensely emotional. I feel some kind of chill running through my body. The pastor's loud prayer through the microphone is mixed with the sounds of the fervent prayers of the devoted, who order the demons out of their bodies and affirm their victory in the name of Jesus. There is an impressive power of collectivity at work.

The spiritual assistants (*obreiros*) wander around with attentive eyes. I feel my face stiffen: my eyes tightly closed and my forehead wrinkled, evidencing the tension of the muscles. I feel nervous, and get goose-bumps. Apparently, the way I look draws the attention of the assistants: they believe they have found a person with demons to be expelled. They approach me, and my tension increases. They seem to have no doubt that there are demons inside me. The *obreiro* presses my forehead with one of his hands, and with the other he holds the nape of my neck tightly. Forcing my body to move in a circle, he commands the manifestation of the demon, which is assumed to be *Pombagira* or one of the other deities from Afro-Brazilian religion.

But there is no demon being manifested. Instead I feel an intense desire to laugh; this is a ridiculous situation to me. A sarcastic and nervous laughter wants to come out but I hold myself together: such laughter would probably be interpreted as another diabolical manifestation. The assistant screams into my ear: 'Get out in the name of Jesus, get out, get out!' When the prayer is finished, I am really relieved, although not in the sense that IURD would have it. The relief does not come from the soul, but from the withdrawal of the pressure of having someone yelling at my ear. This relief does not last long, however, since other assistants seem to agree that there are still demons inside me. I feel the expression on my face becoming more and more tense.

As I show more anxiety, the chances of my having evil spirits in me seem even greater to the pastoral assistants. I am exorcised three more times. Difficult demon, does not want to manifest . . . Now the pastor shouts: 'There are still hidden demons here! There are still hidden demons here!'

The tension increases. If I am in any way frightened, it would be of the thought that the assistants could produce a demon in me. I wonder how other persons in the room feel, persons with a stronger faith and confidence in the words of the pastor: 'Those of you who have participated in religious cults, those who have used objects of Afro-religions, those who have eaten food offered to demons, those who have done any kind of witchcraft or have been a victim of witchcraft . . .' The pastor goes on and on with a long list of possible ways in which the demons could have entered someone's body. There are so many possibilities! Hardly anyone escapes from suffering the great, evil power of the demons.

Finally the pastor asks for silence. The period of strong tension has lasted for thirty minutes. Now, there are enough demons manifested. Nine women possessed by demons are taken to the platform. The pastor asks the rest of us to return to our seats.

At this moment an exorcism process starts at the platform. The pastor chooses one of the possessed women to be interviewed. We can all hear how the demon growls, foams and shivers. The woman's body is bent and her hands are behind her. The assistant remains close to her, giving her support. The congregation is now extremely tense, and everyone is invited to participate in this battle against the Devil. We all shout in order to expel the demon: 'Burn, burn, burn . . . !' The battle lasts for a long time. When the demon who had possessed the woman has been shouted to, even interviewed, and then expelled, her husband is exorcised too. Three times the public is asked to hold hands forming a great chain and shouting to the demon: 'Burn . . . burn . . . burn . . .'

The environment is still tense. People pray simultaneously, their arms stretching out in the woman's direction and commanding the devil to get out. After almost an hour of intense battle, the possessed woman kneels down and finally says, in Spanish, what the pastor had ordered: 'I am defeated in the name of Jesus.' The public is thrilled, and they clap their hands vibrantly.

The woman is interviewed again and speaks in a clear Portuguese, with a calm voice. She claims to feel as if she was just waking from a deep sleep and she feels fine. She tells about pains in her body that she used to feel. Now she does not feel them any more. The pastor has the woman and her husband publicly reconciled. He tells her to look in her husband's eyes and say that she loves him. The woman says to her husband: 'I love you.' The pastor asks them to kiss for everyone to see. Great applause – for the couple, and for Jesus.

The pastor now speaks about the power of the Devil and assures us how hard it is to win this spiritual battle. Therefore, he says, it is so important to be with God and attend church.

Then it is time for tithing and offering. The assistants also distribute invitations for coming campaigns. New offering envelopes are handed out, after three pastors have lain over the envelopes and prayed. The envelopes are distributed according to a hierarchy: first for those who commit themselves to give R$100 (around US$35). Then for those who will give R$50, R$20, R$10 and finally R$5 (which is around 2 dollars). The pastor tells the people to pass the envelope over their bodies, and to do this repeatedly during the coming week, especially on places where they believe there is some kind of harm or pain. According to the pastor, the envelopes are anointed by the sweat from the bodies of the three pastors that lay over them. In a similar manner, insoles to be used inside the shoes until Sunday are also distributed. People should bring these back for the Sunday meeting. Another offering is collected. This time the purpose of the offering is that God should open doors for the person offering his or her gift.

The meeting ends with one final request to offer. We are asked to give everything we have at the moment. We are called to hand in our offerings passing through a great wide wooden door. In fact, everyone can pass through the door, even those who are not giving anything in this particular offering. Some people touch the upper part of the wooden door. Before passing through the door all of us return the 'circle of deity' to the assistants and pastors.

We leave Brazil and arrive in Europe. We are in Lisbon, Portugal, at Alameda Don Afonso Henriques, 35, the former cinema Cine Império. Around 2,000 people are present here. It is a Monday. We are attending the so-called 'Meeting of Prosperity' or 'Congress of Businesspeople'. The bishop runs the meeting with impressive authority, showing extreme self-confidence. He shouts: 'If a person does what I tell her to, this person will be prosperous. I will also cure this person. I will pray and you will be cured and will be a prosperous person with my prayer.'

He then asks the people to come forward to the altar and take the envelopes to 'plant their seed'. The bishop insists: 'If you want money, you must plant money. Do not put a potato in the envelope because that is not what you wish for. You want money, don't you? So, plant money!' The envelopes are to be returned on the same day the following week. The bishop assures us: 'The greatest expression of faith is when somebody's pocket is touched. The church is persecuted because it requests offerings. But God does not need your money. Your money shows your faith; it shows that your heart is not set on money. People are saved with your money.'

Next week's offering should be at least 5 euros. 'But in the name of Jesus, you will give much more; you will double your offering. Do not give the minimum offering if you can give more. The greatest poverty is to have poverty in your mind. Do not think that you are poor, that you cannot give much. Think big and you will be big. If you don't have money, make an extra effort, sell something in order to be able to give, and give your best.'

We leave Europe and head to the United States of America. Queens: a Hispanic area, in New York. The huge and comfortable temple, with a capacity of 600 people, is crowded. It is a Sunday morning. The 10 o'clock meeting is considered the most important and lasts about two hours. I will not describe the whole meeting. I wish only to mention some words used in the bishop's speech.

After a long period of simultaneous praying where everyone speaks at the same time, crying a lot and demanding prosperity and a solution for all problems from God, the bishop preaches about the difference between natural and supernatural faith. He emphasizes that super-natural faith is the kind that leads to victory, to prosperity, to success, to cure, to the solution to everything, and ultimately to happiness. In the middle of his preaching he explains the importance of attending the Monday meetings. He claims that those meetings are not meant for everyone. They are only for those people who wish to progress, to prosper and to become successful.

He makes it clear that 'it is not a sin to be ambitious; for the Bible teaches that it is good to have ambition'. Therefore, those who wish to achieve something must attend church on Mondays. He also reminds everyone that, 'in order to keep what someone has achieved, it is necessary to be faithful and obedient to what the Bible teaches: to be a son of God and have spiritual authority'. He explains that the church will teach people how to become prosperous and to handle money successfully, becoming competent investors and, thus, making more money.

## IURD as a Response to the Needs of People Affected by Globalization

This experiential approach to worship in IURD congregations in Brazil and beyond calls for a critical reflection from the perspective of the psychology of religion. Interestingly, although there is much research on IURD, this perspective has not been pursued in any depth, to my knowledge. In fact, psychology of religion is not a strong discipline at all in Brazil, despite its being known as a very 'religious' country. The religious dimension neglected by psychology has left a gap on a theoretical level as well as on a practical level. But one could say that in praxis, IURD has filled this gap. On their television pro-grammes people continuously give testimonies about IURD 'Spiritual Therapy' and of how much this therapy has changed their lives, making them happier. One of the most watched programmes is named *Speak, and I Will Listen to You!* On Saturdays IURD offers the 'Therapy of Love'.

Psychology of religion focuses on the study of the religious dimen-sion of human beings, that is, what the human being does with religion and what religion does with (and in) the human being. It is concerned with the analysis and understanding of the religious element present in the processes of subjectivity production. This means that it concen-trates its efforts on comprehending the impact, the effects and the role of religion in human behaviour regarding the individual and/or social dimensions.

IURD often presents itself as a 'Centre of Spiritual Help' or a 'Centre of Collective Help'. What kind of help does it offer? It offers help in dealing with all kinds of suffering experienced by people today: depression, panic syndrome, headaches, anxiety, unemployment, loneliness, alcoholism, drugs, family problems, debts and even serious diseases, such as cancer and HIV/Aids.[1] These are all global sufferings and are not particular to countries less favoured by the process of economic globalization, although obviously these countries experience the consequences to a greater level, such as increasing unemployment, bankruptcy of small businesses and problems with debts and legal processes.

To an increasing amount of people the globalized world is a world of constant struggle for survival, a world in which there does not seem to be room for everyone. 'The winner takes it all' seems to be the order of the day. In such a world interpersonal relationships become competitive and individualistic. There is a constant feeling of mutual threat. There is also a constant feeling of the need to protect oneself from the others. The feeling of loneliness becomes common. The level of stress, anxiety, uncertainty about the future is developed to a higher level. Such diseases as panic syndrome and some kinds of phobia become more and more frequent, and the number of people with depression increases.

In such a world IURD promises happiness. It draws people to the meetings through the slogan 'The Meeting of Happiness'. Many of the temples around the world exhibit the motto 'Stop Suffering'. The church assures that 'after being aided, those who really seek the presence of God change their behaviour towards life and find a solution for all their problems. They can, finally, find happiness . . .' In this context it is to be noted that IURD centres are open every day, all day long. Depending on the country, three to seven meetings are held each day.

As a devoted mother who gives her baby a sense of completeness, IURD constitutes itself as an employment agency, a business consultant, a general hospital, a psychiatric hospital, an attorney's office, and a psychotherapy clinic, all at the same time. It even plays the roles of a travel agency offering tours to the Holy Land, and a matrimonial agency. In other words, it presents itself as a multifunctional space, which offers services to those who suffer, flavoured with a religious diversity taken from Afro-religions, Catholicism, Protestantism,

Pentecostalism, and the New Age 'non-religion'.[2] This, in my view, is the way IURD positions itself as an object of desire, as a 'dream of consumption' which will fulfil what is missing in a person. Only this church may bring a sense of happiness, the ultimate sense of life. An idealistic transferring relationship is established: 'It has all the happiness and power that I need.'

Where can we find this 'complete object', this 'dream come true'? Addresses and telephone numbers of Centres located in every Brazilian state, Europe, South America, Central America, Africa, Asia and North America are available on the internet. IURD is present in almost 80 countries, with around 40,000 pastors all over the world.

Why has IURD become such a great force of expression and expansion? What kinds of subjectivity and religiosity are produced in a church with such characteristics? In my view, it is necessary to look at the interrelationship between the kind of religiosity promoted by IURD and the present globalized capitalism. In doing so, I offer the following tentative observations.

## IURD and the Spirit of Globalized Capitalism

IURD emphasizes the development of a 'speculative spirit' with the purpose of attaining financial-economic success. The 'Congress of Businesspeople' (Monday meetings, see above, p. 57) promotes the desire to have one's own business. The idea that the person's worth is not in what s/he *is* (including ideals and character) but in what the person *possesses* is thus reinforced. This reveals that the human ideal propagated is the one with a greater capacity for consuming. The more a person is capable of consuming, the greater the sensation/illusion of being adapted to the external world. The happiness sought is intimately connected to the capacity for consumption and to a person's self-perception: 'I consume, therefore I exist.'

Success and prosperity are the results of one's own effort. They come from exercising an individual faith. Participation in meetings with a great number of people has an effect of mirroring and recognition, rather than the promotion of collectivity. The other person present in the meeting is necessary only as a mirror for me, where I recognize myself, but with whom I do not establish any significant relationship. What is sought is thus a state of completeness without the necessity of another person as an alterity, as an interacting being. One merely sees into another person (and consequently reassures the idea) that s/he 'has rights and must demand them from God'.

This role of mirroring enables an extraordinary sort of practice that could be called 'Mass Therapy'. The therapeutical practice common in IURD centres is one that treats everyone as a great mass. In this sense, it can be seen as being in accordance with the capitalist slogan 'Time is money'. Time and space are optimized. The same solution is offered for all kinds of sufferings. The technique used is not at all focused on individualized listening, although some people do seek an individualized assistance. No matter what the problem is, the solution is the same for all people. Although IURD meetings gather a great number of people, there is no group formation process taking place, since interpersonal exchanges are not observed. The praxis in Spiritual Help Centres reveals an appropriation of different therapeutic techniques: cognitive therapy, psychodrama, group therapy, systemic therapy. But in IURD context these techniques are 'blessed'; they operate with the power of faith. In addition to this, they set up a sort of predominantly magical thought produced mainly through the usage of magical objects, considered magical because they are anointed. The results are amazing, in the sense that the mirroring elements are activated and people become dependent on the system. Yet, if there is no 'I' in the mass therapy, how is it that one finds such strong individualism?

I suppose the 'I' who disappears in the mass finds a form of expression through the offerings of sacrifice (as well as through 'Positive Confession'[3]). The person who comes to the Centres is frail and vulnerable, often feeling worthless, with low self-esteem, low self-confidence and with a wounded narcissism. When the church presents the sacrifice as a condition for prosperity and happiness, the person must let go of a passive attitude towards suffering and make a 'self-investment'. This process involves a strong decision. The greater the offering of sacrifice, the greater the profit. Here, the act of self-sacrifice does not mean resignation. On the contrary, when the person gives more than he/she possesses, he/she is overestimating him/herself. So, a frail and worthless person leaps to a status of worth, since he/she is making a self-investment.

This changes the way the person stands before God to whom the sacrifice is made. The prayer request now includes an additional value, a monetary value. It can be said that money is what identifies persons in a capitalistic society. 'Those who have money have power.' When money, the highest symbol of value in this context, is added to being, the feeling of worthlessness is changed into a feeling of power. The person feels more worthy of obtaining something from an Almighty Being.

This process of becoming 'more' of a person (by adding money) through the offering of sacrifice has an immediate effect on the person's subjectivity. It has an effect of personal empowerment. The 'I' that seemed to disappear in the mass reoccurs, or meets him/herself again in the act of sacrifice. However, this meeting now takes place with a transformed self due to the relation established, through the sacrifice, with the almighty God, who 'certainly' will answer the person's request.

The certainty, interpreted as faith, is conditional on the effectiveness of the sacrifice. The feeling of empowerment towards life and sufferings, which takes place in a person, proves the effectiveness of the technology of sacrifice. This can be observed through a great number of personal testimonies. This whole process reinforces the idea that everything depends on the individual person. The group together, the collectivity as such, will not cause social or environmental changes. It all depends on individual faith and personal effort. In this way a positive attitude towards sufferings is 'all' that it takes. Sacrificing is enough. A kind of sacrificial ethics is thus produced: Do you have financial problems? You should sacrifice on Mondays! Health or emotional problems? Sacrifice on Tuesdays!

The person tends to connect with archaic narcissistic elements more easily, because of the vulnerability of self resulting from what he/she has suffered. As a part of IURD Spiritual Therapy, it is common to see people in the meetings express themselves in a childish way. A frequent scene is people stamping their feet on the floor, punching in the air and shouting to God 'I don't accept poverty . . . I don't accept this . . . I don't accept that . . . I am determined to be victorious!' It is a typical reaction of a child infuriated with the limits imposed by the external world. This represents a paradox. By verbally expressing the resistance to an unacceptable life condition, vulnerability is recognized and the possibility of recreating internal and external reality takes place. Meanwhile, the recognized uneasiness is repelled. As the person says 'I don't accept . . .', this expresses resistance, nonconformity, a potential reality change. As this is stated publicly, in a loud voice, with the whole group, it also has the power of constituting the person itself. As Lacan reminds us, 'the word is essentially the means to be recognized' (Lacan, 1996: 273). Here, the paradox is revealed. Through 'positive confession' the discontentment is recognized, and it is, actually, the potentiality to create a new reality.

However, this power of desire for recreating is captured by the dominant process of subjectivation and leads to an adjustment of the subjectivity of capitalistic values, the ones socially diffused. The discontentment, which is the potential for recreation, is exorcised by IURD, since it is considered evil. At the same time, however, the sense of omnipotence and grandiosity of self is strengthened (narcissism). The person becomes potent to face concrete sufferings of life today, such as diseases, unemployment or drug addiction.

Why do those words become so effective and (together with the offerings of sacrifice) mark progress in the person's existence? Lacan replies that the verbalization has a creating function and bears the thing itself (Lacan, 1996: 275). Paraphrasing this author, one could state that 'the ultimate sense of what the person says before God is the person's existential relation towards the object of desire' (Lacan, 1996: 276).[4]

It is frequently stated that we are living in an 'Era of Pleasure' in which feelings of guilt have no room. In this era salvation is a synonym of prosperity, a feeling of well-being, and is supposed to be experienced here and now, not in a distant future or after death. In this sense, there is no room for guilt, discontentment or any kind of suffering. Apparently it is not nice to suffer. In the same way that medical pills and drugs promote an anaesthetization of pain and provide pleasure, at IURD we enter into a universe of sensations in the search for pleasure and exorcism of evil and suffering, in a public space of catharsis. In the IURD universe, suffering in the world is not a result of human action. There is no personal responsibility for this; suffering is not the result of one's own failure or mistakes. Evil and suffering have an external cause. They are caused by demons, evil spirits, witchcraft, entities of an invisible dimension that possess people's bodies and minds. Therefore, there is a great need to exorcise evil. Evil is external to the person.

## Final Considerations

Many people who attend IURD eagerly testify that they have become happy: 'I had a very bad life, with depression, was addicted to drugs, had debts, was unemployed, family problems . . . and when I came to IURD and did what the pastor told me, and when I offered sacrifices, everything changed. Today I have my own business, I have a brand new car, get along with my family, I'm happy.'

When IURD states a pluralism of truths and a cultural and religious diversity, it goes further than constituting itself as one more among several existent truths in the market, it introduces itself as 'the' truth, since it embodies the speech of others. In a world of uncertainties and a deep feeling of insecurity, IURD offers certainty, security and the feeling of well-being: a return to a primitive narcissistic state of completeness and total absence of pain.

'I believe IURD is the last door for people to open their eyes to life.'[5] This statement confirms that part of IURD's success is due to the fact that it produces a sort of religiosity that fulfils certain human necessities contemporaneously. Undoubtedly, it transforms the lives of many people who are suffering. The 'theology of prosperity', as Bobsin well puts it, 'provides the excluded people with symbolic means which present some effectiveness in the struggle for survival' (Bobsin, 1995: 36).

IURD evidences a typically postmodern religious production, well adapted to neoliberal values: syncretistic, flexible; individualistic; narcissistic, seeking well-being and happiness at any price; without a boundary between sacred and profane; emphasizing the person's internal resources and minimizing the necessity of interaction. This last characteristic brings important consequences in relation to the constitution of subjectivity, which becomes more individualistic, and in relation to society, which becomes bereft of solidarity. Its ambiguous discourse 'con-fuses' itself with the market, in a double movement of secularizing religion, making it banal and sacralizing the market, elevating it to a condition of 'ultimate validity'.

Despite all that, it is also a religion that involves itself with suffering, and around the world, keeps its doors open almost 24 hours a day, every day, prompting the minimizing of suffering and making people more potent towards life. Does it take advantage of human suffering? Apparently, yes. Does it promote the person's simple adjustment towards life? Several psychotherapies are also accused of that. Is it alienating? Other Christian religions are too.

Kohut calls our attention to the role of religion as 'supporter of self' (Kohut, 1988: 232). In this sense, IURD finds space connecting to the human narcissistic elements, which seeks completeness, satisfaction and well-being. The spirits of the globalized world, which are also present at IURD, could be named Narcissus and Dionysus. The Holy Spirit, then, seems to be in a 'terminal phase'.

Religion as a survival strategy and technology of subjectivity adjustment to the status quo: Is this *all* a contemporary subject could invent in terms of religiosity in a globalized age?

*Notes*

1  www2.arcauniversal.com.br/arcanews/integra.jsp?cod=23959&codcanal=36 Accessed on 20 April 2004.

2  What about education, is that offered too? Interestingly, the answer seems to be no. Although always encouraged 'to use your intelligence', in the IURD preaching you are simply taught 'to put your faith to work'.

3  Positive Confession 'literally refers to bringing to existence what we declare with our mouths' – *Dictionary of Pentecostal and Charismatic Movements* (Romero, 1993: 6)

4  He states: 'the ultimate sense of what the person says before the analyst is the person's existential relation towards the object of desire'.

5  http://www2.arcauniversal.com.br/arcanews/integra.jsp?cod=23959& codcanal=36 Accessed on 20 April 2004.

# 5. Indentured Theology:
## White Souls/Black Skins? Decolonizing Pentecostals within the Indian Diaspora

### SAROJINI NADAR AND
### GARY S. D. LEONARD

## 'Indian' Pentecostals in KwazuluNatal

In his Foreword to the 1999 study of global expressions and adaptations of Pentecostalism across five continents, entitled *Pentecostals After a Century: Global Perspectives on a Movement in Transition*, Harvey Cox can admit that in his lifelong study of religion and religious movements, he has come to believe two essential things: *first*, that 'religious movements can never be understood apart from the cultural and political milieu in which they arise' (Cox, 1999: 11) and *second*, that religion can act as a very accurate barometer, often providing 'the clearest and most graphically etched portrait in miniature, of what is happening in the big picture' (Cox, 1999: 11).

In this study we will seek to critically engage and explore these two 'working' premises within the context of the Pentecostal churches among the Indian/South Asian community within the South African province of KwazuluNatal (KZN).[1] As we are socially engaged and religiously located practitioners[2] within this Community, our study will be one that has intimate knowledge of the 'public and hidden transcripts' (cf. Scott, 1990) that exist within a community and movement that has only recently emerged from 134 years of British colonial and White Afrikaner Nationalist racial oppression, marginalization and injustice.

We will argue that the majority of established 'Indian'[3] churches are *phenomenologically* tied and *ideologically* entrapped within the 'classical' form of 'Mission' Pentecostalism, under which it was paternalistically subsumed, and from which it has only recently begun to emerge. More particularly, we will seek to show that this has resulted in a pro-Western (or better, imperialist) cultural and religious disparagement and spiritual disjunction, providing in its stead an overt and uncritical reliance upon a globalized and essentially American fundamentalist Neo-Pentecostal faith movement, a modality that it shares with a growing number of the other Pentecostal/Neo-Pentecostal and charismatic streams present in South Africa.

## South African Pentecostalism's 'Classical' Proto-history

However one reads the proto-history of classical Pentecostalism, the name of William Joseph Seymour (1870–1922)[4] features prominently. His name and that of the Azusa Street Apostolic Faith Mission have long featured in the strongly held lore of the movement especially in its classical form, as has the name of Charles Fox Parham (1873–1929).[5] The son of emancipated slaves, Seymour's religious and theological roots can be traced to the Black Holiness tradition (Synan, 1988: 780; Lovett, 1988: 76–84) among emancipated slaves in the American Deep South.

The historical beginnings of Pentecostalism within South Africa can be traced to a virtual flood of Pentecostal missionaries that came to South Africa from North America following the Azusa Street Revival in 1906. They were to arrive during a particularly volatile period of political foment and tension as Anglo and Boer struggled in their passage towards Union,[6] and what Davenport has rightly called 'the shaping of white domination' (Davenport, 1991: 201). Chief among these was John G. Lake, his name being synonymous with the formation of the Apostolic Faith Mission of South Africa (Die Apostoliese Geloof Sending van Suid-Afrika – AGS/AFM) the first, and currently largest, of the 'classical' Pentecostal mission church denominations within South Africa.[7]

## The Origins of the South African Indian Diaspora

South Africa reportedly holds the largest component of the Indian Diaspora. Originating in the main from this system of indentured labourers,[8] their recruitment and introduction into the Colony of Natal came after its British annexation (1843), and establishment as a Crown Colony (1856) and after concordat agreements passed into law by the Natal Legislative Council and the Indian Colonial Government in 1859 and 1860 respectively. Under the direction of Emigration Agents, labourers were enlisted chiefly from Tamil and Telugu communities within the South Indian Madras Presidency (now Tamil Nadu) and bound by indentures (contracts of service) for a specified period of five years to work on Natal's tea, coffee and (in particular) sugar plantations under what were harsh and oppressive working conditions, for a menial wage, plus food and lodging. At the close of this initial indentured period they were entitled to remain, continuing their labour under privately arranged contracts. Following a further five years, such labourers were entitled to free passage back to India, or at the discretion of the Governor of the Colony, a grant of Crown land in lieu of repatriation.[9] Most of the Indians however remained as 'free' labourers after their indentures had expired. In total some 152,184 indentured labourers were brought to the British Colony of Natal between the years 1860 and 1911 (Brain, 1983: 4), after which Indian immigration to the Colony came to an end.

## The Operational Historical and Theological Rationale

It is not surprising – given the socio-political conditions of the time – that the newly established Pentecostal Mission Church would soon become engrossed in questions of race. Among the overt historical and theological mechanisms utilized by the white Pentecostal mission church leaders to justify racial segregation, were the so-called scriptural precedents set within the Bible, whereby it was boldly asserted that the white race was mentally, emotionally and spiritually superior to that of the 'non-white' races (Anderson, 1992: 34). Indeed, the apartheid regime was so comfortable with the AGS/AFM position on race, that it invited Pastor Gerrie Wessells, then Vice-President of the National Church, to serve as a State Senator in 1955 – a particularly important appointment in the light of J. G. Strijdom's decision to enlarge the Senate in order to gain a two-thirds majority in Parliament necessary to remove the (so-called) coloured franchise in the Cape from the common voters' roll.

Another significant indicator is the formal amalgamation in 1951 of the Full Gospel Church with that of the largest and oldest US-based Pentecostal churches, the Church of God (Cleveland, Tennessee), thus extending its name to that of the Full Gospel Church of God in Southern Africa. Historically, the Church of God was a predominantly white, Pentecostal mission church, with its roots firmly in the South. Maintaining racial segregation policies from 1926, these were not eradicated from their church statute books until 1966 – most probably as a result of pressure exerted by the struggle for African-American civil rights.

Other racist indicators could be referenced, the most blatant example within South Africa being that of historical revisionism, the basis of which was the concerted effort to put forward Charles Parham rather than William Seymour as the progenitor of the modern Pentecostal movement – for how could a white apartheid church have a black as its founder! Hence F. P. Möller, a past President of the AGS/AFM, is prepared to simply write off Seymour on the basis of his presumed (black?) ineptitude. 'Later', Möller could write, 'Seymour was replaced by more able people and the different races ceased to worship together.' The present President of the AGS/AFM, Dr Izak Burger, is as deliberate in his racial bias. In his 1987 University of Pretoria D.Th. dissertation he asserts that the idea of Pentecostalism's origination being within a black church is a 'warped, one-sided conclusion'. He further contends that the racial segregation that was soon to take place at Azusa Street through the ministry of Parham and others was actually a 'natural and spontaneous' development.[10]

## Black Pentecostal and Black Consciousness?

The year 1974 was to become a watershed for Pentecostal historiography. In this year, Walter Hollenweger, the acknowledged doyen of Pentecostal Studies, began emphasizing the historical connection between the development of organized black resistance in North America and that of the Azusa Street Mission. His words were radical for the time, 'Black Power cannot be seen as a contrast to the African Pentecostal movement. Both movements are religious and revolutionary and it is difficult to draw a dividing line between the two' (quoted in Anderson, 1992: 25).

Within South Africa, such historical, sociological and theological reconstruction only began to appear towards the latter years of the apartheid regime, when three small, but significant groupings made their Pentecostal voices of conscience and resistance known.

First among these was a group of some 132 'Concerned Evangelicals', when in 1986 they published what became known as the EWISA statement (EWISA, 1987). In the face of the apartheid regime's escalating brutality, alongside that of the more radical *Kairos Document*, came forth an equally innovative theological statement critiquing South African evangelicalism. Of the signatories, 30 were from the AGS/AFM; 17 from the International Assemblies of God; and 3 from the Full Gospel Church. In all, nearly 38 per cent represented core 'classical' Pentecostal mission churches!

In 1988, a group of Durban metro-based Pentecostals, calling themselves 'Relevant Pentecostal Witness', published the booklet *A Relevant Pentecostal Witness*. Among the members of the small interim steering committee were a number of 'Indian' Pentecostals, emanating from the Full Gospel Church and Assemblies of God. Desiring not 'to duplicate that which has already been stated in the Evangelical Witness' (*Witness*, 1988: 5), they commented on the conspicuous silence of Pentecostals, in comparison to that heard from among the ecumenical denominations:

> Our silence lends support to this make-believe situation and betrays our blindness to the true context. Our silence is a wilful support of an ideology that is irreconcilable with the Holy Scriptures and with our Christian Faith. In repenting of this sin we are forced to re-examine our theology. (*Witness*, 1988: 6)

Examining the core teachings of the 'classical' Pentecostal mission churches within the context of the prevailing political situation, they would conclude,

> For the most part, the Pentecostal church has thrived under the Group Areas Act. It has no qualms about having separate so-called Indian, Coloured, African and White sections within the Church. Is this a true testimony to the one Spirit who unites us? (1 Corinthians 12:13). (*Witness*, 1988: 9)

Most importantly, especially within the context of the thesis of this study, there was evidenced a clear understanding of the important role that American evangelists, both past and present, played in compounding the ideology of racism and imperialism within the 'classical' Pentecostal mission churches of South Africa.

It came from abroad, notably the USA. When the early Pentecostal missionaries came to evangelize, they did not find it necessary to analyse the South African context. (This is still the practice today of Pentecostal pastors, evangelists and missionaries who come to South

Africa to preach and to evangelize.) They found it expedient not to jeopardize their position with the government of the day. Therefore, they did not get involved in any matter that seemed political. As a result, their message was conservative and upheld the status quo.

Finally, mention must be made of a third document, published in 1991 by the Relevant Fellowship of Concerned Christians, *The Apostolic Faith Mission Church: A Challenge to Action by the RFCC*, signed by 82 black pastors and members of the AGS/AFM. It pulled no punches in describing the approximately 83-year history of the church's overt racist policies:

> The white AFM – an imperative dichotomy – has up to today embraced apartheid policy as God-given policy or ideology. It did not see any evil or heresy in the abhorrent system. It has constitutionally and otherwise approved and endorsed racial discrimination, and as far as it is concerned the scriptures could not find anything wrong and ungodly about the system. (RFCC, 1991: 3)

In promulgating a 'challenge to action' it called all members of the AGS/AFM

> To open dialogue with the white section, aimed at negotiating a new unitary, non-racial AFM Church . . . To put strong pressure on the Presbytery, to dissolve the composite structure and replace it with a more credible unitary structure that will represent the disenfranchised masses within the Church. To set up strategies which will facilitate the process of re-defining Pentecostal theology in terms of our concrete situation, that is to say, contextualising our Pentecostal theology. (RFCC, 1991: 20f.)

## Colonization and Indian Mission Work

Turning our discussion now to the Indian Pentecostal community, it is important to reflect on the possible reasons for its acceptance and continued phenomenal growth among a community that was/is essentially Hindu.[11] These beginnings come as a direct result of the 'classical' Pentecostal mission churches.

In typical dualistic fashion, and in line with other African cultural-religious settings, new Hindu converts within classical Pentecostalism are required to make a complete break with what is considered their 'heathen' past. The Pentecostal pastor visiting the home of a potential convert would require that the *Camatchee Vilakku* (a prayer lamp used in family worship), *thali* (a yellow piece of string tied around the neck indicating marriage) and the *bhotu* (a red dot indicating marriage worn on the forehead primarily by women) as well as other Hindu cultural/religious accoutrements be removed and even destroyed, the would-be convert being persuaded that these objects of veneration and devotion are agencies of the Devil, 'an understanding which does not allow for Hinduism or any other non-Christian philosophy to be a possible *praeparatio evangelica*' (Pillay, 1994: 186). For Pillay, the reaction of the new convert was 'often so strong that not only was the former religion rejected but so also were many purely cultural features' (Pillay, 1994: 187), resulting in such a destructive tension being created between the old and new that it 'provided the mentality that stimulated innovations within Pentecostal thinking' (Pillay, 1994: 187). Hence for Pillay these new innovations – only possible within a Pentecostal setting – provide the vital clue 'to an understanding of the character of the movement and to an understanding of the reasons why Pentecostalism communicated more successfully with the Indian than "established" Christianity did' (Pillay, 1994: 187).

In many ways, this search for the divine that takes place within Indian Pentecostalism, whereby humanity reclaims God by experiencing the mystical immanence through the Spirit, finds resonance with Cox (1999: 7), when he eloquently states,

Have not Pentecostals vigorously reclaimed many of these spheres as places where we are invited on a daily basis, to 'walk with God'?

This thesis was extensively worked out in his well-received *Fire from Heaven*. For him, Pentecostalism plays an increasingly important role in reshaping religion in its global relationships, in an age where people especially within Western societies have been beset within the 'Secular City' (Cox, 1995: 83).

For the first forty years of their existence these churches were under the sole paternal tutelage of white missionaries. Under their control and direction these churches expanded their membership throughout the 1940s and 1950s, consolidated that membership well into the late 1960s and early 1970s. Their struggle for structural autonomy only began during the late 1970s.

## The Faith Movement and American Imperialism

The twin concepts of faith and healing represent core teachings within classical Pentecostalism. It is no surprise therefore that the faith movement took hold so forcefully, particularly among white South Africans who shared a similar pseudo-religious ethos of success and material prosperity with North Americans.

The faith movement began life essentially as a parachurch movement consisting of, in the words of Chappell, 'a mixture of evangelistic revivalism, fundamentalist literalism and Pentecostal experientialism' (Chappell, 1989: 186). Central figures in the early theological development and history of the movement were the American healing evangelists of the 1940s and 1950s – William Branham (1909–65), A. A. Allen (1911–70), Oral Roberts (1918–) and T. L. Osborn (1923–). They were to be followed by the faith and prosperity teachers of the 1970s and 1980s, Kenneth Hagin (Sr), Kenneth and Gloria Copeland, Jerry Savelle, Marilyn Hickey and Lester Sumrall, to name but a few.[12] Each had an enormous influence upon the South African Pentecostal mission churches.

During the late 1950s both Branham and Roberts were invited jointly by the AGS/AFM and Full Gospel Church to conduct mass 'healing campaigns' mainly among South African whites. The ensuing wave of 'enthusiasm' soon spread to the mission 'Sections' of the church, conveyed through the teaching of their white Missionary Superintendents, Evangelists and Pastors. In the case of the formative period of the AGS/AFM 'Indian' mission such white Missionary Superintendents as Charles Flewelling, J. T. du Plessis and Charles Kantor are important, all of whom to some extent had features in common with the 'latter rain' 'signs and wonders' healing stage of the movement – before it entered its second and later Neo-Pentecostal phase of material prosperity.

With the rapid development from the late 1970s onwards of the semi-autonomous Neo-Pentecostal networks of Rhema, Durban Christian Centre and a plethora of other smaller 'white' so-called charismatic groups, the 'wealth, health and prosperity' gospel was to take on almost hegemonic proportions. By the middle to late 1980s these movements first began to accept coloureds and Indians into their services, under the slightly questionable title of 'multi-racial' services. This enabled a cross-over to take place, whereby 'Indian' churches, within both the 'classic' Pentecostal mission structures, and the growing number of autonomous Indian churches, began adopting the style of worship and rhetoric common to these groups. With countless teaching videos and audio tapes, booklets, and later evangelical crusades, the faith movement was to epitomize the very psychology of the Indian church, where positive confession as a means to wealth, health and prosperity was taught as a spiritual law and an essential part of God's perfect 'will' for humankind.

## A Search for Meaning

Turning our attention once more to the South African Indian Pentecostal churches, we set out to explore to what extent this 'faith gospel' impacts the churches as they stand at present. In our search for meaning then, we utilized the methodology of contextual Bible study (as discussed in West, 1999; 2001) as the most appropriate vehicle for researching their prophetic-political potential. Our intention was to gain an understanding through empirical research, of the extent to which

- Indian Pentecostalism places reliance upon a globalized Neo-Pentecostal 'faith/word gospel' form of individualistic spirituality, piety and practice; and
- this has ideologically enabled or hindered it to respond to pertinent social, political and contemporary issues, such as HIV/Aids, gender justice, children's rights, culture.

To effectively answer these questions we developed three Bible studies related to HIV/Aids; Gender Justice and Children's Rights; and Ethnicity and Culture. Space will not allow us to provide a detailed analysis of the Bible studies, but in what follows we will seek to examine in brief the contributions of the participants to our research workshop, and thereby provide an attempt at analysing their understanding and interpretations in the light of the 'glocal' issues present within the Indian community, and wider South African setting.

## Group Dynamics and Process

The plenary group of the research workshop which we set up consisted of 22 recognized leaders and pastors from the Indian/South Asian Community of KZN. Eight were from the three classical

Pentecostal mission church denominations, namely the Full Gospel Church; AGS/AFM; and Assemblies of God. Fourteen were from autonomous and semi-autonomous churches and networks. All participants however had had their beginnings within at least one of these classical Pentecostal mission churches. They consisted of 19 males and three females. None of the three females were ordained ministers. The group was randomly divided into three smaller Bible study groups. Each group comprised approximately six members, and each was assigned a facilitator.[13]


## Forging a Theoretical Basis for Analysing the Bible Studies

Our interest in facilitating these Bible studies was to discover to what extent the reading of the Bible enables *first*, the hegemonic to become ideological; *second*, the unconscious to become conscious; and *third*, non-agentive power to become agentive power (Comaroff and Comaroff, 1991: 22–9).

The Comaroffs (1991) have stressed that hegemony becomes unstable when confronted by ideology. They show this by placing hegemony on a continuum with ideology, with the two at opposite poles; and unconsciousness and consciousness parallel to the hegemony–ideology continuum, with unconsciousness lying on the hegemony side of the continuum, while consciousness lies on the ideology side of the continuum. Framing both these parallel continuums are the concepts of culture and power.

Hegemony, according to the Comaroffs, is

That order of signs and practices, relations and distinctions, images and epistemologies – drawn from a historically situated cultural field – that come to be taken for granted as the natural and received shape of the world and everything that inhabits it. (Comaroff and Comaroff, 1991: 23)

More significant to our analysis is the Comaroffs' observation that,

. . . power has so often been seen to lie in what it silences, what it prevents people from thinking and saying, what it puts beyond the limits of the rational and the credible.

In our analysis of the Bible studies which follow, we will use the Comaroffs' three continuums, shaped by culture, as a measure of the extent to which the hegemonic can become ideological through the process of the Bible studies, using the critical tools of the contextual Bible study method. We will further explore to what extent the hegemonic in becoming ideological enables transformation within the communities, that is, the likelihood of non-agentive power becoming agentive power.

## Bible Study 1: HIV/Aids

*Text: Mark 3.1–8*
- What is the text about?
- What image of God do the Pharisees have?
- What is the Pharisees' view of synagogue tradition?
- What image of God does Jesus have?
- What is Jesus' view of synagogue tradition?
- What is the disabled man's image of God?
- What is the disabled man's view of synagogue tradition?
- What image of God do people living with HIV and Aids have?
- What is their view of Pentecostal church tradition?
- What resources does the Pentecostal church have to deal with HIV and Aids?

## Bible Study 2: Gender Justice and Children's Rights

*Text: 2 Samuel 13.1–22*
- Read the text aloud to the group as a whole.
- Summarize the story.
- What is the theme of this text?
- Who are the main characters in this text and what do we know about them?
- What is the role of each of the male characters in the rape of Tamar?
- How does Tamar respond throughout the story?
- Are there women like Tamar in your church and/or community? In small groups answer the questions from the case study (see Case Study 1, p. 84).
- Respond to T. D. Jakes' commentary (see Case Study 2, p. 86) on this story. What are the issues of children's rights that come up in his commentary? Should it come up at all? What are the issues of women's rights that come up in his commentary?
- What resources are there in your area for survivors (women and children) of rape?

In addition to these questions the participants were given two handouts, a case study on violence against women and a narrative on the Bible text by Bishop T. D. Jakes.

## Bible Study 3: Ethnicity and culture

*Texts: John 4.7–23 / Mark 7.24–30*
- Read the text aloud.
- What is the text about?
  – What is the theme about?
- Who are the main characters in this text?
  – What do we know about them?
  – How do we come to know about them?
- What is the theology of Jesus in this passage?
  – What is the theology of the Samaritan woman?
  – What is the theology of the Jews?
- Are there Samaritan women and men within the Indian community?
  – What are some of our encounters with them as Pentecostals?
  – Are Hindus/Muslims the modern equivalents of Samaritans?
- Do you think Jesus is dispossessing the Samaritan woman of her religious and cultural traditions?
  – On the basis of Jesus' dialogue here with the Samaritan woman and the Syrophoenician woman (Mark 7.24–30) is there a place for respecting the religious and cultural traditions of others?
  – What does Jesus' conversation tell us about his attitudes towards others of different ethnic and religious backgrounds, and what light does this shed on South African interracial relationships particularly within the Church pre- and post-apartheid?
- What does this say for the Church's past acceptance of relocations under the Group Areas Act on the part of Indians, policies of segregation, white missionary control, etc.?
  – Is there a place for an 'Indian' contextualized gospel? Do you think that that gospel preached by American and African American Evangelists/Teachers is contextualized within the American and African American cultural experience or is universal?
  – Does it 'fit' well within the context of the South African Indian experience – particularly within the previous 'Indian locations' of Chatsworth and Phoenix?

The first few questions in each of the Bible studies were specifically aimed at gauging the extent to which each group was able to gain distance from the text. This exercise was well suited to the textual questions that the contextual Bible study method advocates. By focusing on the content of the narrative, rather than on a strict analysis of its form, context, evaluation or history, the aim was to familiarize each group with reading the 'text as text' before reading the 'text for evaluation'. Each group struggled to stay 'true' to the textual questions of the contextual Bible study method, a factor which at least one of the facilitators noted with frustration. Finally, each group was asked to gain critical distance from the text, but that in this process they would actually get closer to their own readings of the text, and be able to see not only why they interpreted the text in that way, but why previous interpreters experienced the text in that way as well.

In all three Bible studies it was interesting to note that it was difficult for the participants to gain critical distance from the text at first. Indeed the most striking observation in all three groups was the inability of the participants to stay focused on the 'text as text'. In other words, it was easier for the pastors to 'evaluate' the text and thereby prepare a sermon, than to read the text as a literary unit. Though it must be said that once the facilitators began to encourage familiarity with the methodology, the pastors were able to grasp the objective better and thereby begin to look deeper into what the text itself was saying rather than what they thought, or to draw upon previously held interpretations. As a result, all three groups were enabled to carry out a detailed textual study of their given passages, and were able to realize interesting observations which opened up opportunities that led well into what West calls 'community consciousness' questions.

The 'community consciousness' questions were deliberately formulated not just to encourage the groups to make the links between the biblical text and their context; but in terms of the research that we were conducting, to pose specific questions as to how Indian pastors from the classical Pentecostal mission tradition perceive their tradition engaging with the pertinent questions that arose out of these Bible studies, such as HIV/Aids, gender and culture.

## Of Responses and Reactions

The responses received from the groups in terms of the textual Bible study were in a way 'model' answers. As one facilitator could say: 'It seems as if I am speaking to the converted here,' in response to the very bold and innovative answers that were given by the groups in response to the questions posed by the Bible studies. For example, in Group 1, when posed with the question of what the Pharisees' image of God was they were all quick to see that the Pharisees' image of God was that 'God was a God of ritual', and that the Pharisees believed that 'God was a legalistic God'. They were also clearly able to see that Jesus' image of God from the text was that 'God is flexible', that 'human need is more important than the law', that 'to do good is better than to observe outdated rituals', and that 'if Jesus is typifying what God is, then God is confrontational!'

Similarly, in group 2 the responses to the questions concerning the roles that male characters played in the rape of Tamar were met not with a wall of defence, but rather with openness. Indeed the thought was expressed that each of the male characters in the story was in some way complicit in the rape of Tamar. They argued that Jonadab was as guilty as Amnon because he advised him to pretend that he was sick; they further asserted that Absalom was held responsible because he covered up the rape in order to protect the family's integrity: 'be quiet for he is your brother'. They traced the main problem to David, who they thought was in a way paying for his 'ungodly' behaviour towards women, as for example Bathsheba, so that his family was also corrupt. They even went further to empathize with the pain that Tamar went through and acknowledged that her pain was also caused by laws of the time, specifically those regarding virginity. So, the group was able to grapple with the textual issues of rape and to see gender injustice very clearly within the text. Although probed on the issue of children's rights by the facilitator, the group focused more on gender injustice, which perhaps in their minds was a separate concern.

Group 3 was also able to grapple with the issues presented by the text in some way. They saw very clearly that the texts of the Samaritan and the Syrophoenician women's encounters with Jesus were directly related to issues of ethnocentricism. They were able to point out that Jesus through his encounter with the women was breaking barriers, 'breaking cultural and ethnicity bondages'. They acknowledged that the women, particularly the Syrophoenician woman, had challenged Jesus to such an extent that he 'changes his mind', and rewards her. They were able to point out that through Jesus' encounter with these women he was breaking stereotypes of other cultures and even gender stereotypes. It should be noted that later within plenary, the idea that Jesus could have been persuaded to 'change his mind' was totally rejected, the pastors preferring to consider this to have been a pre-ordained device.

Most of the responses elicited from all three groups with regard to the textual questions showed clearly that even though in the minds of the facilitators clear hegemonic lines were drawn with regard to the way in which these texts are usually read in the Pentecostal churches known to the facilitators, the Bible studies somehow managed to allow for the hegemonic to become ideological.[14] In other words, the pastors in these groups were able to see and accept interpretations of the texts which ordinarily they would not relate. As a result they were able to become more ideological about the issues which the texts were raising. This then led well into the latter set of questions which required that the ideological enable non-agentive power to become agentive power. In other words, this part required a step further from the ideological.

With these sets of questions a very clear ambivalence with regard to 'how far we could take the interpretation of these texts' arose in each of the groups, in some more than others. For example, in Group 1 with regard to the question about what people who live with HIV think of God, they were quick to mention shame and guilt, and that for people living with Aids (henceforth PLWA), images of God were largely mediated by the Church. They admitted that the Church was judgemental and did not do enough to address the issue of HIV/Aids. Some related experiences of PLWA whom they knew of, who had become alienated by the Church, due to the stigma that was attached to the pandemic particularly because of its connectedness to issues of sex and sexuality. They were also able to see that the Pentecostal church's exclusive focus on physical healing through signs, wonders and miracles as opposed to holistic healing contributed strongly to giving PLWA false hope and hence making them feel even more alienated.

So although there was general agreement that the classical Pentecostal church had failed in its ability to deal with the issue of HIV/Aids in the community, the group was extremely ambivalent as to how to deal with the issue. Hence although acknowledging the Pharisees' judgemental attitudes and their inability to see beyond tradition, most of this group were unable to move beyond their tradition. Hence, when speaking of commercial sex workers who contracted HIV, and their view of God, one of the pastors could exclaim that the sex worker would probably think that 'God had let her down' considering that she was in this line of work to put food on the table for her children, but at the same time she would or should be able to see that this is what happens 'when I live outside the will of God'. Another pastor still understood HIV/Aids as a punishment from God for conducting a sinful lifestyle and could state with utter conviction that 'the apostle Paul tells us that the wrath of God is revealed from heaven upon all men [*sic*] who are unrighteous and do not walk in the will of God.' Still another pastor pointed out that even the 'Job disclaimer' about HIV not being a punishment from God does not apply in most of the cases because Job was a righteous and innocent man. Despite the group's endorsement of these opinions they were willing to concede that, notwithstanding, God was a merciful and forgiving God, and that the Church needs to give this hope to PLWA.

When probed further by the facilitator about the weaknesses and the strengths inherent in the Pentecostal tradition that could hinder or help in the struggle against this disease, the group was willing to acknowledge again the weaknesses of the Church. For example it was pointed out that in the Pentecostal understanding the measure of healing one received was directly related to the issue of faithfulness to God. One pastor pointed out that a person who was diabetic was told: 'Be faithful to God and He will heal you.' It was further pointed out that another weakness of the tradition was the Church's lack of a holistic theology regarding healing. In other words it was believed that God could only heal in miraculous physical ways and not in other ways, for example through less stigmatization or the ability to cope with and handle the illness.

The discussion then moved on to the Church's limited understanding concerning issues of sexuality and the Church's inability to engage with issues regarding sexuality such as the use of condoms. One pastor was met with severe resistance when he suggested that the Church should be dispensing condoms. The group disagreed strongly, saying that this was unbiblical and that it would encourage promiscuity. One pastor stated that instead of teaching the ABC of the HIV/Aids education programme (Abstinence, Be faithful, Condomize) he rather taught Abstinence, Be faithful and Christ. The group was extremely concerned that the Church should emphasize conduct and not condoms. In other words there was a distinct reluctance 'to give people permission to be sexually active outside of marriage'.

So although acknowledging the value of the Bible study and the lessons that it taught them, the participants in Group 1 were not willing to move beyond their tradition, with regard to what it said about HIV/Aids but more particularly about sexual practices. The extent to which the ideological was able to convert into agentive power seemed to be applicable only on a superficial level, as the group seemed to be still ideologically trapped by the theology of the classical Pentecostal mission church tradition. Interestingly all of them pointed out that their churches were simply not able to deal with the issue effectively. An AGS/AFM pastor pointed out that although it had a document regarding their stance on HIV/Aids, the ideas contained therein remained in the document and did not filter through to the people in the pew. A Full Gospel Church pastor related a similar experience and cited the fact that the denomination was still largely 'white controlled' and therefore they did not view this as 'their' problem. The fact that Indians saw the disease as an African disease further exacerbated the problem. It was the autonomous churches who asserted that they could do most because they were not bogged down by institutional 'bureaucracy'. So it seemed that the ideological gains made in the Bible study could very well remain in the Bible study unless a serious introspective study is done by the Indian Pentecostal church regarding its theology of HIV/Aids.

With regard to the step from the ideological to the implementation of agentive power among Groups 2 and 3 with regard to issues of gender justice, children's rights and culture and ethnicity, a similar pattern to that of Group 1 could be observed. In other words, although the groups were able to move beyond their hegemonic understandings regarding the texts and become ideological about their interpretations, the translation of that into praxis was a larger and more difficult step to make. This was clearly truer in Group 3 than in Group 2.

Group 2 were far more able to see the limitations of the typical interpretations of texts in their churches through their evaluation and critique of the commentary given to them on the text by an icon in the movement, Bishop T. D. Jakes (see Case Study 2, p. 86). The group was able to distinguish between what was genuine theological and exegetical interpretation and what could simply be termed as 'motivational speaking'. They pointed out that the weakness of the Pentecostal tradition was often realized in sermons where the focus was more on arousing passionate responses through colourful rhetoric and exaggeration than making the message relevant to the issue at hand. They saw the graveness of the situation through the case study (see Case Study 1, p. 84) that they were presented with regarding an issue of domestic violence, and were appalled to note that Jakes in his commentary on the Tamar text focused more on getting 'a great sermon' through his use of pulpit rhetoric, than on focusing on the issue of rape. They were also dismayed by the fact that he seemed to lay the blame at Tamar's door.

In terms of the case study they were freely willing to acknowledge that many Pentecostal pastors were ill-equipped to deal with these issues because of their lack of theological and exegetical training. They were opposed to what they called 'SAPs' – Self-Appointed Pastors – those that founded congregations without any prior theological training, but were simply 'called by the Spirit'. They also pointed out that pastors needed to redefine their theological and biblical interpretations in the light of such issues as violence against women and children.

Overall, this group seemed to understand the need to translate the ideological into agentive power. However, even they slipped into the hegemonic sphere towards the end, where they declared that they still thought that divorce was wrong, and that the Bible was right to teach against it, but in this particular case it could be the best option.

Group 3 also seemed to understand the need to translate the ideological into agentive power. The group acknowledged that the Bible study had enabled an understanding of the way in which Indian culture has been marginalized by those who presume to have sole ownership rights to the 'gospel' and the 'truth'. The group was able to offer very creative suggestions as to how the cultural and ethnic identity of Indians could be re-established within the Church, such as through the use of Indian music and symbols. They also acknowledged that there were many Samaritans and Syrophoenicians in the Indian community too, represented by the Hindus and Muslims and other faith groups. They acknowledged that the classical Pentecostal mission church had 'demonized' these groups and that Indian Pentecostals had been 'brainwashed' by the American televangelists with regard to this issue.

So, Group 3, more than any other group, we would suggest, were able to see clearly the hegemonic pull of the Pentecostal understanding with regard to issues of culture and ethnicity and were able to become more ideological concerning their own stance. However, in terms of translating this new-found ideology into agentive power, this group, like Group 1, had to acknowledge their inability to do so. Although longing to implement a more Indian understanding of the gospel into their churches, they said that if they had to do this, they would lose 'more than half their congregations'. The Indian Pentecostals in South Africa had become so steeped in American ideas of the gospel that these had become 'godly' norms; and that any deviation would be regarded as sinful and demonic.

## Hegemonic Entrapment or Black Liberation?

To conclude this brief appraisal of the Bible studies, it can be said that the extent to which the Bible studies allowed the hegemonic to become ideological was significant. However, the entrapment of the 'faith gospel' and its accompanying theology is so powerful that it does not allow for even those with a keen understanding of the ideological issues at stake to translate this into praxis, because that would mean giving up an essential part of what being Pentecostal is understood to be all about.

Having said this, it is also important to point out that we still believe that forms of critical consciousness as espoused in these Bible studies are necessary so that the Indian Pentecostal community can forge their own language of resistance. We recognize though that while explicitly avoiding romanticism and idealism, regarding the contribution of the Indian Pentecostal community to the issues presented by the Bible studies, we also have to avoid minimizing or rationalizing their contribution (West, 1999: 37).

## Towards a Conclusion: Triple-Indentured Pentecostals at the Crossroads?

To conclude, as with Dalit Christians within the Protestant Church in India (Oommen, 2000), Indian Pentecostals in South Africa have experienced a triple indentured alienation. *First*, as indentured labourers under the British colonialist-ruled Province of Natal, and the later Christian Nationalist apartheid regime; *second*, under Afrikaner civil religion in its supposed a-political Pentecostal and unapologetic racist guise; and *Third* (and currently), through the imported North American 'faith gospel'.

With their uncritical adoption of right-wing American faith gospel teaching, Indian Pentecostals continue to exist as indentured labourers for what is a 'white' kingdom, the systemic nature of this faith gospel ensuring that its legacy is still being realized, ten years after democracy – a legacy that continues to promote:

- a reliance upon a faith gospel which promotes God as white, successful, male and American;
- a willingness to be co-opted ideologically in white paternalist missionary terms;
- a reliance upon classical Pentecostal forms: moralistic, pietistic, individualistic.

Is it too much to argue that Indian Pentecostals in the light of such an indentured theology remain both ideologically and spiritually trapped, having white souls, yet black skins?

As Cox has clearly defended (Cox, 1995: 303),

> The great irony of Christian fundamentalism . . . is that it shares the same disability that plagues and cripples the modern rational mind – literalism. . . . Fundamentalism is not a retrieval of the religious tradition at all, but a distortion of it. The fundamentalist voice speaks to us not of the wisdom of the past but of a desperate attempt to fend off modernity by using modernity's weapons.

In many ways South African Indian Pentecostalism has realized within it a certain irony – that of a syndrome of dependency. Our workshop clearly demonstrated this phenomenon. The pastors moved full circle. They became ideological, but when pushed to apply what they had seen, they retreated back to the security of their psychology of a colonized mind. For transformation to take hold, a determined process of decolonization must begin. If Pentecostalism is at the cross-roads as Hollenweger contends, our research of Pentecostalism within the Indian diaspora firmly bears this out.

> From its own ranks there comes the challenge first for a critical historiography . . . secondly, there is a challenge for a social and political analysis . . . Then thirdly, there is the challenge for a more differentiated treatment of the work of the Spirit and for spirituality which does not blank out critical thinking . . . (Hollenweger, 1999a: 33)

### Case Study 1: Kayla's Story

Kayla has been married for sixteen years now, and has two children (boys aged 15 and 9). Her husband, Peter, has been beating her periodically, for a number of years. They both come from working-class backgrounds, with little education. She works in a shoe factory and he works casually. He is an alcoholic. She gets paid more than he does, and before acquiring this job he was also unemployed for some time. However, in order to make ends meet they need even his meagre wage. The whole family lives with Kayla's mother, a widow living on a state grant in a council flat. They belong to an evangelical church, one that does not ordain women, nor allow them to participate equally in the life and activities of the church. Kayla is asthmatic. Her youngest son is also asthmatic and epileptic.

The last beating that Kayla received from her husband was particularly severe. X-rays showed that she had a crack in her skull. She decided that she wanted to end this marriage. Because they were living with her mother, she asked Peter to move out. The pastor and the elder immediately came over to visit, telling Kayla that:

1  The Bible says that divorce is wrong.
2  The man is the head of the woman therefore she is supposed to submit to him.
3  By not cooking and doing other household chores which a wife is supposed to do for her husband she inevitably brought on the abuse.

Then Kayla's sister comes along and gives her good sisterly advice. 'You see, Kayla, according to our culture, you are not a good wife. You should wake up early in the morning and pack lunch for your husband. Peter says that you don't iron his trousers with a neat lining – how many times has mummy taught us how to do that? His clothes are not washed, ironed, folded and put into his cupboard on time so that every morning he has to look for socks. He also says that his food is not ready when he comes home really hungry. Kayla, you should really try to be a better wife. Then maybe Peter won't beat you so badly.'

Kayla protests that she leaves home two and a half hours before he does, while it is still dark. She says that she comes home only after him therefore it is difficult to have food ready on time before he is home. She says that sometimes she has to take leave from work and spend the whole day in a public hospital with her youngest son who is asthmatic and epileptic. She protests that she is often very tired and very sick . . .

Her protests fall on deaf ears. Her sister tells her that she should return to her husband, and learn how to be a good wife. Her pastor tells her that she should return to her husband, pray for him, and submit to his will. Her friends at work tell her that it is very disgraceful for a woman to leave her husband: 'What would people say? Return to him,' they tell her.

She does. The following week he punches her in the face again.

## Group Activities

1  Identify the forms of abuse you can find in this case study.
2  Substantiate your identification with sentences from the text.
3  Discuss how you would have advised Kayla if you were her:
   • pastor
   • friend
   • sister

## Case Study 2: Tamar's Story (2 Samuel 13.1–20)

Commentary by Bishop T. D. Jakes, in *Holy Bible, Woman Thou Art Loosed Edition* (1998)

She lay among the soiled and wrinkled linen, the room in total disarray, her garments tattered and torn, her future changed forever. Her femininity had been crushed like a rosebud. Tears ran down her face like rain on a windowpane. She was weeping, not just because of her torn flesh, but because of her shattered trust. She had tried to help a man in need, and instead of receiving his gratitude, she had been brutally abused and assaulted.

She had entered into the relationship as his sister, but she had tried to be his friend. She was Tamar. Her brother Amnon was ill. He needed her, he said. You know how it is when a man needs you. Sometimes your maternal instincts take over, and reason goes out the window. Besides, Tamar thought that she could cure her brother by caring for him. Little did she know that what ailed him could not be cured by any woman's gentle nurture.

While she stirred the soup and prepared to minister to him, he plotted her demise. Somewhere in the process of trying to help him, the tenor of the relationship changed. The tempo escalated, and before she knew what had happened, Amnon had raped her and left her bleeding and humiliated.

Be watchful, my sister. Be careful, because you may not realise the moment a relationship changes. It can happen in the blink of an eye, and you will wonder why you didn't see it coming.

Tamar wailed, but no one answered. She cried, but it seemed no one cared. She needed compassion and sympathy, but all she found was loneliness and despair. Bad enough that the one she had trusted had betrayed her. Worse still, that he had rejected her as well. 'What you did at the end is worse than what you did in the beginning,' she told him (2 Samuel 13.16). Who would have ever thought that something so innocent could have brought such evil results?

Just when it seemed she could not bear the shame and disgrace a moment longer, another man entered. It was Absalom. He lifted her from her crumpled state, wiped her hair from her face, kissed the tears from her eyes, and brought her into his house where she could recover.

Be wise, my sister. You may have the best of intentions, but I must tell you that good intentions may not prevent a broken heart. Still, every man is not like Amnon. And just because you were violated once doesn't mean that you can't learn from your experience. It doesn't mean that you can never be loved.

So take courage. If no man comes to assist you, pick yourself up and walk on. Walk right past the agony of the first man and listen for the knock of the second. It will come. The knock may not be delivered by a human hand, but it will come. It will be the knock of Jesus – your Bridegroom coming for you, His beloved.

*Notes*

1 According to the 2001 South African Census, of the 798,274 Indian/South Asian population group resident in KwazuluNatal, some 67,847 (or 8.5%) are described as belonging to Pentecostal/charismatic-based churches. This is by far the largest grouping among Christian churches within the Indian community, the second being the Roman Catholic Church which registered 10,099 adherents (1.27%). The third largest grouping is what the Census refers to as 'Other Apostolic Churches' – a diverse and somewhat heterodox group of churches, registering 10,067 (1.26%), and including the 'Old' and 'New' Apostolic Church, some of which although not 'classical' in the sense of Western Pentecostalism, may indeed be represented as 'Spirit-based' churches. Other 'mainline' colonial-originated denominations do not even register into single percentage points. A feature that must be noted within the Census was the number that registered as belonging to 'Other Christian churches', namely, 105,541 (13.22%). Taking into consideration the innumerable small autonomous and semi-autonomous church groupings holding prayer and Sunday services in private homes, school rooms, sheds, tents and garages scattered throughout the province in what were previ-

ously designated 'Indian areas', most, if not all, Pentecostal in nature, the true number of Pentecostal-type churches within the Indian population may actually be nearer 22% of the total Indian population. http://www.statssa.gov.za/census2001

2 Sarojini Nadar grew up within the Full Gospel Church of God, Phoenix, Durban, and teaches at the University of KwazuluNatal. Gary Leonard served as a Pastor within the 'single (white) division' of the Apostolic Faith Mission (AFM) (1983–94), and for ten years taught at the AFM 'Indian' Bible College, Durban. He used also to be a regular preacher in the Indian congregations for many years.

3 In terms of South Africa's apartheid past, terminology is difficult and even treacherous territory upon which to journey. Hence the somewhat nefarious, and politically-loaded appellative terms 'population group', 'race', 'Indian', 'coloured', 'white', black', are admittedly problematic but unavoidable within our present discussion.

4 Consisting of a majority of blacks, and a 'sprinkling of whites', the non-racial character of the so-called 'Azusa Street revival' has often been emphasized, whereby 'the colour line was washed away in the blood' (Anderson, 1992: 22).

5 It is from Parham that 'classical' Pentecostalism gained its defining religious, racial and doctrinal features.

6 During the Boer War, Britain had claimed to be fighting for the freedom of black Africans from 'Boer slavery' in the Transvaal and Orange Free State Republics. Indeed, the British had promised that after the war, the franchise system operating in the Cape would be extended north to the former Boer Republics. The ratification of the Act of Union by the British Government ('The South Africa Act') on 10 May 1910 was to belie this promise. In line with article 8 of the Treaty of Vereeniging, virtually all political power remained in the hands of whites. The limited franchise among a few property-owning blacks in the Cape of Good Hope was to remain, yet they could only elect white candidates. Blacks could only be elected to the Cape Provincial Council. Within the Transvaal, the Orange Free State and Natal, whites alone would own the franchise.

7 As with its North American beginnings, the historical and sociological roots of the AGS/AFM were primarily among disenfranchised blacks.

8 Apart from Indentured labourers, a number of 'free' or 'passenger' Indians who held British travel documents arrived from north-west India, settling in the Colony of Natal at their own expense as merchants. The largest of these were Gujarati-speaking Muslims from the Bombay area and Gujarat.

9 Only 50 grants of Crown land were in fact made, mainly within remote areas (Pampallis, 1991: 90).

10 The overt ideological inclination towards Parham expressed by Möller and Burger is further bolstered by the fact that Parham was known to be sympathetic to the Ku Klux Klan (cf. Lovett, 1975: 135).

11 According to the 2001 South African Census, Hinduism, with 443,987 (or 55.62%), still maintains the majority share of the population, with Islam claiming a further 117,424 (or 14.71%). http://www.statssa.gov.za/census2001

12 Such American Neo-Pentecostal evangelists/teachers freely visited South Africa throughout the 1980s – at a time when the ecumenical churches rightly shunned South Africa, supporting political isolationism and economic sanctions.

13 The facilitators of the Bible studies comprised the two authors of this

study and Prof. Gerald West, Head of the School of Theology, University of KwazuluNatal, and sometime leader within the Assemblies of God (AOG). In essence each of the facilitators represented at least one of the classic Pentecostal mission churches with which we were dealing, namely the Full Gospel Church, AGS/AFM and Assemblies of God.

14 This may indeed be attributed, in part, to the nature and the design of the contextual Bible study method which is aimed at transformation.

# 6. Global Warfare and Charismatic Resistance:
## The Case of George Khambule (1884–1949) and the Book of Revelation

### JONATHAN A. DRAPER

### 'I am Greater Than Him'

In his groundbreaking book, *Zulu Zion* (Sundkler, 1976), Bengt Sundkler describes a fascinating prophetic movement led by a Zulu from Telezeni near Nqutu in Zululand, George Khambule. His indication in the footnotes to this chapter that there were 600 pages of handwritten Zulu manuscripts from the prophet whetted my appetite and curiosity. The cache of documents preserved in Sundkler's archives proved to be a very rich, if rather enigmatic, source of insight into the emergence of the Zionist movement in South Africa in the early twentieth century, on which I have reported elsewhere (Draper, 2002a; 2003a; 2003b; 2004; 2005).

Among the prophecies and visions, one recorded for Friday 5 April 1929 seemed at first to be bizarre. Khambule has a vision in which 'I was before King George V and he was reading a letter which was talking about me, praying for me about everything with all his strength. Because I am greater than him' (Diary 1: 99B–100A).[1] This seems at first sight to indicate a profoundly misguided ego: a rural Zulu listening to King George V of England praising him. No more startling, however, than the prophetic word to Khambule that the power of all the prophets has been written upon him: 'They all have been written upon you. That is why Jehovah said, "All the nations shall bow under you, the black and the white." It is so!' (Diary 1: 4A). This view of global significance and worldwide scope for the obscure Zulu movement seemed at first hard to explain.

Fieldwork interviewing the former followers and family members of

Khambule, however, provided the missing link. George Khambule had been a soldier in the First World War in the South African Native Labour Corps (SANLC). He had almost certainly seen and heard King George V in person, when the king paid an official visit to the Front and made a speech to the SANLC thanking them for their service. The vision of King George, then, is not at all unrealistic. In fact, Khambule's vision stands as a reproach to the king who could praise the Zulu people for their help in England's hour of need, only to abandon them to the growing institutionalization of racism in the Union of South Africa. The 1914–18 War, where massed armies and powerful weapons beyond every nightmare turned men into expendable ciphers, opened the eyes of Khambule and others to see things on a worldwide scale, and they were not slow to make their own deductions, something the colonial authorities had been afraid of all along (Clothier, 1987).

This chapter explores the role which world wars may have played in the formation of a global religious consciousness. Perhaps the participation, voluntarily or involuntarily, in two world wars, multiplied across the previously isolated and unconscious indigenous communities of the colonized world, may have contributed to fostering the consciousness of religion as a worldwide rather than a local phenomenon also.

## George Khambule (1884–1949)

George Khambule came from a prominent Westernized Methodist family, originally from Edendale near Pietermaritzburg in South Africa (Draper, 2003a). They had a record of alliances with the colonial authorities in Natal, fighting alongside the British in wars against Langalibalele, Cetshwayo and Bambatha. However, George's father left Edendale to join the mercenary Sotho Chief Hlubi and his followers, who had been given land carved out of the formerly independent Zulu Kingdom near Nqutu for his role in fighting against Cetshwayo. The Khambule family intermarried with these *Amahlubi* families, with whom they formed an alliance. His father Isaac Khambule became a headman (*induna*) under Chief Hlubi. Hence, George was born in one of the most isolated and traditionalist areas of Zululand, even though he and his family prided themselves on their status of exemption from Native Law, for which they had to apply individually (Welsh, 1971).

It seems that George Khambule was originally named Garden Mtshokobezi Khambule, and it is not clear when he changed his name from 'Garden' to 'George' (as he appears in his application for status as 'exempted native' in 1918), probably after his time in Europe. It would appear to me to have been inspired by the visit of King George V to the SANLC during the First World War, to which we have already referred. He appears for his elderly father, and is cited as 'headman', in the magistrate's negotiations around who should succeed Chief Hlubi after his death in 1912. He is listed as one of those in favour of Chief Isaac Molife's succession, but the latter seems not to have appointed him headman after the death of Khambule's father in 1916, it would appear, since Frank Khambule is named as headman in the hearing of 1924. Nevertheless, he inherited his father's land, which he tended very successfully. The value of the crops and improvements when it was expropriated was £250, which was regarded as excessive in Pretoria. He also inherited his father's gun and applied successfully for a transfer of the licence. In line with the tradition of his family, George applied in 1918 for the status of an Exempted Native, which was granted after a tussle in 1919. His exemption papers record that he was educated up to Standard 4, probably at the famous Anglican mission school of St Augustine's, Nqutu. He worked on the mines as a police captain, was literate and competent at the secretarial work required by his job, dressed impeccably, also made money as a music teacher in Johannesburg. More fatefully, as we have seen, he volunteered for the British forces in the First World War as a volunteer in the South African Native Labour Corps, probably in 1917.

## The South African Native Labour Corps (1916–18)

The white settler government of the Union of South Africa was reluctant to allow black people to volunteer for military service. The offer in August 1914 of the South African Native National Congress, the forerunner to the African National Congress, and strongly dominated by *Amakholwa*, to encourage volunteers was rejected by the Secretary for Defence (Gleeson, 1994: 10–12). There is no doubt that the government feared the prospect of armed and well-trained black soldiers returning to South Africa after serving abroad. It was only once the disasters of the Somme Offensive and Delville Wood had stretched the Imperial Government and the Union Forces also that the colonial government agreed to the enlistment of African soldiers in the newly formed South African Native Labour Corps. However, they were to be unarmed and kept from direct military action. A total of 15,000 served in the war theatre in Europe. The irony of this situation is evident, if we examine its impact on someone like George Khambule, whose father, grandfather and great grandfather at the very least had served the colonial government in an armed capacity and who himself possessed a licensed firearm. Many of the volunteers were educated Christians (*Amakholwa*), who enlisted out of the same kind of idealism as drove the white volunteers. A volunteer, Stimela Jason Jingoes, writes:

> I followed closely the progress of the war, as our papers wrote it up, and I felt growing in me the conviction that I should go away and help in some way. (Clothier, 1987: 212)

Yet they were sent in unarmed to perform menial tasks such as cooking, dockyard duties, trench-digging and so on. They were kept separate from the other South African forces in a special barracks surrounded by barbed wire. They were forbidden to fraternize with white soldiers and were placed under the command of white officers (Clothier, 1987; Gleeson, 1994).

There is no doubt about the impact of the First World War on those who participated in it. Its impact has been analysed in a masterful way by Eric J. Leed in *No Man's Land: Combat and Identity in World War I* (Leed, 1979). He has discovered a remarkable consistency in the experience of enlisted men of all ranks and races and backgrounds and units, and on both sides of the conflict, which he describes as 'a coherent, unified, historical experience' (Leed, 1979: ix). I am sceptical about the claims of such universality, especially with regard to the participants in the SANLC, but there is evidence that there was still commonality of impact, despite the unarmed and separated status of the black soldiers. Their officers were affected in the same way as those of all the other serving units, being transferred in and out of the conflict. Their sense of frustrated aggression and inertia, highlighted by Leed, was in some ways heightened. Since they were employed digging trenches and docking among other things, they would have been in contact with the horrors of the war. They were also in the line of fire from the unseen enemy and victims of the technology of war, in some of the same ways as those in the trenches, only without means of defence, as Jingoes complains:

There we had a hard time, because nearly every evening we were attacked by the enemy planes and we had nothing to defend ourselves with. Only the whites were given arms. This camp was twice in flames during enemy attacks. (Gleeson, 1994: 36)

Their responses seem to follow some of the same patterns of trauma and neurosis (Clothier, 1987: 134–7). Yet their experience of racism and inertia, leading to repressed aggression, would have been even stronger. Their sense of alienation and dissociation from the society to which they returned would have been greater.

## The Effects of the First World War on the Soldiers

The impact of the First World War on the participants was traumatic and formative for their subsequent lives: in many ways it served, as Leed argues, as a rite of passage through the liminal space of No Man's Land. Yet they did not experience the re-aggregation and status elevation which normally accompany such rites of passage. They returned to a society which had changed and was afraid of these returning and traumatized soldiers, whose experience it could not understand:

The greatest danger to any society lies in the possibility that the warrior may begin to practice against 'friends' and kin the activities which are proper only against enemies and strangers. This danger, and the anomalous project of battle, is ameliorated by the ritual definition of the warrior as a man who has been temporarily separated from his social roots, set apart and placed together with strangers in a moral betwixt-and-between. If he wants to return to the life of settled domesticity, he must be re-adopted precisely as a stranger is adopted into a family or clan. (Leed, 1979: 14)

Leed explores 'the cultural repertoires of meaning drawn upon by participants to define felt alterations in themselves' (Leed, 1979: ix), but only within the limited confines of Western European culture. Their ritual experience of liminality was, in Victor Turner's terminology (Turner, 1969: 94–165), one of existential *communitas*, and their experience after demobilization was one of enforced normative liminality, with all the tensions and incompatibilities of that state. In a situation which contradicted and disconfirmed their worldviews, they attempted to reconfigure and reinterpret them in a way which made sense.

This attempt to force meaning on chaos by means of a reconfiguring of the deep and often hidden cultural values of the soldiers became more and not less intense in the years following their experience of combat:

> But with the ending of the war the pattern of discussion breaks down, for the cessation of hostilities did not mean the end of the war experience but rather the beginning of a process in which that experience was framed, institutionalised, given ideological content, and relived in political action as well as fiction . . . [so it ends with] an attempt to explain why the war experience was something which could *not* be resolved, reintegrated, and covered over with the exigencies of civilian existence. (Leed, 1979: xi)

The real problems which emerged after the war ended in riots and many other forms of violence, especially in 1919, the year of the 'khaki riots'. The returning soldiers were also prone to take part in and organize new social, religious and political movements, which appealed to their sense of human solidarity and community on the battlefield, yet their allegiance and commitment was evanescent and fickle.

Besides this sense of marginalization and continuing liminality, two of the defining characteristics of the war were especially formative for the combatants: the first was that of the domination of human beings by technologies and machines. The war was largely fought against an unseen enemy, waiting, inert, hiding underground, dehumanized and grotesque. Its destructive power was awesome beyond anything which had been experienced in the world before. The predominance of technology left its mark in a number of ways in a redefinition of man over against machine. Secondly, the continuing and ever-present reality of death and the horror of bombardment by an unseen enemy led to a widespread and continuing neurosis among soldiers even after their return, the experience of being buried alive, of dying and then returning slowly to life:

> It was so common that for a period during the war hysterical paralysis as a result of premature burial earned its own pathological category as the 'burial alive neurosis.' What is significant about this experience is that it was often felt to be an experience of death from which the victim slowly returned to life. (Leed, 1979: 23)

Finally, there was a widespread feeling among returning soldiers of having a secret which those at home could never understand. They are characterized by a burning sense of having changed into something new and that their 'secret' knowledge gained in such traumatic fashion was not easily communicated to those who had not shared it:

> Always the disorder, chaos, fragmentation of 'cherished categories' and the juxtaposition of normally separate things and moods is designated as the source both of the knowledge that characterizes men experienced in war and the incommunicability of this knowledge. Men issuing from the dark door of war are normally characterized as 'silent,' and this silence might be a mask for bitterness or for 'secrets'. (Leed, 1979: 28)

For returnees from the SANLC, there was the even more poignant experience of being confronted with a profound ambiguity. They experienced both the solidarity and existential community of the liminal wartime experience and also the racial discrimination of their unarmed and confined status under white officers with a starkness that contradicted that experience at the same time. They had a visit from a French parliamentary delegation which included a black member of the government (Clothier, 1987: 138) and were told that there was 'no discrimination in the French colonies'. They slipped out of camp to join in the makeshift nightlife of the trenches. They were visited by King George V of England, King Albert of Belgium, French Government delegates and General Smuts, as well as other high-placed people, and lectured on the importance of their contribution and persons. For the *Amakholwa* among the soldiers, who were educated and understood what was going on, this was an even more transformative experience than for the uneducated. Their experience of Europe in crisis changed their perspective on the racial inequalities back home in South Africa, as can be clearly seen in one documented instance, where a black soldier refused to be called a 'native' by his white officer, on the grounds that neither he nor the white officers were 'natives' in France. This led to a court martial, in which the black soldier, Jingoes, was acquitted, somewhat fortuitously (Clothier, 1987: 128–32). The impact of these experiences was not lost on the settler government in South Africa, who decided to terminate the SANLC even before the war ended, and there were riots at the docks and on board ship on the way home for the last contingent (Clothier, 1987: 160–3; Gleeson, 1994: 42–4).

## The Effect of this on George Khambule

During his work on the mines, after his wartime experience, Khambule and his girlfriend in Johannesburg were struck down by the Spanish Influenza which spread around the world after the First World War, killing millions. He had a vision of his girlfriend in the fires of hell, but he himself was saved by the intervention of his dead sister Agnes, who cried out to God that 'His time has not yet come!' A great wheel turns in front of him with the words of the Lord's Prayer on it, which stopped when it came to the words, 'Forgive us our sins as we forgive those who sin against us.' He stands accused of murder and of sexual misdeeds. Interesting in the light of his recent return from the Western Front, where the SANLC fought unarmed, he denied having killed anyone, a denial which is rejected in the vision: 'Then I saw the corpses of many people whom I had murdered, and then I spread my hands saying, "Lord I have never handled poison." The voice said, "You killed them with your mouth"' (Mhlungu, 1941: 14–17).

Khambule died and rose again, having been given a second chance on the appeal of his dead sister Agnes, whom he had helped put through school. In another prophecy, a liturgical performance celebrates Khambule's entry into heaven and fixes it in the memory of the community:

> *Priest:* Peace be with you. In 1918 on the eighteenth day of the tenth month it became dark at Khambule's place.
> *Congregation:* Today St Itengirrah is present.
> *Priest:* The gates were opened and one of us went with her through the twelve gates because he was worthy.
> *Congregation:* Itengirrah overcame death. (Diary 2: 85)

Note the language of being 'worthy', which echoes Revelation 5.2, 4, 9, 12, a foundational text for Khambule (Draper, 2002a; 2002b; 2004). His death and resurrection experience led to his attempt to build the New Jerusalem. He returned to his village at Telezini near Nqutu, summoned there by a local teacher turned evangelist, John Mtanti, who had heard of his conversion, and he began to preach repentance and practise healing and exorcism, setting up a new and exclusive community (Sundkler, 1976: 120–5).

In many ways, Khambule fits the profile common to ex-servicemen after the First World War in various countries, but it takes a different form in the cultural configuration of his own Zulu traditions. He has a vision for a New Jerusalem come down out of heaven to earth and a holy community living the life and worship of heaven. In the process he adopted and transformed the traditional Zulu understanding of kingship, with himself in the position of king, the embodiment and viceregent of Jesus on earth, 'You must know this. You have taken upon you the likeness of the Lord Jesus' (Diary 1: 7A). That 'Garden' Khambule became 'George' Khambule is an aspect of his royal aspirations. Indeed, as we have seen, he receives a vision in 1929 of King George acknowledging him and praising him, king to king!

He has come as God's king and judge on earth, being in some ways possessed by the spirit of Jesus, an incarnation of Jesus:

> Things in heaven stand like this. Now, it is the description of mystery. Now everything is coming together. Truly this is a mystery. Things begin to be hidden above. It was really the king himself who comes here, carrying many names in his hand. But do you not know? No! Listen now. The Judge will know how to discern between the tricky people and those who are sincere. They mentioned them yesterday. I kicked them out, according to Jehovah. It is the end of matter. Now, is it an explanation of the hidden things about you? The hidden things have come to pass now. Now the things, which are destined through you, are in the hands of *uTixo*. (Diary 1: 14A–14B)

Hence all nations will ultimately acknowledge George's sovereignty under God:

> The word of Jehovah *uTixo*: In this scripture all the nations shall be saved through you. It was written, 'Will and kingship, Lord Jesus Holy!' Part of the house was written, S.I.J.N.H.D.A.I.E.E. All the power of the prophets was written about you. These are their names, beginning from St Samuel up to the forefathers. OA! They ascended with a fiery chariot E & E. They all have been written upon you. That is why Jehovah said, 'All the nations shall bow under you, the black and the white.' It is so. [page 4B] They will follow you, those who believe in miracles. They are being attracted now, say St Gabriel and St Michael.

His converts were married to Jesus as the Lamb: they went through a marriage ritual after the traditional period of seclusion and entered the royal *isigodlo* or harem, in accordance with Zulu custom (Draper,

2002a). They were now forbidden to eat food of unbelievers (food offered to idols in Revelation) or to have sexual relations, even with their own spouses, since they were married to Jesus. Each of the members of the new community received their own guardian angel and were called by their own angelic name, rather as if the 'marriage of the Lamb' was also a marriage with a heavenly being. They received power over evil, which was physically located in a stone taken from the riverbed at Telezini. This was their *izikhali* or weapon against Satan. Khambule himself never was without his ritual stone in his hand, even when eating (Interview with Bra' Joe Mncube, 27 December 2001). They had a ministry of healing which was widely recognized among the community, even by one of the local magistrates, whose son was healed by Khambule. The worship of the community was premised on the understanding that it was an entry into heaven: 'The throne of God is established on earth through the victory of the Lord the Judge' (Liturgy 3: 4–5). The glory of the clothing and the dignity of the worship had to reflect this: 'The one who speaks with God must be adorned for heaven' (Diary 1: 44A). The angels are a felt but unseen presence all around in the worship of the community: 'We thank the holy ones (angels) of the Church. Yes, they cannot be seen. Let peace be among you. This is the new throne which came down' (Liturgy 3: 3).

Ultimately, the success of Khambule's movement in drawing members – several thousand at its height – also brought its downfall. The community at Telezini were outraged when their wives, daughters and sons left home to join the community, refused to eat any longer the food provided there and refused to marry or have normal sexual relations. A protracted and complicated legal process led to Khambule's expulsion from Telezini and the movement never really recovered from the loss of their New Jerusalem, despite the characterization of the new temporary homes of the community as 'Elim', the place of refreshment in the wilderness wanderings of Israel (Draper, 2003a: 57–89).

## The Ritualization of Memory

I have used the concept of the 'ritualization of memory' in a combination of the ritual theory of Victor Turner and the social constructionism of Berger and Luckmann (Berger and Luckmann, 1966). I am not really working with psychological theory of trauma here. Rather I am examining the way in which Khambule, after the transformative liminal experience of the Western front, reconstructed his social universe, combining elements from Zulu culture in new and fantastic shapes with the images and experiences of the war. I am also examining the way in which he attempted to construct the new community by the oral technique of ritual performance to create a communal memory out of his own personal experience and memory. Fundamental to this process for Khambule is that the experiences and visions on which the community is built are turned into liturgies and hymns sung, recited, performed by the members of his *iBandla Labancwele*, Church of the Holy Ones (cf. Draper 2005). Each oracle is dated, and often the place of the experience is recorded and also the angel through whom it was given. The oracle is then turned into liturgy and recited year by year and month by month, often day by day in the daily morning and evening prayers of the church.

## Ritualization of Death and Resurrection

We have already examined the death and resurrection experience of the war veteran which provides the starting-point for the New Jerusalem. This is celebrated in a hundred different ways in the hymns and liturgies of the church. So the death and resurrection and entry into heaven of Khambule is continually performed in this liturgy, as in this 'Hymn the Judge received from the Lord when he attacked the nations', which is 'affirmed by the four angels':

Halleluiah! The rest of the angels!
You will be brought before Caesar
Behold your God gives you all the people
Who walk with you.
You were taken to Paradise
And heard words which are not to be uttered. (Liturgy 3: 15)

The precise date of Khambule's visionary entry into heaven on 18 October 1918 is celebrated and fixed in time in many of the ritual performances. This is part of the process of solidifying and healing the personal death–resurrection neurosis and of creating salvation history for a new community. Through this 'secret' knowledge and experience of Khambule, the community themselves enter heaven and worship with the angels.

### The Ritualization of the Field Telegraph

A second aspect which emerges here, and is completely misunderstood by Khambule's only interpreter, Bengt Sundkler, is the 'telephone' or 'wire' (*ucingo*). This is one of the technological aspects of trench warfare: the encripted telegraph, so vital to survival and communication on the front. A message from an unseen power which a person can hear and decode is able to move whole sectors of an army, or order devastating firepower. It is likely that Khambule had purchased one of these war-surplus instruments himself after the war. He sees this as the medium of communication of the angels:

18th June 1925: This is the work of that angel who was seen by *Umshushisi* (the Prosecutor), who had put the wheel of the machine over the head of *Umshushisi*. (Diary 1: 18B; cf. 19B)

However, he seems to have been somewhat ambivalent about this machine, as if uncertain if the technology is or is not a necessary aspect of the oracular communication:

The faith of *Umahluli* [the Judge, i.e. Khambule] on the day he met *iNkosi* [the Lord] and then there were written in him in truth their faith and wrath of God which will conclude everything in this place about the matter of the machine, so that it will never be talked about again. It is needed that everything which has been done does not matter if this matter of the machine does not happen. Whereas the angel who speaks comes from God, who arranges everything, it is not an inheritance. (Diary 1: 21A–21B)

It seems that he finally resolved his unease by burying the machine with his first female assistant, Joanna Ndluvu, who died probably of polio in 1926:

Saturday 2/1/26 7:30pm: With regard to the matter of the machine, which belonged to a white man, St. Agrinneth Khambule had received from Nazar [Khambule], today it is handed over to Joanah Ndlovu to be hers, as she is St. Agrinneth's [Khambule's sister's] child. It is like this. There is no dispute today about it. It has gone out of the hands of *Umahluli* [Khambule] today. It is so. (Diary 1: 47B)

Although the 'machine' continues to be spoken of even until the end of the Church, no-one after the death of Khambule in 1949 was able to explain what it was, other than to insist that Khambule could talk to God by means of it. The text of his diary and the robes of the leaders of the church are full of encrypted letters in the early days.

The word of the Lord is delivered in code and then interpreted by Khambule: 'The word of Jehovah *uTixo*: in this scripture all the nations shall be saved through you. It was written, 'Will and kingship, Lord Jesus Holy!' Part of the house was written, S.I.J.N.H.D.A.I.E.E.' (Diary 1: 4A). Sometimes we can observe him working out the codes:

A. B. C., three stars, they are present today. They stand for God F. God S. God H. They were written to you, the power of the Trinity, but you did not know. These stars existed before anybody else. 'This is why all the nations shall be under you,' says Alpha Omega swearing. 'It is so I.K.S.P.T.' 'Is he the king, priest and God?' Here is the answer, 'No,' says Jehovah Immanuel, God with us. 'Who is the judge?' 'The coming Judge is Jesus. Know therefore that it is He who is the Judge. *uSimakade* [the Eternal One],' says Jehovah. 'This is the Scripture. It says about you, that you are what you are.' (Diary 1: 4B–5A).

At other times the coding is completely opaque to us: '4th June 1925 6 pm–9.30 pm: The General of the Lord and prosecutor I.K.Y.I.Y.K.A. The glorious morning star, the stone on which all the apostles are written (Stones of the 12 Apostles).' Or although we see them written on the ritual stole of Joanna Ndlovu, we cannot really understand any significance at all beyond mystery: 'Y.-S.P.A.J.Z.J. F.B.T.M.J.A.L.T.S.K.-S.O.S. These are the names that were written on the glorious morning star' (Diary 1: 8A).

### The Ritualization of Command Structure

The military experiences of Khambule in the First World War seem to be primarily interpreted by means of the Apocalypse (Draper, 2004). The experience of the prophet and his community are seen as a kind of holy warfare against the unseen forces of Satan. The iconography of the community makes this plain. For instance, in the photograph of Khambule with his two female assistants, Joanna Ndlovu and Fakazi Mhlungu (printed in Sundkler, 1976: plate facing p. 140), the stole of Ndlovu is inscribed with the title, 'General of the Lord', while

the stole of Mhlungu is inscribed, 'The General's Clack [*sc.* Clerk] of
the Lord and Prosecutor' (the Zulu word *uMshushisi* is frequently
used). The latter is a reference to the Presiding Officer at a Court
Martial, which was a very real experience in the life of a front soldier
(see Jingoes' account of his own court martial, in Clothier, 1987).
Khambule himself wears a crown entitled 'Camp of God', and is
entitled, 'The Beginning and the End', 'Alpha and Omega'. All three of
them carry weapons (*izikhali*) in the form of stones carefully wrapped
in white cloth to contain their power and holiness, just as a Zulu
*isangoma* carries his divining materials. Besides the decipherable
names, all three wear mystic encryptions of prophecy.

These titles, together with other titles like *Captenis* (Captain), who
marshals the *isigodlo* (royal harem), 'Bearer of the Ark', *Umahluli*
(Judge) and many others, create a command structure and ritual order
which incorporates the battlefield as well as the heavenly home of the
New Jerusalem. Status and hierarchy are clearly set out and formulated. Members of the *iBandla Labancwele* are called 'Volunteers' and
wear uniforms and hats with this written on them. One of the key
aspects of the community is the organized 'hospital' (*isibhedlela*),
which uses the stone 'weapons' and water with ashes mixed in, to heal
the sick, with the healing group carefully arranged in cross formation.
There are also the 'labour gangs' (*amaGang*, language surely taken
from the SANLC, the black Labour Corps on the Western Front) or
prayer groups of the community, who resist the power of Satan in
organized fashion.

As a final hint of the returning soldier behind the mask, I would like
to return to the vision with which we began, received when things
were going badly wrong for Khambule. The white magistrate had
finally succeeded in destroying his New Jerusalem and dismantling the
church building as well. He has not yet settled into his final home at
Spookmill. His vision is of King George V, who had visited the
SANLC at Abbeville on 10 July 1917, and had addressed the troops
earnestly. He also spoke to troops on a boat going home on the same
occasion. Jacob Koos Matli, one of the volunteers, writes that the King
had 'addressed us personally and thanked us for the services we had
rendered. He told us that we were going home within a few days, and
when we reached home we must tell our Chiefs and fathers how he
had thanked us' (Clothier, 1987: 139). There is a photograph of the
King addressing the SANLC (Gleeson, 1994: 41), which is poignant
when placed beside this vision of George Khambule, to which we have
already made reference in our opening remarks:

Friday 5/4/1929

Nazar, what I have seen tonight is great indeed. Why? Because I was before King George V and he was reading a letter which was talking about me, praying for me about everything with all his strength. Because I am greater than him. I cannot remember all the praise names which he was giving me and those which I was giving him. Indeed there were many things which he spoke about his own white people, that they know about me but they have forgotten and they did not do all that they were supposed to do. He was talking and praying with all his might and with all he has. Indeed there is great joy. He was jumping for joy, appreciating me very much indeed. I thank my God very much. I don't have the power to praise him. (Diary 1: 99B–100A)

### Ritualization of Weaponry

Along with the other adopted metaphors of the war taken up in Khambule's system is the ritualization of weaponry. The stones used in healing, exorcism and protection in the war against Satan are called *izikhali* or 'weapons'. The term can also have a cultic sense and is often used to refer to the crossed spears and shield, which might be placed prominently in a home (usually in the ancestral shrine or *umsamo*) to ward off evil magic. Red-black volcanic stones taken from the riverbed at Telezini are held in the hand, wrapped in white cloth to protect the user from their power. These are passed over the sick in the hands of the *isibedlela* or hospital or held to mediate power in prayer (Draper, 2003a; Mhlungu, 1941). Former members of the church and family members recount that Khambule was never without his 'weapon' in his hand, even when eating at table.

### Race Conflict and Holy War

Another ambivalence in Khambule's position is his transitional position between the rural traditional people of Telezeni and the urban setting of Johannesburg and the mines. He, and ultimately his followers as well, commute between two worlds, between the mechanized, commodified world of the city and the traditional world of rural Zululand, just as he spans the divide between the educated, westernized *Amakholwa* of Natal and the illiterate, largely traditional religious practices of Zululand.

His experience of war and white officers produced the same

repressed anger that can be found widely in front soldiers, but transposed now into a spiritualized cosmic warfare:

> He will defeat Satan. The ark will come out from the camp to fight the Philistines. The camp should fast because Satan will be proud, so it is good that we should be strong. It will go with Captenis and the staff before you. (Diary 1: 35B–36A)

When he is tried before the magistrate for 'causing trouble' in the reserve, he sees the process as a holy warfare, in which the angelic armies are triumphant against the Philistines and the Ruler of Babylon. The vision seen on the occasion on 27 April 1926 is transcribed into liturgy as 'The Prayer of the Church of the Holy Ones of April 1926 for Victory over the Philistines at Nqutu Babylon. *Through St. Itengirrah*', copied several times and performed in the worship of the community (Liturgy 3: 86–91; Diary 2: 7–12; the full text of the vision may be found in Draper, 2003a: 76–7). It describes the hearing before the magistrate of Nqutu as cosmic conflict between the Philistines and the ruler of Babylon on the one hand, and Khambule 'dressed in the clothes that he was dressed in the day he fought Satan' and the angelic powers on the other hand. Khambule before the colonial magistrate is portrayed as reversing the roles in the court, by giving judgement to his judges according to the 'scale' of justice which he holds: 'He gave everyone their due.' At the beginning of the hearing, heaven stands silent like the 'folded scroll' of Revelation. Even the sun and the moon stand silent, until Khambule's accusers enter, and they are miraculously put to confusion: 'The first Philistine put his foot inside, all the angels turned their back, and when all the Philistines entered, they lost their minds. They quarrelled with each other.' The members of *IBandla Labancwele* look to the north, the south, east and west praying for peace, but at midday, the angels enter and put the enemies of God to rout:

> Then at 12pm the cherubim entered, whom no one could stop. They were with their leader St Gabriel. They sang and said, 'Be opened you eternal gates, so that the King of Glory may come in.' They said, 'Give them power, God.' At that moment the form of St. Nazar was like the sun. His voice was like the sound of rushing waters. Then the ruler of Babylon went mad and he surrendered. (Liturgy 3: 89–90)

The language of the Scroll visions of Revelation 7, where the seventh angel holds back from opening the seventh seal until the right moment, informs the depiction of the whole courtroom drama. The colonial authorities have become Rome-Babylon, the material expression of the rule of Satan. The hearing, which led ultimately to Khambule's expulsion from his New Jerusalem after a further three-year-long drama, is depicted in terms of holy war in which heavenly victory is already assured. It is ritualized here in an attempt to construct the social universe of the new community.

## Conclusion

A study such as this can only map out tempting lines of interpretation. There are 600 pages of Zulu script, containing diaries, hymns and liturgies. There is a hypnotic quality about them and, certainly, field visits to survivors of the movement quickly rekindled the excitement and sense of joy and awe experienced by Khambule's followers. What is performed becomes real to the performers. There are angels, there is the New Jerusalem. Satan is defeated by the weapons of the 'hospital' (*isibhedlela*). This is a rich field for studying the interface between the worlds of Africa and Europe, Zulu tradition and Christian inculturation. The movement failed for a number of reasons, but in its attempt to construct the new and alternative community in the interface between these worlds and with the experience of the trauma of war, it retains its fascination. Ironically, in my research, I found that a different (probably related) George Khambule fought also in the Second World War (Private N30728), *plus ça change, plus c'est la même chose.*

## Note

1  All references to Khambule are from Khambule, 1925–49.

# 7. The Dark Side of Pentecostal Enthusiasm:
## Abraham's and Sara's Sacrifice in Knutby, Sweden

JONE SALOMONSEN

## Faith with a Licence to Kill?

There is always a dark side to religion, as there is to any human, social configuration. In this chapter I will reserve the adjective 'dark' to the fact that Pentecostal beliefs and worldview sometimes are used to legitimize practices that are in radical disjunction with contemporary social norms, such as taking somebody's life. It will also refer to the fact that when such severe transgressions are known, they seldom seem to trigger any substantial or critical self-examination of basic theological paradigms, of the ethics of inter-human relations or of spiritual authority in the Pentecostal movement as such. To the extent that self-reflexive utterances are heard, they tend to be limited to a rejection of unhealthy or isolated leadership, or to blaming a single individual's unfortunate failure to gain a *correct* understanding of completely harmless theological propositions that are purely aimed at healing and empowering ordinary people and bringing them close to God.

But is this true? Is Pentecostalism really only about vitality, prosperity and direct communion with God? Hasn't the movement *always* balanced on a very difficult edge between, on the one hand, proclamations of God's wonderful love for all, promising rewarding spiritual gifts to anyone who listens to their heart and makes Jesus their Lord, and on the other hand a rather aggressive form of a hermeneutics of suspicion, not applied to written texts or biblical interpretative traditions, but to people and their moral faculties whenever they would be disagreeing with Pentecostal authority? In such certainty of being God's elect, executors of God's so-called revealed 'will', does not

Pentecostalism risk being totally occupied with modifying, engineering, 'fixing' – fixing personal destinies, fixing away evil, fixing up the world – and thus ending up supporting very cold and aggressive forms of 'love'; forms that do not hesitate to break personal autonomy or to invade a person's psychic and bodily space, if called to do so by a higher power?

To substantiate my allegations, I shall present three legal cases of total bodily invasion to the point of death, although the actions were legitimized with traditional Pentecostal rhetoric of doing 'good' or following 'orders' from God on high. The first case is from California and pasted almost directly from Carol Delaney's book *Abraham on Trial* (Delaney 1998). It is a finished case, researched and analysed in depth by her. The next case is from England, and the third and most recent one is from Knutby in Sweden. To my knowledge, scholarly research has not yet been published on the two last cases. Thus, the data available to me for description are court decisions, inquiry reports and public media. The latter are not always trustworthy, neither in detail nor amplitude, but I will use them as carefully as possible and cross-check the information I pass on.

While I do intend to investigate what it means to kill someone out of love of God or obedience to the Almighty in a Pentecostal setting, I will just briefly touch upon the personal and psychological motivations for committing such a horrific act. People who seek out the Pentecostal movements as adults do not come empty-handed. Among many things they bring former religious upbringing, moralities and local cosmologies. Their process of entering a Pentecostal community is, therefore, less a process of reception than of active appropriation: they blend new beliefs with old, and integrate this mix in a number of different ways, depending on who they are, where they are, and how they have become all that they are. In the cases to be discussed, I have no access to data that may help us understand really deeply the complexity of reasons that make a particular associate of Pentecostalism in a particular context end up as a criminal. Having said this, we should still take notice of the following: the three acts of killing were in every instance intertwined with certain interpretations of some very central textual traditions or biblical themes that eventually also were used as model or alibi for the fatal actions. The themes are:

1  Abraham's obedient almost-sacrifice of Isaac.
2  Joel's prophecy that one day, God will pour out the spirit on all flesh, so that your sons and daughters will prophesy, old men have

dreams, and young men see visions (Joel 2. 28–9) – a prophecy which, according to Peter in Acts, is fulfilled when these spiritual gifts apparently are bestowed upon the apostles and the believers (brothers) at Pentecost as sign and effect of the coming of the Holy Spirit (Acts 2. 14–21).

3 The Gospel 'evidence' of Jesus' and the disciples' power to cast out demons, thus legitimizing (gnostic and/or shamanic) models of the body as jar or container, waiting to be filled or emptied by outside (good or evil) agents.

In addition, Pentecostalism represents a form of experiential or primeval spirituality not exclusive to Christianity (Cox, 1995). If we resort to analytical language, we may say that Pentecostals modulate the sociality of ordinary space and time through more or less ritualized forms of *strong prayer* (performative prayer with body movements), *channelling* (speaking in tongues, receiving messages from being online with God), *chanting* (simple, repetitive singing), *trance-work* (ecstatic singing, praying and dancing intended to induce an altered form of consciousness) and *healing* (depossession through powerful speech/naming/witnessing, or moving energy through the laying on of hands).

These ritual elements, encountered cross-culturally, are usually far more important for the crafting of a holy, corporate, Pentecostal body than any Christian sacrament, including Baptism. In fact, Pentecostals share many features with the so-called New Age movements and may, to a certain extent, be categorized as a post-Christian or post-traditional phenomenon within Christianity. There are three basic characteristics of this contemporary religious trend: first, a nostalgic turn towards an ancient literary past to help redirect the future, morally as well as socially, by using highly contested textual strategies; second, overwriting Christology with a mystical, beneficial Creation theology and/or advocating direct communion with divinity as a path to salvation and/or self-realization; third, reclaiming a magical world-view in order to gain power with/over life in contemporary society (particularly over suffering, illness and death) (Salomonsen, 2002).

In the case of Neo-Pentecostals, they turn towards an imagined biblical past at the same time as they blend into and invoke the authority of a Gnostic, dualist worldview of a Manichaean bent. The Gnostic God of the world is a powerful Creator/Warrior God who continuously is at war with an almost equally powerful Satan and his army of demonic spirits. Consequently, the willingness to employ demonology rather than Christology when seeking out the religious meaning of affliction and death is stunning in the communities to be discussed. The suffering, dying, resurrected Christ is reduced to the 'name of Jesus', a name made powerful through a historical 'bloody sacrifice' in Jerusalem. Yet, 'Jesus' has become a cultic name to be used invocatively and performatively to cast out demons and induce healing and well-being.

These allegations will be substantiated and discussed in the second part of the chapter. First, however, I will present the three cases that set the background to my claims and critical discussions.

### Case Study 1: California.
### 'How Can You Say No to God?'

The first case to be considered is narrated by Carol Delaney (1998). On 6 January 1990 in California, a middle-aged bus driver, called Cristos Valenti, by Delaney, took his youngest child, his most beloved daughter, with him in the truck, to faithfully accomplish what the voice of God had told him to: sacrifice the one he loved the most. They drove to a place he had been directed to, and he told her that she soon would meet God. As they prayed, 'Our Father, who art in heaven', he took the knife and killed her. He sat next to her body and prayed for several minutes. When he looked up he saw her star shining brightly in the night sky; he saw two stars moving closer together. He knew then he had fulfilled her destiny, he knew he had done the right thing. He picked her up and took her home. When his oldest daughter opened the door she saw her father holding the child, like a *pieta*. 'Call the police,' he said. 'I have given her to God' (Delaney, 1998: 35).

Cristos never admitted to murder, even though he knew he had committed a legal wrong. Otherwise he would not have asked his oldest daughter to call the police. In court, he argued that to kill your own child does not mean that you are either evil or insane. According to Delaney, he said: 'How can you say no to God? Everything is his. We all belong to him. It was an order directly to me from God; God asked me for her. You can't back out. I had no choice.' When the court-appointed psychologist questioned Cristos about the law, why laws are necessary, Cristos answered: 'Laws are for everybody because there's a lot of trouble around out there.'

Psychologist: 'Thou shalt not kill, what about that law?'
Cristos: 'That's God's commandment.'
Psychologist: 'Did you break that law?'
Cristos: 'Yes and no. I did break it because the Bible says that, but I didn't break it because God told me to' (Delaney 1998: 58).

The psychiatrists called Cristos' experience an 'auditory hallucination', and the jury sentenced him 'not guilty by reason of insanity', and ordered psychiatric treatment. Delaney reports that almost everybody in the courtroom cried upon hearing this verdict. They felt betrayed on behalf of the murdered child and the mother who gave birth to her and had now lost her.

Cristos grew up as a Catholic, but had left the Catholic Church and moved to a charismatic, Pentecostal church with his wife and six children. Neither the prosecutor nor the public defender called the minister of this church to the stand as witness, but Carol Delaney interviewed him at his church when researching the case. The minister did not think Cristos was insane even though he claimed to hear voices. Rather, he felt Cristos struggled between good and evil forces, between the voice of God and the voice of the Devil. But which is which? During the autumn prior to the murder, the church's Bible study group had studied Genesis 22. According to the minister, 'Abraham laid the wood on Isaac as the cross was put on Jesus' (Delaney, 1998: 46). But now, he went on, 'God has no need for sacrifices any more. Jesus is the final sacrifice'. The minister took no responsibility for having contributed to Cristos' confusion and evil action through his preaching; neither did he feel that the tradition had any responsibility. He claimed that the story of Abraham is a model to be followed, exactly. And according to the model, Isaac was saved. But, as Delaney observes, the minister fails to recognize that it was not Abraham who prevented the sacrifice, but God. Cristos, too, was following a command from God, not the biblical model, and *his* God did not tell him to stop.

Furthermore, the voice of ethical reason is in the tradition expressed by the figure of the Devil. As Delaney notices, both Jewish midrash and Muslim legend are explicit when letting the Devil say to Abraham: 'How could you possibly think of killing your precious son? This is the son God said would make you the father of many nations.' The point of both midrash and legend, says Delaney, is that the Devil is trying to tempt Abraham away from his duty to God by arousing his compassion for his son. Abraham's duty was to follow God's command.

But, as Delaney points out, in the twentieth century, the minister felt that the voice telling Cristos to do the deed could not possibly have been God's. Cristos obviously disagreed with his minister in this effort to limit what God possibly can say and not say, even today.

Delaney then asks: how did Cristos get the idea that the child was *his* to sacrifice? One answer is that the concept of paternity in the Christian tradition is embedded in a theory of procreation in which only male seed is regarded as generative, whereas maternity means passive soil into which the seed is planted (Delaney, 1998: 157). That which is generated by the male belongs to the male – although in the end it must return back to God, to whom everything really belongs since he is the Father and creative power of all (a further presentation of this very important section of Delaney's book is beyond the scope of this chapter).

## Case Study 2: England.
## 'She Would Not Cry at All'

On 25 February 2000, a black girl named Victoria Adjo Climbié died from severe abuse and hypothermia in London, eight years old. According to a governmental inquiry report published in January 2003, she had 128 separate injuries on her body and virtually no hair when she died. Nearly 18 months earlier her parents had sent her from home in a shanty town in the Ivory Coast to live with her great-aunt, Marie, in Tottenham, North London, in the hope that she would get a good education and a better life. After a short while, her aunt became convinced that witchcraft had followed the girl from the Ivory Coast, and that evil spirits possessed her. This belief, which may or may not have served merely as an excuse for the abuse, was nevertheless the reason Marie and her boyfriend, Carl, gave for beating the girl daily and keeping her tied up in a plastic sack in an unlit, unheated bathroom for long periods of time. One sign that the stubborn spirits continued to inhabit her was that 'You could beat her and she would not cry at all. She could take the beatings and pain like anything', as Carl explained in his written confession that was read in court when the couple were tried for murder (*The Guardian*, 6 December 2001).

Not succeeding in exorcising the evil spirits themselves, even though they obviously tried to fight with them physically, Victoria's abusers took her to a series of evangelical and Pentecostal churches. Here, the girl was made to repeat the story that she was possessed by demons and that Satan was making her injure herself. Pastor Pascal Orome at the 'Mission Ensemble Pour Christ' in Borough, south-east London, met her six months before she died, in late August 1999, and was apparently convinced that the girl's injuries and bruises were the result of demonic possession. He exorcised her, seemingly with no results. When the pastor saw the girl again in October, Marie provided 'new evidence' that she still was possessed: the eight-year-old was incontinent, put excrement into food, burned herself and 'made a mess' at home.

In the period immediately before her death, Marie and Carl brought the girl to the pastors of the Brazilian-based but worldwide Universal Church of the Kingdom of God at the Rainbow Theatre in Finsbury Park, north London. As we know from Furre's and Esperandio's contributions above, the church offers a 'deliverance service' for those whose health is troubled by spirits. Here they met with Pastor Alvaro Lima and Marie Thérèse explained her witchcraft thesis to him. Even though he was not fully convinced that witchcraft was the real problem, he apparently agreed that the girl had 'spiritual problems' and that he would fast and pray for her. He also suggested that they returned for the more powerful Friday service, at which they would try to cast out the evil spirits. But when pastor Lima saw the girl again, she was barely conscious. He realized that the girl was sick, probably from 'neglect', and asked Marie to take her to hospital. It was too late. She died the next day.

On 12 January 2001, Marie and Carl were convicted for having murdered the girl and jailed for life. They did not receive the verdict 'not guilty by reason of insanity', as did Cristos Valenti. In Cristos' case, it was impossible for the prosecutor to present any minister from any recognized Christian congregation who would defend child sacrifice as a legitimate outcome from having formed a personal covenant with God and promised to obey his orders. Sacrifice as such is understood as a closed avenue since Jesus is proclaimed to be the final sacrifice. A sacrificial scheme that demands the killing of organic life, the actual shedding of animal (or human) blood as a necessary intermediary in order to obtain blessing, balance out sin, propitiate God's anger or perform an act of obedience, which once had a place in Israelite religion, even in Judaism, has no place in the Christian tradition. Even though traditional Christian theology makes no sense without recourse to a sacrificial language, it is purely a case of 'sacrifice in a spiritual sense', for example offerings to God of a pure heart, a broken conscience, good deeds towards fellow human beings. This is also why it was concluded that Cristos Valenti was mentally ill. He took what he heard literally and performed, against all sense and habit, an act banned by the tradition as cruel, irrational and heathen.

This was not the case with Marie and Carl, rather the opposite. They reasoned and acted according to a learnt magical worldview that has reified people's experiences of good and evil into an external war between God and the Devil, a perpetual war that takes place simultaneously on a macro (cosmic) and micro (social) level. This fight may, in addition, intrude itself into the otherwise bounded space of the individual body, causing all kinds of misery. The situation, however, according to such a worldview is not without hope, since certain 'specialists' can settle the war temporarily through exorcism of the evil, as can for example Jesus and the pastors of his church. Marie and Carl share this worldview with millions of other fellow Christians, a worldview that is well and alive, and not banned by any international Christian consensus. Contested, yes, but not banned. Their crime, therefore, was to take too far the option of exorcising the Devil, not to invent the option itself, or the Devil. This, at least, is a possible explanation why they could not be diagnosed as mentally ill, but rather had to be treated as two ordinary citizens, totally responsible for their own acts, which were to have used their beliefs as an excuse to torture and literally 'beat the hell out of' Victoria as if she was a demon.

However, when the Universal Church of the Kingdom of God advertise on their web page for 'spiritual release gatherings' on Friday nights, offering 'strong prayer to destroy witchcraft, demon-possession, nightmares, curses, envy, bad luck, etc.', they reproduce and confirm a socially meaningful world similar to that of Marie and Carl. Thus, the difference between them is only one of degree, not of kind, since it all comes down to disagreement on the legitimate methods to reach an otherwise common goal: authentic, prosperous living in a clean body, filled up with the Holy Spirit, depossessed of inauthentic, evil spirits causing illness, unemployment, broken families, jealousy, alcoholism, despair, poverty, bad luck. The crucial question that set the Universal Church apart from the two black immigrants is this: by what means may the Devil be purged? What means are proper, which ones are improper, inefficient, and unethical? Symbolic beatings in terms of strong prayers or fights upon a podium, that is, the church altar, are legitimate, as are incantations and devocations spoken by a person of authority. Physical beatings, on the other hand, are not legitimate, at least not in public, and at least not to the point of death. Resort to such means is a sign of superstition, of having too little faith, of having paid (sacrificed) too little money to the altar, typical of the poor and uneducated, or perhaps a manifestation of pure evil: the Devil in human form, trying to exorcise/extinguish the God-given life of an eight-year-old girl. The church, of course, can take no responsibility for such misuse. Or can it? Let us see what happened.

The killing of Victoria Climbié was extremely brutal, happening little by little, day by day. Yet, what happened was not hidden from public eyes. Many people, among them social workers and Pentecostal pastors, met the suffering girl several times and had a chance to stop the abuse and save her life. Why didn't they react? To understand this and to estimate whether criminal charges should be brought against more people, a public inquiry into her death began in September 2001. The chairman of the inquiry, Lord Laming, handed his report to the Government on 6 January 2003, and it was published on 23 January 2003. The report revealed that there had been at least 12 chances for the social agencies involved in her protection to save her life. As a result, two social workers were suspended. Yet, none of them admitted to having done anything wrong. One shared Marie's worldview and stated she had been the victim of a 'witch-hunt' since the true reason for her failure to intervene was poor supervision by her seniors. The other one, a senior social worker manager, denied all charges. Marie and Carl also gave evidence in the inquiry. While Marie claimed to be innocent and the victim of a conspiracy (she had done what she did out of love for the girl), Carl apparently apologized for his part in the poor girl's death and said the child protection agencies could not be blamed for her suffering. This is not surprising. After all, Marie and Carl were convinced that evil spirits possessed Victoria and that she brought the dangerous spells of witchcraft into their tiny flat in Tottenham. Consequently, they did not ask any social worker for help, they asked Christian ministers in the Pentecostal tradition who explicitly offer, to a wide public, exorcism and deliverance from troubling spirits.

The statutes of the Universal Church of the Kingdom of God maintain that a pastor is one of God's elect and not subject to criticism from the congregation, only from God himself. Having incorporated such a leadership model, it is not surprising that neither the Universal Church in London nor its pastors were willing to take any responsibility for perpetuating or feeding on a simplistic, double-edged worldview that historically, at least in the West, has helped to kill so many people (so-called 'heretics' and 'witches'). Pastor Alvaro Lima admitted to being unconcerned about Victoria's medical welfare, and that he failed to contact the police or any child protection services about his concerns. But that's all. An official investigation into the church even concluded that there was no evidence that the Universal Church ever had claimed to be able to heal individuals or purge them of demons, nor to cure them. They just offer prayers to help people overcome their illnesses for 'only God can heal' (www.rickross.com/groups/universal.html, 9 May 2003).

## Case Study 3: Knutby, Sweden.
## Lethal Text Messages from God

The last killing to be considered here took place in January 2004 in a Pentecostal community in Knutby, a small town of 600 inhabitants just outside Uppsala, Sweden. The court trial started in mid-May and ended on 30 July 2004 when the two suspects, Helge Fossmo and Sara Svensson, were convicted for murder. Helge Fossmo, however, did not accept the verdict and appealed to a higher court. On 12 November 2004 he lost and was sentenced to jail for life. He then re-appealed to the Supreme Court, but on 4 January 2005 the court dismissed the case.

This case is more complicated to represent since one of the convicted, Helge Fossmo, has not admitted anything and therefore has told us nothing. It is nevertheless possible to draw a simple outline of the events by using the testimonial highlights processed in court as well as the basic arguments in the legal verdict that was passed. My main source is the numerous news reports that documented the case in detail, in particular the highly regarded Swedish newspaper *Dagens Nyheter* which printed extensive, tape-recorded 'word by word' documentation from the court proceedings. My main goal is to portray a way of thinking and acting that is legitimized by a theological discourse that claims power over any aspect of life – social, ritual, sexual, legal – and hence a divine right to modify any of these institutions 'if necessary', even the right to live.

Early morning 10 January 2004, a 26-year-old former nanny, Sara Svensson, killed Alexandra Fossmo (23), step-mother of three and wife of Helge Fossmo, while asleep in her own bed. Helge Fossmo (32), who at the time was a senior pastor in Knutby Philadelphia Church, slept in another room and – according to what he claimed in the trial – did not wake up from the gunshots. After having killed Alexandra, Sara went to the neighbour's house, rang the bell and shot

Daniel Linde (30) as he opened the door, and then ran away. Surprisingly, Linde did not die although he was severely injured. Some months later he was even able to testify in the trial. Daniel is married to Anette Linde (26), and both are members of the congregation.

Two days after the murder, Sara confessed that she had committed the crimes, and that she had done it alone. However, it soon came out that Sara had been pastor Fossmo's mistress for several years. For six months she had even lived in his bedroom, while his wife slept on a couch in the living room. In 2003, Helge and Sara's relationship changed from affection to abuse, and in the autumn Helge started to have nightly visits from another woman: his neighbour, Anette Linde. Sara was 'degraded' to the basement, although she continued to deliver sexual services to the pastor daily.

Sara was obviously humiliated and most probably jealous, too. But, if so, why didn't she kill Helge Fossmo or Anette Linde? Why did she kill the pastor's even more humiliated wife, Alexandra, the one exiled from the marriage bed to the couch? And why attempt to kill Daniel, who already was being let down by his wife, Anette Linde? Probably because jealousy was *not* the motive. And clearly, about two weeks after the murder, on 30 January a new picture started to emerge. Helge Fossmo was arrested, suspected of being a collaborator. Two months later the charges against him were extended to include suspicion of murdering his first wife, Helene, as well, the biological mother of his three children. Helene had died five years earlier under very strange circumstances.

In April 2004 the public was informed that in the two months leading up to the murder of his second wife, Alexandra, Helge and Sara had exchanged more than 2,000 text messages, and a phone call 15 minutes after the crime was committed. In fact, on the day of the murder they sent each other 18 messages and spoke ten times on the phone. Sara protected Helge until the police proved to her that he was the real author of those anonymous text messages she had believed were sent to her phone by God himself, instructing her in the killing and pushing her forward.

The trial started on 18 May 2004, and both Helge and Sara were formally charged with murder. Yet the prosecutors' theory was that Helge the pastor was the main perpetrator while Sara the nanny was manipulated by Helge, herself a victim of severe mind control and ideological/theological seduction. What was this theory based on? In addition to interpreting field research, confessions, testimonies and technical findings, it was deduced from a critical 'reading' of the story hidden in the case. The following is a short version of this story, based on my interpretation of the prosecutors' 'reading'.

In the early 1990s, the Philadelphia Church in Knutby went through a process of rejuvenation and growth due to the charismatic pastor Åsa Waldau, at that time 26. She had moved from Uppsala to Knutby because of her husband-to-be, Patrick Waldau, who is ten years younger than she. Although one of six pastors, she soon became the leader due to her rare gift of attracting lots of young people who decided to move to Knutby because of her prophetic abilities and probably also counselling skills. Together, she and they created a community that newcomers said they felt radiated care, love and joy, a place where people dared to show their brotherly/sisterly love through hugs, kisses, touch and fond words. As is common in Pentecostal groups, they built their relationships through singing and praising, spontaneous witnessing, strong prayer, prophetic speech, visioning and dreaming, Bible study groups guided by the Holy Spirit, and obedience to the Lord(s) both in heaven and in the home.

The fact that the community accepts a female pastor should not be mistaken as sign of any tacit feminism. It is rather a result of this congregation having been inspired by the controversial community ideals of the Australian pastor David Cartledge (who has been visiting both Sweden and Norway). Basically, these ideals are (1) Apostolic leadership, meaning that the leaders are chosen directly by God, and therefore responsible only to God. They are leaders *because* of their direct communication-lines, and therefore have absolute authority in spiritual matters. (2) Equality between the sexes *in* the worship since the Spirit comes to all and the Bible says Jesus had female disciples, meaning that women are welcome into the ministry. (3) Non-equality between the sexes *outside* the ministry since the Bible says woman is created as helper, and man portrayed as her head. When Helge Fossmo told the court that it is a woman's duty to please her husband sexually whenever he wants, to obey his word and not be rebellious, there is nothing exceptional about his sayings from the point of view of this community. So, yes, Åsa Waldau can be a charismatic leader in church, but she is still a woman and must therefore obey her husband Patrick at home. According to witnesses, there are written rules in Knutby instructing women and men how to behave in relation to each other. These rules aim at reinforcing a hierarchical, patriarchal family model, and may seem very strict to an outsider, though apparently authored by Åsa herself. The existence of these rules and everybody's stated agreement to live by them, have been confirmed by all the witnesses brought to the stand.

However, this 'loving' community was knit together even more tightly, and its hierarchical, gendered bi-polar (or dualist) worldview confirmed even more strongly, when the pastors started to help arrange marriages between spiritual brothers and sisters they felt were fit, or that would benefit the husband in his growth process. Apparently, they did not feel obliged to consider whether the couple were in love or not since God would 'fix' such 'details' if they just prayed for it to happen and otherwise obeyed His word. Some refused and ran away, others agreed, such as Sara, who in 2000 married a man she did not love because the pastors said it was the right thing to do.

Marriage in Sweden is customarily regulated by exogamic kinship rules; that is, rules saying you should marry outside the (extended) family. It is also governed by bilateral, egalitarian family ideals according to which children belong to both their parents' kin groups, and husband and wife are legal co-partners. In contrast, the Philadelphia community in Knutby started to develop a new endogamic family structure inspired by biblical models. Endogamy means marrying inside the clan or extended family, preferably a cross-cousin, which in societies with patrilineal descent normally creates strong generational bonds between male siblings and cousins, producing what are also known as sibling-societies (Todd 1985). The bond between husband and wife is equally weak, usually being both hierarchical and segregated. Yet, the goal with endogamic family models is not to build a marriage-partnership or a single household, but to perpetuate or expand the clan and the larger tribe by circulating human, spiritual and economic capital strictly within a rather closed group of kin.

Patrilineal, endogamic family models and their associated cousin/ brotherhoods are typical of Semitic cultures, in particular Palestine, according to the French social scientist Emmanuel Todd, whereas the Roman kinship system of the early Latin Christians was patrilineal and exogamic. Exogamy does not create strong cousin/brotherhoods, but more independent households under a common lineage, usually headed by an extremely powerful *pater familias*. They rely on clients more than brothers. In fact, brothers and blood-relatives may even go to war, helped by their friends.

When charismatic Christian communities start to develop androcentric, endogamic family patterns (not patrilineal in this case, since it was not in their power to change the Swedish inheritance laws), they probably look upon themselves as *one* spiritual family or clan, who prefer intermarriages rather than mingling with the world. Having noted this, we should look once more at the *dramatis personae* in Knutby. Then we may discover that it is probably no coincidence that Anette Linde is Patrick Waldau's sister, and that Patrick is the one married to Åsa Waldau, just as it is of utter importance that the murdered Alexandra, married to Helge, was Åsa's sister. If Helge has orchestrated the murder(s), and if it is correct that endogamic family patterns are about to develop among them, his real target was probably the spiritual head behind these two women, namely Åsa Waldau, who is related to Alexandra by blood and to Anette through marriage: Daniel is Åsa's brother-in-law, married to her husband's sister Anette, who then is Åsa's sister-in-law. So, Helge probably arranged to kill Åsa's sister (Alexandra) as well as her brother-in-law (Daniel), in addition to defiling her sister-in-law (Anette) through marital infidelity. He also abused Sara, of course, in a number of ways. In the end he sacrificed her life and dignity by persuading her to commit murder, thus sending her away too, not 'home' to God, but to prison.

Helge Fossmo (who is Norwegian by birth) came to this community in 1997 with his wife Helene and three children, apparently because of his brotherly and spiritual attraction to Åsa Waldau. He soon became a co-leader with Åsa, and gained authority and respect through his so-called Bible knowledge and prophetic faculties: he could speak in tongues, see future events, and had dreams that came true. For example, he claimed to have dreamt seven nights in a row that Helene died in the bathtub as a punishment for her disobedience towards him, a dream cycle he apparently shared with several witnesses. Some time later it happened, she died in the bathtub. Shortly after, Helge married Åsa's sister Alexandra.

Interestingly enough, Helge also developed a new theological understanding of the 'Bride of Christ' metaphor. Rather than being a symbol of the Church, he claimed that it pointed towards a living person of flesh and blood, namely Åsa Waldau. Since Christ obviously waited for his bride, Åsa would not live very long, she was soon to die. They therefore established a prayer group to ask that her death would arrive soon, that she would be taken home and meet her real groom, Jesus. In the meantime, she – the elevated one – had to keep secluded from the community in order to keep her purity intact. Åsa Waldau now claims that she did not understand until her sister was killed that this obscure theological construction was merely a means to gain power over her and keep her out of the way. But she was quite clear in her testimony that this is her understanding today.

Helge met Sara in this prayer group for 'the quickening of Åsa's death', so to speak. He fell in love with her, or acted as if he fell in love with her, early in 2001. Honoured by the pastor taking such an interest in her, she started to have the same feelings for him. Helge called their affection a divine love between siblings, and said God wanted a covenant to be set up between the two. Afterwards they had to seal the covenant through sexual intercourse. When Sara's husband got suspicious and it became hard for them to meet, Helge all of a sudden got very sick: he acted as if he experienced some form of possession. We are told that he had daily fights with the Devil, and that he needed assistance from a spiritual nurse. Thus, Sara was called to move into his house, and every night they celebrated that he had survived yet another day's fight by having sex. According to the news reports she did not leave the house for six months.

When Helge told the five other pastors that he had a revelation in which God said he should marry Sara, the group did something unusual: they opposed their senior minister and said: 'No, you are wrong.' This was probably because Åsa first said: 'Your dream is not from God, be faithful to my sister Alexandra.' From that moment the love affair between Helge and Sara was over, although they continued to have sex and she continued to love him. But it was no longer mutual. Instead he started to treat her as a slave and abuse her psychologically, telling her she had no value, that she was so evil she had lost God's grace, accusing her of having tempted him into infidelity, which of course is *the* sign of a fallen woman. But, he offered her one way out: if she was willing to obey God's will no matter what, even if it was to kill another person, she could be saved. But first she had to pass this test.

She asked if he meant 'like Abraham', as his faith had been tested through his willingness to sacrifice Isaac? Helge said she could not compare the two, because she lived today. But Sara did make the comparison. So when Helge told Sara that he had dreams and revelations that Alexandra had to die because she was too rebellious, that her time on earth was over, he got Sara to take it upon herself to assassinate her. In doing so, she both believed that she released Alexandra and sent her 'home', just as she hoped to be one of the elect as Abraham once had been: She would be tested, but God would interfere and stop her in the last minute, just like he did with Isaac. But God did not. Instead, as Sara saw it, God sent text messages and told her to continue (*Dagens Nyheter*, 18 May 2004; *Dagbladet*, 19 May 2004).

When Sara finally was able to hear the truth, she was relieved that it was not God who had ordered her to kill, but a human being, that God after all was recognizable to her. But we do not know if it has ever occurred to her that in Helge's universe, she never played the role of Abraham, but rather that of Isaac, the one Helge was willing to sacrifice for a larger goal: becoming Master Minister in Knutby, controlling everybody, even Åsa Waldau. And in this perspective, one could say, God certainly intervened: God rescued Sara, as God once had rescued Isaac, from disintegration, defilement and death. From this perspective the hidden script, the fight between Helge and Åsa, takes on an almost metaphysical dimension, quite similar to the warrior plots in science fantasy literature.

The tragic events in Knutby received a lot of attention from media, both in Sweden and in Norway. Critical analysts in search of explanations pointed to authoritarian leadership, the congregational principle of Pentecostal communities that isolates them and shuts them up for surveillance and control, the male misuse of power through sex, religion and ministry, and so on. The Knutby congregation have also voiced their concern, not in any self-critical *theological* sense, but by recourse to a familiar form of hermeneutics: we were too naive; we were too loving and trusting; evil spirits deceived us. Helge Fossmo was not God's messenger, he was the Devil. As always when confronted with evil, they tried to exorcise it, expel it from the community, park it outside. But they took no responsibility for the fact that two women have been killed, one man seriously injured, another woman facing ten years of forced psychiatric custody, or that three children have lost everything, including parents, trust, love and meaning. Acting like a typical sibling-society, holding no real adult responsibility, they consider themselves purely as victims too: victims of a cosmic war between good and evil, manifested in their midst as a fight between a White (Åsa) and Black (Helge) Magician. This was a fight Helge almost won by slipping into Knutby in disguise, throwing a flattering spell on Åsa, calling her 'Bride of Christ'. But she finally woke up, just in time to prevent the whole congregation from disintegrating into confusion, being installed once again as their Holy-Sacred-Beacon.

## Theological Underpinnings of the Crimes

If we do not believe that people got killed in Knutby because God continuously fights the Devil in outer and inner space or that God decided to send the Devil to test this particular congregation, how may we then explain why such a terrible thing could happen among young Swedish people, people whose only reason to settle in Knutby was a positive yearning for love, community, sensuality and meaning – a 'longing for Jesus', as they probably would have put it themselves?

Many commentators have diagnosed Helge Fossmo and suggested that he is a psychopath. Even though we may never know exactly who he is, there is no doubt – according to the legal verdict – that he is responsible for acts that most people regard as simply 'wicked'. Yet, such diagnoses will *not* fully explain how and why he managed for so long to get away with killing, seducing and manipulating right and wrong, without taking into account the theological factor. A fatal problem was, in my view, that Fossmo did not meet any real resistance to a theological discourse that became more and more disturbed.

For example, Alexandra's former fiancé told the jury (*Dagens Nyheter*, 7 June 2004) that when he was still engaged to her, Helge Fossmo informed him of a special dream that returned to him seven nights in a row. In that dream Helge was married to Alexandra. Since the witness believed that Helge could foresee the future, he broke the engagement. He did not ask Helge to stay away from his woman, as is expected from a Swedish man; he just backed off. Neither is Helge's 'wickedness' enough to explain how Sara could be impregnated with the same idea as Cristos Valenti (see above, p. 110); how she really could believe that God tested her faith and obedience, almost like he did with Abraham, only not by asking for a child sacrifice, but by ordering her to 'release' someone from life and 'give them back' to God.

I argue that it is impossible to understand Knutby and other similar tragedies if we resort purely to external, instrumental or non-theological explanations, and I hope my presentation of the cases above has made this evident. Sara worked as a nanny, a caretaker of children. She grew up in a Christian family and claimed always to have had a strong belief in God and to have found great comfort in her faith, not least since her mother died when she was still a young teenager. Sara may have been naive, and definitely in search of love, community and authority to make up for her loneliness, but there is no evidence that she was or is mentally ill or has any criminal leanings. Hence, it is unlikely that she could have been manipulated to kill if a *rationale* for acts that might even include bloodshed had not already been foundational to the community ethos and beliefs that everybody already shared, including Sara. This rationale is first and foremost constituted by a deep commitment to listen to God's messages and by a strong urge to follow God's orders – no matter what. Both attitudes are in addition acutely intensified by the sincere conviction that there is a continuous, ongoing war between good and evil in the world, calling all Christians to take sides. Following God's commands without objections is a sign of being on the right side, of being an obedient friend of God, a loyal, non-deserting servant/soldier in God's Holy War.

However, as I see it, the situation in the congregation in Knutby was aggravated even further by two additional theological interpretations, which in Sara's case were crucial: (1) a notion of sexual difference as inborn *essence*, constituted through and manifesting as gendered dichotomies and hierarchies; (2) a home-made notion of blood-sacrifice as *deed*, a deed that still may be demanded by 'God on High' (although only under certain circumstances), thus implying the possibility of being an act in *positive* conjunction with acts otherwise associated with the 'God of Love' and, therefore, in conformity with the Christian prototype of 'good works'.

First, the particular worldview legitimizing this 'Holy War' is magical and dualist: it conceives of cosmic and social life as interconnected and interdependent, and of every living creature (except Jesus) as embodying two opposing, elemental forces of which one is good and the other evil. If elemental, the two forces are of necessity also congruent in some way with those essences believed to constitute sexual 'difference', since this differentiation is said to keep the world going by adding new generations to God's creation from the beginning of time. If we combine these elemental/essential forces in magical pillars (of correspondence), we get well-known pairs of opposition that are related, or may interact, in a rather dramatic sense: a higher divine force, good in essence and destined to win in the end, is fighting against a lower devilish force, evil in essence and destined to lose. The alleged sexed nature of this set hierarchy is not necessarily explicit or stable in terms of cultural codes and meanings since the process of gendering fixed space is open to social negotiation and, thus, to logical and cultural variation. Yet, in cultures informed by the symbolic hierarchies of biblical religion, masculine is higher, feminine lower. Another well-known strategy in our hemisphere is to represent the masculine as crude nature eternally in need of culture, and turn the feminine into a romanticized, purer nature with educational capabilities in regard to perfecting this 'man', who is the main character of the plot. Thus 'woman' is put upon a life-inhibiting pedestal (like Sara, who was made 'spiritual nurse', and Åsa, the 'Bride of Christ'), but from which she is always threatened to be put down. Yet, the subject in charge of this unequal cast is not female. The person in charge of defining figures and their configurations will in this particular plot hold the subject-position of a social male (although 'he' may be a 'she' put in male office, as in the case of Åsa, who wrote Knutby's marriage rules from the position of a 'minister'). The pure, fragile woman is a male fantasy that may eagerly be used as a means to envelop women and keep them away from 'real (public) life', 'real (political) decisions', 'real (intellectual) thoughts', 'real (moral) responsibility' – hence domesticated and under control.

Second, the flawed notion of sacrifice we have encountered in the reported cases enters the scene because of these particular Pentecostals' refusal to work with theological hermeneutics (which, of course, is much more than simply reading the Bible and preaching around a text). In two of the three cases presented, reading Genesis 22 *with* Joel/Acts proves fatal. Also, to read the promise of an indwelling spirit as being the core meaning of Genesis 22 changed the theological focus from the meaning of sacrifice to the meaning of possession. Instead of asking *what* a sacrifice is; *how* it is different from ritual killing; why an *intermediary* was necessary between Abraham and God on High in order that a privileged, patriarchal nation could be born, the Pentecostals in question seem more occupied with Abraham's direct speech with God. Thus, they read the text purely in this order: *First* Abraham and God were 'on-line', *then* Abraham was commanded to sacrifice his son. The command itself – including its function, meaning and silent, underlying gender relations – seems not to be the important part. But being in communion with God by virtue of having the Spirit, taking orders and acting out, this – apparently – is what is perceived as important. Such a reading strategy implies a significant twist to Genesis 22 since it fails to understand that the covenant between God and Israel is built on the consecration of the firstborn son, not on licence to kill, and that the duty to sacrifice is something very different from the legal right to kill (Young, 1979). As observed in the three cases above, this aberrant interpretation had very dramatic consequences when applied to real life. Yet, it gained authority through allusion to a most traditional Christian take on Abraham as overall interpretative horizon for the Christian faith:

Abraham's obedient willingness to sacrifice Isaac is canonized by the tradition to constitute both a definition of God, a model of faith and a prefiguration of the crucifixion, as well as an indisputable typology for making sense of Jesus' death. This interpretative horizon, I hold, needs revision, irrespective of how it is used or misused by some Pentecostals.

Even though the three cases above represent the *dark* side of Pentecostalism and, therefore, cannot be read as a just description of the movement in general, my critical remarks are probably relevant to any Christian denominations that cultivate 'charisma' and 'pneuma' in their worship-service and community-building activities, *in so far as they also and simultaneously embrace* the horizon of a dualist, magical worldview. In addition, the cold light shining from Los Angeles, London and Knutby is a critical lesson to be taken seriously by all Christian churches, not only the Pentecostals: leaning on the same biblical traditions and flirting with the same dualist heritage, there are no innocents here.

Summing up the above cases, the Pentecostals in question failed in terms of social irresponsibility and in lack of respect for personal autonomy and the integrity of the living body for a number of reasons. It seems, however, that the refusal to work seriously and critically with theological hermeneutics, ethics and inclusive models of leadership/ authority turned out to be most critical. I will end by commenting – briefly and admittedly in rather general terms – on why these three fields are particularly important.

## Theological Hermeneutics

It is deeply problematic that some Pentecostal groups refuse to work with theological hermeneutics, and that they refuse to learn from or take seriously the accumulated knowledge of local moralities, cultural wisdom traditions and practical, ritual skills in 'handling' spirit possession in context, or in setting up clear limits and rules so that spirit-manipulation is not misused. This refusal is probably linked to a simplistic understanding of literary texts (whether biblical or not) and a failure to distinguish between 'text' and 'lived life'.

Such a refusal usually goes in tandem with a sweeping invalidation of critical reason and of mundane (or non-Christian) wisdom: this world only holds the status of a temporary 'airport terminal' for the transition of the elect to the world to come, the hoped-for kingdom of

God. If 'distance to the world' in addition signals a lack of creation theology, the result may be socially disastrous, not only because there is no Christianity without God the Creator being included in the Trinity, but also because the lack thereof may have devastating effects on the mentality and ethicality of religious communities of a Pentecostal bent. It may, for example, help strengthen the idea that the 'kingdom' of God is an event that loyal, obedient Christians may help create through their 'moral' lives, 'godly' communities, 'just' states-manship and 'righteous' warfare against the ungodly and corrupt (within social reality, metaphysical reality, or the interior of individual bodies) and thus weaken the belief that the Kingdom is taking place here and now, graciously and across time and space, offered to all as pure gift. There is a delicate balance between 'passively receiving' and 'actively responding' in the Christian tradition, and reinforcing one at the expense of the other always seems to have unwanted social implications.

## Ethics

It is deeply problematic that the implicit morality of a dualist, antago-nistic worldview, as we may encounter it in Pentecostal circles, is per-mitted to live on in Christian churches without due resistance. Manichaeism was a non-Christian, Gnostic movement, but may also be used as a transhistorical prototype for a way of thinking that splits the world apart into moral antagonistic categories that are unceasing-ly at war. This reality is utterly reinforced when Adam and Eve's dismissal from the Garden is read literally as a cosmic event affecting all generations to come. Hence, human society outside the Garden is degraded to a 'polluted' space, deeply conditioned by the 'evil spell' cast over Adam and Eve as a consequence of their sin (disobedience). This is a rather pessimistic worldview in which it is hard to conceive of human potentiality positively, such as being gifted with an innate ability for compassion, or with a real, un-egotistical desire for social justice, *unless* humans are filled up – and daily refilled – with the miraculous Holy Spirit of Pentecost. Thus, to be saved is to be rescued from evil spells and filled up with new power: the power of 'love'.

Not surprisingly, these Pentecostal groups cultivate a reified dis-course on love: love is preached as if it was feeling, a sensation that comes as a consequence of 'having been filled up', a name for some-thing you may 'get' like you get other magical things. Against this view we could argue that love in biblical traditions is not primarily figured as feeling or a/effect. Rather, love is the law, the ultimate horizon and measure of all human activity (and of all supernatural activity, if any), meaning that it is set between us as norm, aiding us in shaping relationships and community. To the extent that God is Love, love is also the law. In fact, the Decalogue teaches us to fear God, that is, to fear Love, that is, to have fear and respect and treat cautiously above anything else that divine principle that sustains, renews and heals all life (Christian or not) in a thousand visible and invisible ways in order that we may grow and thrive, not decay. This force of creation takes on the personae of Father, Mother, Sister, Brother, Friend, Lover, etc., and without it we would not be. Furthermore, it is essential that the first commandment tells us to love God/Love, and that *communion* with God/Love is not even mentioned in the two tablets – except indirectly, as social behaviour circumscribed and directed/limited.

## Leadership

It is deeply problematic that some Pentecostal congregations choose to organize around very authoritarian and hierarchical leadership models, although this 'choice' can be seen as a logical outgrowth of an apparent unwillingness to work seriously with theological hermeneutics and ethics. Leadership models in religious communities are always connected to definitions of the divine, to perceptions of morality or of a moral order, and to interpretations of those spatial constructions called person, family, community, congregation, society, nation, cosmos, universe, nature. They are therefore always also related to gendering and kinshipping. In the three cases discussed above, we have witnessed male authority cults with women and girl children as main victims. This is not to be underestimated; neither is the fact that male authority and hierarchical leadership are widely accepted as 'apostolic', apparently in line with an acclaimed biblical model of the world and its particular take on sexual difference and the obligations of kin. It is also crucial to note the ease with which the public has accepted the suffering of women and children when it has been exposed (through media): despite some accurate and critical voices, public discourse in general seems more offended by the fact that misdeeds have been acted out in the name of religion than with wanting to understand why gender and age have been central to these crimes. In fact, only one newspaper article so far has (to my knowledge) mentioned Helge Fossmo's children. Only one has asked what will happen to them, one out of several hundred articles.

## The Constructive Challenges of Pentecostalism

The three cases discussed above are not a representative portrayal of Pentecostalism as a spiritual movement, either historically or today. I have primarily discussed a small segment within this movement that may be said to yearn for 'a-historical, patriarchal and demonological' solutions to the tasks of theology and the troubles of human life. It means that I have primarily looked at forms of discourse and sociability that seem to help engender a legitimate framework for individuals and groups that are attracted to immediate and authoritative forms of spiritual/moral practices and that seek out demonology in order to explain misfortune and evil. Thus, the ability of Pentecostalism to engender constructive gifts and important challenges to all Christian churches has therefore been neglected. I cannot totally make up for that now, but it is important to somehow balance the dark side of Pentecostal enthusiasm in order to make a fuller picture. If we rephrase the most important challenges inherent in Pentecostalism with the intention of presenting them to theological traditions that are critical of a-historical, patriarchal and demonological worldviews, they may be articulated like this:

> How may we *commune with divinity* in a meaningful sense in the modern world and sometimes feel vibrantly alive and at peace after having worshipped? How may we commune without being abusive, individually as well as communally, through forms, symbols and institutions that are in agreement with the social cosmologies, norms and aspirations of people living in the twenty-first century, and not with the priestly norms of preliterate, patriarchal chiefdoms; nor with the kinship systems and sacrificial schema of pastoral, endogamic sibling societies; nor with the utopian horizons of those brotherhoods that attempted to overturn feudal kingdoms and patron–client relationships in early Renaissance Europe?
>
> Furthermore, how may we *commune with each other* with sense and sensibility in the modern world? How may we, for example, develop forms of worship that combine the singing, the shaking and the ecstasy – what Harvey Cox (1994) calls primeval spirituality – with an utterly intellectual faith tradition, a mature social consciousness and a highly developed ritual and moral competence?

These challenges face all theologians, across denominations, and represent the constructive gifts of Pentecostalism to any contemporary faith tradition, Christian or not. Yet, as argued in this chapter, we are not permitted to accept gifts naively. Theologians are not permitted to be naive in anything that pertains to religion, rather the opposite. It is our duty to be fully and critically aware of the dark sides lurking on any scene, religious or political, whenever a person is requested to wilfully suspend her own will in order to be 'taken over' or 'filled by' a higher power.

Religious people have always heard God's so-called voice. Yet in traditional society there were strict social schemes as to how this voice ought to be interpreted and how inter-communication ought to take place. Before the birth of the autonomous, free individual, persons were persons in community and obliged to each other in set networks of reciprocity and hierarchy. Reference to an inner dialogue with God or to the authority of one's own consciousness as a valid argument to break common sense/law was a privilege of the wealthy, the learned and the crazy only. It was not yet a human right. There are many good historical reasons why this is no longer the case, why every man, every woman, has been granted the position of priest vis-à-vis God. This freedom, however, does not mean that we can dispense with form and proceed to a level where we can relate to God or to each other unmediated, without socially accepted intermediaries, as pure essences – at least without risking resorting to new forms of abuse and power.

*Webpages accessed June 2004*

www.dn.se. (*Dagens Nyheter*, search 'Knutby')
www.dagbladet.no/print/?/nyheter/2004/05/19/398516.html (*Dagbladet*, report from Sara Svensson's testimony in court)
www.guardian.co.uk/ (*The Guardian Unlimited*)
http://society.guardian.co.uk/children/story 0,,1161987,00.htm/ (The Guardian's news reports on the Victoria Climbié case)
http://www.victoria-climbie-inquiry.org.uk (the e-publication of the 28 January 2003 governmental report on the Victoria Climbié case)
www.uckg.org.za/ (homepage for the Universal Church of the Kingdom of God)
www.rickross.com/groups/universal.html (private webpage with critical comments on new religious movements, including the Universal Church)
http://home.c2i.net/DeGamleStier/artikler/trosrotterteol.html (private webpage with critical comments on 'Livets Ord', a neo-Pentecostal church in Sweden with many similarities to the congregation in Knutby)

# 8. Charismatic Mission, Miracles and Faith-Based Diplomacy:
## The Case of Aril Edvardsen

ODDBJØRN LEIRVIK

It is often observed that in the age of globalization religions have come to play an increasingly important role in political tensions and violent conflicts (Stålsett and Leirvik, 2004). Because of this (perceived) reality, religious communities and leaders are often called upon to contribute to reducing the potential for conflict inherent in all religious traditions, and to commit themselves to peaceful dialogue between different faiths.

Many observers would be accustomed to seeing commitment to interfaith dialogue and generous attitudes towards other religions as characteristic of a modern, liberal type of Christianity. According to this perception, interfaith dialogue is linked with certain other issues that loom high on the agenda of liberal Christianity. For instance in a recent book by Marcus Borg (who writes from a North American context), it is suggested that the three most divisive issues among the churches today are (1) the ordination of women, (2) the attitude towards gays and lesbians and (3) the theological attitude towards other religions. According to Borg, liberal Christians typically take a liberal, accepting attitude in all these issues – underpinning their view with a historical, dialogical and metaphorical understanding of the Bible (Borg, 2003).

The conservative strands of Christianity, both fundamentalists and charismatics, have so far not been known to participate very eagerly in peace-building dialogue through mutual understanding and co-operation between religions. There are signs, however, that this is about to change. The present chapter aims at shedding light upon this significant shift, by looking at recent developments in the ministry of a prominent charismatic missionary from Norway, Aril Edvardsen, the founder of the Proof of Faith World Mission ('Troens Bevis Verdens Evangelisering'). Edvardsen is rooted in the Pentecostal movement and has to a large extent related himself to Pentecostal networks. However, he professes that he has always felt an ecumenical orientation and, according to his 2004 biography, he does not really regard himself as a Pentecostalist any more (Rem, 2004: 129). He remains, however, a charismatic missionary and miracle preacher, with a worldwide agenda and a growing commitment to faith-based diplomacy.

The forms of faith-based diplomacy in which Aril Edvardsen has engaged should probably not be regarded as isolated phenomena but rather as part of a global trend. There are in fact many indications that as Pentecostal and other charismatic churches and communities gain significance in religious and political terms, at least some of their constituencies and leaders take on greater responsibility for social and political developments even at a global scale. Formerly this would be quite unusual due to charismatic religion's mainly otherworldly focus.

## Conservatives in Dialogue

At least in the Western context, it is an indisputable fact that initiatives towards interreligious dialogue have often come from liberal circles in the churches. But this is not the entire picture. In the case of the Roman Catholic Church, the more generous attitude towards other religions that was expressed in the documents of the Second Vatican Council was indeed indicative of a relatively liberal theological trend typical of the 1960s. In more recent years, however, in international forums we have seen several examples of conservative Catholics siding with conservative Muslims in issues involving so-called 'family values'. In the United Nations, Muslim diplomats have been approached by American Christians who would like to strike conservative alliances in the issues of abortion, homosexuality and combating Aids (Bjartvik, 2002). Combining open and conciliatory attitudes towards other faiths with a strong commitment to conservative family values was in fact a striking feature of Pope John Paul II's ministry.

In a similar vein, a good number of Norwegian Muslims have expressed their support for the Christian Democratic Party, in appreciation of the party's traditional stand on similar issues: restrictive legislation regarding pornography, alcohol and abortion; resistance to homosexual partnership; affirmation of family values; and not least sensitivity towards religious minority rights (Brekke, 2002: 80f.).

Whereas liberal Christians speak of the 'softening impact' of inter-religious co-operation and a corresponding conversion to a relational understanding of religious truth (Ahlstrand, 2003), at least some conservatives distinguish sharply between case-by-case co-operation in the political field on the one hand and human relations (not to speak of theology) on the other. In 2002, the director of a Catholic family- and human-rights institute involved in UN lobbying said that Muslim diplomats could be seen as 'allies, but not necessarily as friends' (Bjartvik, 2002).

It would be far too simplistic, however, to imply that conservative Christians involved in interreligious dialogue and co-operation are merely tactical in their manoeuvres. There is also good reason to question the dualistic notion of pre-packed sets of combined attitudes that could be labelled as either 'conservative' or 'liberal' respectively. In real life, one will often find combinations of attitudes that contradict such simplistic categorizations.

## Faith-Based Diplomacy

Before turning to Aril Edvardsen's current activities in the field of interfaith dialogue, I will take a detour via the recent American notion of 'faith-based diplomacy'. The notion has been launched by Douglas Johnston, who both has an academic, political and military career and is currently the director of the International Center for Religion and Diplomacy in the USA. His book *Faith-Based Diplomacy*, which carries the subtitle 'Trumping Realpolitik' (Johnston, 2003), was a follow-up to a book that received much attention in international discussions of religion and politics: *Religion, the Missing Dimension of Statecraft* (Johnston and Sampson, 1994).

Johnston's vision of faith-based diplomacy positively affirms the return of religion to politics, and highlights the special competence that religious people have in what he terms 'faith-based peacemaking' (Johnston, 2003: 18). Increasingly, Johnston's International Center for Religion and Diplomacy has engaged Muslim partners, perhaps most conspicuously in the Sudan, where a peace treaty between the warring parties in north and south was signed in January 2005. In the Sudan, Johnston's centre has engaged both the Sudan Council of Churches, Muslim leaders and the Islamist government in 'faith-based dialogue' aimed at reconciliation training; the formation of an inter-religious council; the establishment of an independent human rights centre; the involvement of religious leaders in the peace process; the free movement of religious leaders and the protection of holy places. Describing his centre's activities in Sudan, Johnston mentions that its incipient activities were accompanied by Christian–Muslim prayer breakfasts. He explains that their Muslim partners in Sudan have been very comfortable working within a spiritual rather than a purely secular, realpolitik-oriented framework. He also notes that his centre's dialogical endeavours have taken place at a time when normal diplomatic relations between Sudan and the USA were virtually non-existent (Johnston, 2003: 8f., 20f.).

How does Johnston fit into the liberal–conservative pattern? In the USA, Johnston has belonged to the inner circle of the National Prayer Breakfast, which is organized by the so-called Fellowship Foundation of which Johnston was formerly a board member (Getter, 2002). The Fellowship Foundation, which is headed by Doug Coe, has received some critical attention for its blend of conservative Christian networking, interfaith engagement, and secretive 'back-channel' activities in politics. In tune with the vision of Abraham Vereide, the Norwegian-American founder of the National Prayer Breakfast institution, the Fellowship has espoused the idea of change from above and consistently targets top-level politicians, businessmen and religious leaders.

After having lived undercover at their training centre, the journalist Jeffrey Sharlet characterized the members of the Fellowship Foundation as 'America's secret theocrats', with strong visions of changing not only domestic but indeed world politics (Sharlet, 2003). But the change they are aiming at is not supposed to take place under the banner of 'Christianity' and certainly not in the name of 'Christendom'. As the title of Sharlet's critical article – 'Jesus plus nothing' – indicates, the Fellowship focuses its worldwide networking efforts on the person of Jesus Christ, whose prophetic mission and healing power is also (as the Fellowship sees it) recognized by many religions other than Christianity.

In December 2004, the Norwegian newspaper *Dagbladet* published a series of critical articles about alleged links between the ruling Christian Democrat Party in Norway and the Fellowship Foundation (Gjerstad and Ellingsen, 2004). The Christian Democrat member of Parliament Lars Rise, who is co-ordinating a 'Forum for Faith and Values' in the Norwegian Parliament and is also the main person behind the party's relative success among Muslim voters, is part of the international circle around the US National Prayer Breakfast. It was in fact Doug Coe who in 1996 inspired him to make contacts with the Muslim constituency (Brekke, 2002: 79).

The Norwegian 'Forum for Faith and Values' is focused on Jesus as a model for wise leadership (Gjerstad, 2004). In other connections, Lars Rise has referred to interreligious 'Jesus-groups' that have been initiated by the National Prayer Breakfast network and attracted wide interest in leadership circles in Middle Eastern and Asian countries.[1]

## Aril Edvardsen in Pakistan and Sudan: Faith- and Prayer-Based Diplomacy?

Turning now to the Norwegian charismatic evangelist Aril Edvardsen, I will raise the question of whether his combined activities of mission and dialogue fit with Johnston's concept of faith-based diplomacy, and whether or not Edvardsen can neatly be categorized as either 'liberal' or 'conservative'. I will focus on his missionary and dialogical activities in Muslim-majority contexts, with concrete reference to his latest campaigns in Pakistan (1999, 2000, 2002) and Sudan (2005).

Judging from his magazine's reports from Edvardsen's campaigns, his preaching includes classical items such as the forgiveness of sins and reconciliation with God in Christ. Most of the space, however, is devoted to reports of the numerous healing miracles that are said to have taken place at his evangelistic meetings.

There are also other Norway-based evangelists and miracle preachers (such as Bjørnar Heimstad and Svein-Magne Pedersen) who have been campaigning in Pakistan. The distinctive contribution of Aril Edvardsen lies in his additional commitment to interfaith dialogue. Along with large evangelistic meetings and seminars with local pastors, since the late 1990s Edvardsen has staged interfaith dialogue conferences with leading religious and political personalities in Pakistan. As indicated by a 'State leader promo' produced by his organization (Edvardsen, 1999b), his dialogical strategy resembles that of the Fellowship Foundation in targeting top-level leaders. In addition, and as before, he addresses the general public as a missionary and miracle preacher.

When presenting his campaigns in the Muslim world (which are often called 'friendship crusades'), Edvardsen makes no secret of his missionary intentions. But he twists them in the direction of a non-confessional type of Jesus-piety reminiscent of the Fellowship Foundation's insistence on 'Jesus plus nothing'.

Striking examples of how his combination of mission and dialogue works in practice can be found in Aril Edvardsen's reports from his organization's activities in Pakistan. Since 1970, Edvardsen has staged a number of evangelistic campaigns in Pakistan (Fida, 2002: 14; Rem, 2004: 172–206). Then for the first time in 1999, he added a dialogue conference to his evangelistic campaigns. After his evangelistic meetings in Rawalpindi and Islamabad, he staged a dialogue conference in Lahore. Here, he was able to rally a great number of Muslim and Christian leaders under the slightly ambitious heading of 'Universal Peace and Harmony'.

After the campaign, his magazine reported on 'miracles in Pakistan'. The primary miracle was that he was able to preach the gospel to thousands of Pakistanis (most of them Muslims) and also to heal many of them. The second miracle (referred to as such in his magazine) was that Aril Edvardsen was commended by the President of Pakistan's Parliament, Mohammed Rafiq Tarar, for his efforts towards interreligious reconciliation. In return, the President received not a crucifix but a Norwegian flag planted in a Viking ship.

In the case of Edvardsen's campaigns in Pakistan, it is probably pertinent to speak of miracles in more than one sense. The more 'traditional' miracle (in a charismatic sense) was the gathering of thousands of Muslims who in his evangelistic meetings received his charismatic proclamation of the healing power of Christ. Tuning in to widespread expectations in folk Islam of the healing powers of Jesus, Edvardsen was also invited to the home of two Muslim leaders who asked him to pray for their diseases in Jesus' name (Edvardsen, 1999a; Mydland, 1999). As Edvardsen notes, 'Muslims in Pakistan – from the greatest Muslim leaders to ordinary village people – have got an enormous faith in Jesus as a healer' (Edvardsen, 2002a: 9).[2] The healing power of Jesus is in fact a classical feature of Muslim images of Jesus Christ (Leirvik, 1999). However, in folk Islam such expectations are by no means restricted to Jesus and his representatives. On the contrary, Edvardsen's miracle preaching 'in the name of Jesus' corresponds with a much more general expectation of holy men (in particular, Sufi saints) and their healing powers (Ahlberg, 1990: 211f.).

Taking away nothing from the traditional focus on healing miracles, the discursive novelty in Edvardsen's missionary language lies in his additional reference to the Christian–Muslim dialogue conference as a 'miracle'. Since the latter part of the 1990s, interreligious dialogue has become an important part of Edvardsen's agenda. Later in 1999, and as a follow-up to his dialogue effort in Lahore, Edvardsen hosted a Christian–Muslim dialogue conference in Norway, under the same heading as in Pakistan ('Universal Peace and Harmony'). On this occasion, and for the first time in Norway, a large group of Pentecostal leaders visited a Norwegian mosque and received Muslim leaders in their church (Mydland, 2000; cf. Leirvik, 2001: 214). By some conservative Christians in Norway, Aril Edvardsen has been criticized for his open-minded approach to Islam and Muslim faith. Because of renewed criticism prior to the conference, he had to retract his initial plans of praying together with the Muslims during the mutual visits to mosque and church.[3]

Three prominent Muslim leaders (headed by Dr Abdul Qadir Azad who took part in the private prayer session mentioned above) and the charismatic Christian leader Marqus Fida came together from Pakistan to join the conference in Norway.

In November 2000, Edvardsen visited Pakistan again. At the invitation of President Mohammad Rafiq Tarar, who wanted him to pursue his dialogue for peace, Edvardsen hosted a second round of Muslim–Christian dialogue conferences in Pakistan, near Faisalabad and in Lahore (Edvardsen, 2001a). Naturally, he also staged a large evangelistic campaign which he subsequently described as 'the greatest friendship crusade of my life' (Edvardsen, 2001b). As in 1999, healing miracles were a main focus. On this occasion, his magazine could even report of a dead baby seemingly having been brought back to life. In his magazine's reports on healing miracles, there is rarely a critical note. In this particular case, however, one may observe a certain reservation on Edvardsen's part. He emphasizes that as a Westerner, he is not accustomed to this type of miracle. In his magazine, he states that he doesn't really know whether the baby was actually dead – he has only got the baby's grandmother's word for it (Edvardsen, 2001c: 9f.). Nevertheless, both a promotional video and later issues of his magazine continued referring to the resuscitated 'miracle baby' in Faisalabad (Edvardsen, 2000; 2001b; 2002b: 30f.).

However, as in 1999, the reports from his campaign reflect a widening notion of miracles. The video production from his campaign in 2000 gives ample place to Edvardsen's contribution to the strengthening of Christian–Muslim dialogue in Pakistan (Edvardsen, 2000). In the 2000 peace conference, both members of the Pakistani government and the Norwegian ambassador to Pakistan took part, in addition to some 300 religious leaders (Edvardsen, 2001a: 5).

In 2002, Edvardsen ventured a third campaign in Pakistan (in Lahore), repeating his success from 1999 and 2000 in a similar combination of dialogical and evangelistic events (Rem, 2004: 172–206). His biographer Håvard Rem, who accompanied him to Pakistan, notes that posters produced by the local organizers showed Bollywood-style pictures of Edvardsen – either together with the King and Queen of Norway or with healed Pakistanis from previous campaigns (Rem, 2004: 198).

The outcome of his campaign was once again reported in his magazine as 'A historic miracle crusade in Islamic Pakistan' (Edvardsen, 2002a). The bulk of this issue of the magazine is dedicated to a detailed report of all those who were miraculously healed when Edvardsen proclaimed Jesus as the healer of body and soul in Gaddafi stadium in Lahore. One of the local imams reportedly asked Edvardsen to visit his home and pray for his sick daughter (Rem, 2004: 181). According to Edvardsen's magazine, more than 80,000 also received a catechetical follow-up (Edvardsen, 2002a: 13). But as in 1999, his achievements in the field of dialogue are also described as a 'miracle'. In the 2002 dialogue conference, both Muslim, Christian and Sikh leaders took part.

In one of Aril Edvardsen's evangelistic meetings in 2002, even Tahir ul-Qadri, the leader of the organization Minhaj ul-Quran, turned up and stood hand in hand on the podium with Aril Edvardsen and his main Christian partner in Pakistan, Marqus Fida. Tahir ul-Qadri used to be known for his apologetic and at times confrontational approach to Christianity. When ul-Qadri first visited the Nordic countries in the 1980s, the website of his organization boasted that he had totally silenced the Christian leaders whom he confronted, obviously in rather war-like dialogues. His book about *Islam and Christianity* from 1987 reveals much of the same confrontational style (ul-Qadri, 1987).[4] When Tahir ul-Qadri came to Norway in 1999, however, he put polemics aside and staged instead an 'International Peace Conference' in Oslo. Three years later, together with Aril Edvardsen in Pakistan, he appeared in a soft interfaith style, reportedly reading from the Sermon on the Mount (Edvardsen, 2002b: 15, 28).

The main features of Edvardsen's campaigns in Pakistan recurred in his mission to Sudan in 2005. During a planning visit in February 2004, Aril Edvardsen not only met with local Christian partners but also made contact with the very prominent Muslim leader and politician Sadiq al-Mahdi (Edvardsen, 2004c; 2004b). During his conversations with Sadiq al-Mahdi, they reportedly discussed politics and interreligious relations as well as the image of Jesus Christ in Islam. Furthermore, he met with the newly established Sudan Inter Religious Council, which is partly an offspring of the activities of Douglas Johnston's centre. As presented in his magazine, Aril Edvardsen's plans were prefaced by biblical prophecies for the land of Sudan. But they were also explicitly linked to the ongoing peace process in this ethnically and religiously divided country, a peace process in which Norwegian mediators (not least from the Christian Democratic Party) have played a central role (Edvardsen, 2004b: 14).

When carrying out his planned campaign in February 2005 he was able to assemble tens of thousands of listeners in the largest football stadiums of Khartoum and Omdurman. Although thousands of people were said to have run to the podium to accept Jesus as their Saviour, the events focused upon by Edvardsen's magazine indicate once again that miraculous healing was a prime attraction (Edvardsen, 2005).

As in Pakistan, Edvardsen's evangelistic campaign in Sudan was linked with a high-profile peace conference for religious and political leaders. According to his magazine he was afterwards contacted by Somali and Kenyan politicians who wanted Edvardsen to involve himself in peace-building work in Somalia (Edvardsen, 2005: 17).


## Inclusive Jesus-Mission and Faith-Based Diplomacy

How should Aril Edvardsen's activities in Pakistan, Sudan and other Muslim contexts be understood? Is what we see merely missionary activity supported by tactical manoeuvres and camouflaged by conspicuous dialogue events? Or are we witnessing a genuine, dual commitment to mission and dialogue, surpassing the old alternatives of conservative and liberal approaches to religious pluralism (Leirvik, 2004)? And how does Aril Edvardsen legitimize his combined evangelistic and dialogical mission in theological terms?

As for the implied theology of religions underlying his campaigns, Aril Edvardsen clearly does not belong to those conservative Christians who warn against Islam as an evil power or denounce Allah as an idol. For his insistence that in Arab culture, Allah is but the common Christian–Muslim name for the one and only God (Edvardsen, 1997), he has been criticized by fellow conservatives. Although Edvardsen indicates that certain other religions are more liable to the influence of evil than one's own, he can certainly not be counted as a confrontational conservative. According to Edvardsen, any missionary effort directed towards Muslims should first of all confirm how they already believe in God. Only then can Christ be meaningfully proclaimed as the fulfilment of their (and every other believer's) spiritual longings. In tune with this approach, Edvardsen may describe the Qur'an as 'the Muslims' bridge to Jesus' (Edvardsen, 2003; cf. Rem, 2004: 183–95). Edvardsen's views on mission thus inscribe him in the ranks of those who propound a fulfilment type of missiology.

As indicated in the reports from his campaigns in Pakistan and Sudan, healing miracles constitute a most important part of his proclamation of universal promises fulfilled. In a video production from his 2000 campaign in Pakistan, the narrator explains: 'At each meeting, Dr Edvardsen takes time to pray for the sick. The people learn that Jesus not only has the power to take away their sins, but he can also perform the miracles of healing' (Edvardsen, 2000).

However, in Edvardsen's view performing miracles and preaching the gospel is not the same as spreading Christianity. Similar to the National Prayer Breakfast's Jesus-piety and their aversion to the notion of 'Christianity', Edvardsen's missionary vision is formulated as 'an evangelistic revival without the Christianity of the West'. With reference to his TV-transmissions to the Muslim world (through the 'Miracle' channel), Edvardsen underlines that his movement always advises Muslims who accept Christ as their Saviour and Messiah to call themselves 'Jesus-believers' belonging to 'gospel centres', rather than 'Christians' who will inevitably be associated with 'the Christianity and churches of the West' (Edvardsen, 2000: 19).

In his 2004 biography, Edvardsen expresses his expectation of an 'enormous evangelistic awakening' in Islam, a revival that in Edvardsen's expectation will probably be connected with marvellous 'signs and miracles' – and result in a movement of Jesus-believing Muslims that may take distinctively different shapes from that of organized Christianity. In an apocalyptic vein typical of much of his preaching (Rem, 2004: 263ff.), he also suggests that the prophesied awakening may be accompanied by global catastrophes that will lead to an 'explosion' of people seeking God all over the world (Rem, 2004: 194).

In terms of theology, Edvardsen cannot neatly be labelled as a traditional conservative. By some parameters, Edvardsen might indeed seem to belong to the conservative camp. But in his stance on other issues he can hardly be characterized as a conservative. This is true both of his views on the inerrancy of the Scriptures, his avowed interest in eschatology and apocalyptics, and his position in some matters pertaining to 'family values'. But it is in fact very hard to subsume Aril Edvardsen's religious, moral and political views under the dualistic categories of 'conservative' or 'liberal'. For instance, in a 2003 interview with the Norwegian socialist newspaper *Klassekampen* he announced that in the issue of abortion he had given up his former resistance to the free choice stance. Notwithstanding his moral objections to abortion, he now affirms women's choice. In the same interview, he also states that he can see no problem in having women in church positions of any kind. He even indicates that his political sympathies have slid away from the Christian Democrats and back to the Social Democrats which he supported in his youth (Leer-Salvesen, 2003).

In Norway, however, his political backing has primarily come from Christian Democrat-led governments. Previous to his later campaigns in Pakistan and Sudan, Edvardsen was able to obtain political (and some financial) support from the Norwegian Ministry of Foreign Affairs for his evangelistic-cum-dialogical mission in Palestine and North Caucasus (Brekke, 2002: 15–25). In the case of Pakistan, Edvardsen's initiatives have coincided in time with efforts taken by Norwegian Church Aid and sponsored by the Norwegian government, responding to the stated ambition of a number of Muslim leaders to strengthen their commitment to interreligious peace-building, and aiming at establishing a forum for Muslim–Christian dialogue in Pakistan. At a conference in Islamabad in September 2004, this initiative resulted in the formation of the so-called 'World Council of Religions towards Peace, Reconciliation and Justice'.[5] (The process leading up to the Islamabad declaration was first facilitated by Alf Arne Ramslien of the Norwegian embassy in Islamabad, formerly a Pentecostal missionary.[6])

In preparation for Edvardsen's campaign in Sudan, he had meetings with Christian Democrat members of the Norwegian government.[7] In general, it seems that Aril Edvardsen links up closely with the official Norwegian policy of international peacemaking. A video produced by his organization, labelled 'State Leader Promo', demonstrates how successful he has also been abroad in gaining local political support for his peace and friendship campaigns – be it in Sudan, Pakistan, Caucasus or Palestine, where he was able to earn the confidence of Yasser Arafat himself. (Edvardsen, 1999b).

Edvardsen's mission may also have – at least indirectly – some tangible political *effects*, first of all as regards freedom of religion and a more relaxed, interreligious atmosphere in civil society. In his magazine, the Christian leader Marqus Fida praises Aril Edvardsen for widening the scope of religious freedom in Pakistan (Fida, 2001; 2002).

Edvardsen's faith-based diplomacy might seem to correspond well with his self-understanding as a messenger not only of Christ but also of 'universal peace'. However, in the theology of Edvardsen, 'Jesus' and 'peace' appear to be two sides of the same coin. Jesus Christ as the prince of peace seems in fact to be an established *topos* in Edvardsen's evangelistic preaching, as expressed in a video production from his 2000 campaign in Pakistan which also illustrates the combined themes of eschatology and the reign of peace:

> He [Jesus] will come, and he will take the power away from the world ruler who at that time will be Anti-Christ. And when Jesus comes, he will judge everybody on the Day of Resurrection, and there will be peace in the world. Also the Qur'an tells the same and the Hadith also tells that Jesus, Isa, he will come, and he will take the power away from the Anti-Christ, and he will bring peace to the world. (Edvardsen, 2000)

## Conclusion: Pentecostal Mission and Interreligious Dialogue

In my view, Aril Edvardsen's performances in Pakistan and Sudan are more than tactical manoeuvres on the part of a neo-charismatic evangelist. A good indication that Edvardsen is seriously committed not only to mission but also to dialogue is the fact that he has lost some of his followers among fundamentalist Christians in Norway – because of his support for the Palestinian cause and his suggestion that Christians and Muslims basically believe in the same God. In a 2004 issue of his magazine, he warns against all kinds of fundamentalism, be it Christian, Zionist, Islamic, or secular. As for Christian varieties of fundamentalism, he even attacks certain forms of literalist approaches to the Bible (Edvardsen, 2004a; cf. Holbek, 2003).

The political impact of Edvardsen's dialogical mission is hard to evaluate. There is an obvious need for more thorough examinations of how Edvardsen's dialogue conferences and interreligious network-building link up with a growing number of similar initiatives recently taken by governments and religious leaders of different inclinations (especially after September 11, 2001). As noted, in his dialogue initiatives Aril Edvardsen targets religious and political leaders. His communication with the masses seems to be on a different level, tuning in with popular expectations of miraculous healing and a fuller life in countries where large proportions of the population have good reasons for feeling acutely vulnerable in terms of welfare and health. In both the political and religious realms, there is obviously a difference between manifestations of harmony and instant experiences of healing on the one hand, and long-lasting, deep-rooted change on the other.

Edvardsen's congenial blend of attitudes and practices (with their distinctive touch of 'the miraculous') is hard to characterize as either 'conservative' or 'liberal'. As indicated in this chapter, there are in fact many signs that these categories are currently being superseded by much more complicated realities. The list of contributors to Douglas Johnston's books shows that well-known names from the 'liberal' discourse of interfaith relations have no objections to contributing to a book that is edited by a former representative of 'America's secret theocrats'. Or maybe Jeffrey Starlet's label 'secret theocrats' is only indicative of some liberals' reluctance to realize that religion in politics does not necessarily amount to theocracy.

In his explicit critique of fundamentalism Edvardsen certainly parts ways with many forms of conservative Christianity. When in 2003 Edvardsen countered attacks from 'fundamentalist' Christians in Norway, he acknowledged that de-Christianization has gone too far in our society. But his remedy is emphatically not more 'Christian laws' but rather a broad mobilization around what he terms 'Christian values' (Holbek, 2003). Like Johnston in his practice of faith-based diplomacy, Edvardsen's international campaigns indicate that such values could in fact be reformulated on an interreligious basis.

Is that his vision? Or is his vision rather (at the end of the day, not to say of the world) that the entire globe becomes united under Christ?

## Notes

1 Personal conversation, 11 February 2003.

2 All quotes from *Troens Bevis* are rendered in English translation by the author of this chapter.

3 *Dagen*, 23 November 1999, s. 7 ('Kritikk for muslim-bønn'); and *Magazinet* 42, 19 November 1999 ('Felles bønn med muslimer i Pinsekirken in Bærum').

4 Cf. the justified critique in Lønning, 1997.

5 Source: web news posted by Norwegian Church Aid (http://www.nca.no/article/articleview/4112/1/414/)

6  Source: web news posted by Norwegian Church Aid (http://www.kirken.no/ oslo/nyhet.cfm?nyhetid=28707)

7  Source: web news posted by *Troens Bevis Verdens Evangelisering* (http:// www.tbve.no/Nyheter.229+M5d31208b9d6.0.html)

# 9. Embracing Life:
## An Interfaith Dialogue between Confucian Self-Cultivation and Charismatic Christian Self-Transformation

### WAI MAN YUEN

How to live a happy life? Ancient and modern Eastern and Western philosophers have asked this basic question consistently and continually. In order to live happily, humans, whether they come from East or West, seek to bring life to its fulfilment. In Confucianism, *jen* (humanity, goodness) is the key of life; while in Christianity, according to Irenaeus, 'true life comes from partaking in God'. In contrast to the cultivation of the self in order to bring life to its fullness in the East, Christian spirituality emphasizes self-transformation, and the self can be transformed by means of partaking in God. Before we explore the concept of self-transformation in charismatic Christianity, we first turn our focus to Confucian understandings of this concept as a contextual base to start the communicative process.

## Confucian Understandings of Self-Transformation

To embrace life in the Confucian tradition means learning to be human. To be human is a cultivating process by which the self is transformed into an all-encompassing self. As Ch'eng I states,

> The master not only possessed an unusual nature by endowment, but his own nourishment of it was in accordance with the Way . . . His conscientiousness and sincerity penetrated metal and stone, and his filial piety and brotherly respect influenced spiritual beings. As one looked at his countenance, one found that in dealing with people he was as warm as the spring sun. . . He saw penetratingly

and made no discrimination between himself and others. As one tried to fathom his depth, one realized that it was as great as a boundless ocean. (Zhu, Lèu and Chan, 1967: 299)

For Confucians self-cultivation and learning are important to a person for the realization of his/her own true nature. A sage (profound person or holy person) is one who can actualize his/her humanity that is his/her inner self. As the Way is inherent in our human nature, our humanity is to be manifested as the Way. This self-actualization brings a sage to an understanding that self is no longer a private ego but a communal self (Tu, 1994: 180). The ultimate purpose of this process then is to bring the self to become conscious of living in a network of relationships. This network of relationships is based upon the natural order of things in human society: the family, neighbourhood, kinship, clan, state and world (Tu, 1994: 181). Undeniably, to live truly for Confucians is to be able to strengthen the right mind and the right spirit so that humans are sincerely related to one another. Consequently, humanity is one. As Chang Tsai exclaims,

Heaven is my father and Earth is my mother, and such a small creature as I find an intimate place in their midst . . . All people are my brothers and sisters, and all things are my companions. (Chan, 1963: 497)

Thus, embracing life for Confucians means to honour human relations, speak with care, act diligently and be cautious unceasingly until the day of our death. Confucians describe this embracing self as *jen*. *Jen* can be regarded as the key to the process of self-cultivation which is also a spiritual development of the self. In the *Great Learning*, all human beings are called upon to regard self-cultivation as the root of life and the foundations of learning.

What Heaven (T'ien, Nature) imparts to man is called human nature. To follow human nature is called the Way. Cultivating the Way is called education. The Way cannot be separated from us for a moment . . . Therefore the superior man is watchful over himself when he is alone . . . Equilibrium is the great foundation of the world, and harmony its universal path. When equilibrium and harmony are realized to the highest degree, heaven and earth will attain their proper order and all things will flourish. (Chan, 1963: 98)

Within the early Confucian worldview, self-cultivation was a life-long process in which the final goal was to be the achievement of self-transformation and ultimately sagehood itself.

## *Jen* and Self-Cultivation

*Jen* is the key concept that interweaves all schools of thought in Confucianism. We can say that without understanding *jen*, we do not understand Confucianism at all. For Confucians *jen* is an inherent principle in all human beings. Generally speaking, *jen* is defined as love (Chan, 1969: 1f.). However, due to the different interpretations different schools have of *jen*, it has been defined as benevolence, perfect virtue, love, affection, universal love, human heart-mind, impartiality, vital force, consciousness, and forming one body with things (Au, 2002: 149–52). And finally Chu Hsi,[1] the most influential thinker in Neo-Confucianism, summed up the definitions of *jen* into two basic notions: (1) as the character of the heart-mind and (2) as the principle of love (Au, 2002: 152f.). From these two definitions, we can state that *jen* is intrinsic in every human being and only through it can one actualize oneself. Confucius says, 'To master oneself and return to propriety is jen' (*Analects*, 12.1). As Chu Hsi notes:

> The moral qualities of the mind of Heaven and Earth are four: origination, flourish, advantages, and firmness . . . Therefore in the mind of man there are also four moral qualities – namely, jen, right-eousness, propriety, and wisdom – and jen embraces them all . . . For jen as constituting the Way (Tao) consists of the fact that the mind of Heaven and Earth to produce things is present in everything . . . If we can truly practice love and preserve it, then we have in it the spring of all virtues and the root of all good deeds. (Chan, 1963: 594)

Thus in order to activate *jen*, self-cultivation is necessary. Self-cultivation is thus the inner pole of Confucianism.

For Confucians cultivation involves broad education and self-reflection. Self-cultivation requires seriousness. The pursuit of learning depends on the extension of knowledge. In the *Great Learning*, a section of the *Classic of Rituals*:

When things are investigated, knowledge is extended; when knowledge is extended, the will becomes sincere; when the will is sincere, the mind is rectified; when the mind is rectified, the personal life is cultivated; when the personal life is cultivated, the family will be regulated; when the family is regulated, the state will be in order; when the state is in order, there will be peace throughout the world. (Chan, 1963: 86f.)

In Confucianism, the self is the centre of everything. Once the self is set, it can be opened up into different areas of life. In this way, the self should first seek to understand itself by preoccupying itself with the interior experience of understanding its nature. The self seeking to understand itself starts with learning. Through learning, the self can be developed in the direction of sagehood. A sage for Confucians is a person who commits himself or herself to 'the moral responsibility of becoming a person of goodness, an individual who, in reverential attitude, experiences a fundamental unity between himself or herself and Heaven, earth, and the ten-thousand things' (Taylor Rodney, 1990: 56). Simply put, the process from the investigation of things to the rectification of the mind is the moral development of a person. This is a process of self-cultivation.

## Different Theories of Mind in Confucianism

When we talk about self-cultivation in Confucianism, an understanding of the theory of the mind is important (Taylor, 1990: 104). However, there is a broad spectrum of different models of self-cultivation in Confucianism. Basically, one model is from Chou Tun-I's *chu-ching*, mastering of quietude, while suggestive of a certain quality of moral direction and guidance. The other model is from Ch'eng I's *chu-ching*, abiding in reverent seriousness. He recognizes the need for such guidelines and direction to be given to the mind (Taylor, 1990: 103). Based on the understanding of these two models, we recognize that there are two different interpretations of the relationship between human mind and principle. One is from the Ch'eng-Chu school and the other is from the Wang Yang-ming school. The former school holds that principle exists outside of our mind in the sense that by *ko-wu*, extending our knowledge of external things, our mind comes to a point concomitant with the emergence of principle. When our mind coincides with principle, humans act morally, that is, act accord-

ing to principle. Thus 'preserving the mind' through reverent seriousness is important to act out *jen*.

On the other hand, there is another school from Wang Yang-ming
which holds different perspectives on principle. According to the
thought of Wang's school, principle resides in one's mind. That is to
say, humans do not need to extend our knowledge of external things
but rather to search principle inwardly. The extension direction is not
from the outside but from inside. As principle lies within human self,
humans through *cheng-hsin*, rectification of the heart-mind, can act
morally. Thus rectification is important in Wang's school of thought.
*Ko-wu* is then rectification. Wang's school separates mind and principle.

However, whether principle is in the mind or outside the mind,
introspective investigation is important to the process of self-
cultivation. The means of self-reflection is quiet-sitting (Taylor 1990:
93). Quiet-sitting for Confucians is a method of self-reflection through
which *hsing*, the true nature, in *pen-ti*, the original substance, will
manifest itself. *Hsing* is the essence of human nature. In other words,
the goal of self-reflection is to manifest the nature of human beings.
Nature for Confucians means both nature of things and nature of
human beings. ' "The nature is the same as principle." In relation to
the mind, it is called the nature. In relation to events, it is called principle. . . . The nature consists of innumerable principles created by
Heaven' (Chan, 1963: 614). Thus through understanding the true
nature, one comes to understand the Way of Heaven. Fundamentally,
the true nature of being is *jen*.

Although the Ch'eng-Chu school and the Wang Yang-ming school
hold different views of the relationship between principle and mind,
their core concept of *jen* is being concomitant with principle. That is
to say, since *jen* is an inherent principle in all humans, through *jen*,
humans are all related. Thus the web of relationships of the concept of
*jen* is maintained in different schools of thought in Confucianism.
Since *jen* is to be able to relate to others, the manifestation of one's
*hsing* means to activate *jen*. When one acts out *jen*, one's nature is
transformed and perfected. The sagehood of oneself is then realized.
Nevertheless, self-cultivation is a lifetime commitment to build one's
character. Confucius described his own lifetime:

> . . . at fifteen, I set my heart on learning. At thirty, I was firmly estab-
> lished. At forty, I had no more doubts. At fifty, I knew the will of
> heaven. At sixty, I was ready to listen to it. At seventy, I could

follow my heart's desire without transgressing what was right. (Confucius, 1979: 2:4; p. 67)

Furthermore, self-cultivation should also be regarded as a relationship-building process through which human love can be actualized. As we have discussed, self for Confucians is not an individualistic self but always relates to family, community, country, world and beyond. In other words, a self can be a self because it can be well related to others. As Tu indicates, 'Confucians perceive each person as a center of relationships who is in the process of ultimate transformation as a communal act' (Tu, 1994: 183). The set of relationships is built upon the principle of love which is *jen*. All of the specific human relations of which we are a part can be mediated by the Confucian concept of *li* (propriety, rites). *Li* for Confucians is the traditional primarily social mechanism for constituting community and generating its sociopolitical order. Without *li*, human roles cannot properly function.

## The Relationship Between *Jen* and *Li*

In regard to the relationship between *jen* and *li*, *li* 'can be conceived of as an externalization of *jen* in a concrete social situation' (Tu, 1979: 18). *Jen* in the Confucian sense is *moral excellence*. This moral excellence, however, does not depend upon anything. It is a principle of inwardness. It 'is basically linked with the self-reviving, self-perfecting, and self-fulfilling process of an individual' (Tu, 1979: 19). As an inner morality, *jen* depends upon the outward or external criterion for self-actualization. *Li*, then, is this outward or external criterion for one to carry out one's moral self-cultivation in the social context (Ames, Dissanayake and Kasulis, 1994: 182). Cua says, 'If *jen* is to be properly regarded as an internal criterion for the moral relevance of feelings, *li* expresses the outward or external criterion for the relevance or the expressions of these feelings' (Cua, 1978: 59).

In this sense, when one acts out *li*, one is self-actualized. When one can embrace others, one embraces life. Thus the ultimate end of self-cultivation for Confucians is to be *jen* and *li*, which means to turn to life. Tu states,

Self-realization, in this sense, is not a lonely quest for one's inner spirituality but a communicative act empowering one to become a responsible householder, an effective community worker, and a conscientious public servant. (Ames, Dissanayake and Kasulis, 1994: 182)

To turn to life then for Confucians is to be involved in a set of defined roles and mutual obligations. Each person through self-cultivation should understand and conform to his/her proper role. Starting from individual and family, people acting rightly could reform and perfect society.

All in all, we can say that Confucianism can be characterized as not only a system of social and ethical philosophy, but also a faith with its religious dimension. In regard to its religious dimension, Confucianism lays emphasis on *hsin* (heart), which signifies both intellectual awareness and moral awakening. To rectify *hsin* (heart) means to activate *jen* in the sense that the moral activism of one's nature is maintained.

After analysing a Confucian understanding of self-cultivation and its relation to self-actualization, we turn our exploration to charismatics' understanding of self-transformation.

## Charismatics' Understanding of Self-Transformation

The spiritual tradition of Christianity interprets the fullness of life as participation in God. The individual transacts with the divine through prayer and communion in order to live life more fully. It is the spiritual value of divine relatedness that produces the fruits of life for the individual. In other words, experiencing God is important for the Christian's life to be transformed. Different Christian spiritual traditions have different forms of pursuing God. The global phenomenon of Pentecostal and neo-Pentecostal growth in our time makes it particularly relevant to examine more thoroughly the beliefs and practices of charismatic groups.[2] As pointed out by Cox in his introductory chapter to this volume (p. 11), the growth of Pentecostalism is also highly relevant in a Chinese context.

For charismatics,[3] experiencing God is being filled with the Holy Spirit. The initial sign of being filled by the Holy Spirit is glossolalia or 'ecstatic utterance'. Because of the 'latter rain' experience, the lives of Pentecostals are empowered. The baptism of the Holy Spirit has different forms of manifestation, including glossolalia, healing, prophecy, personal testimony and consciously cultivated liturgical spontaneity. Simply put, Pentecostals are those who emphasize the power of the Holy Spirit. Thus when we speak of Pentecostalism, we speak of charismatic experience, which is the work and the grace of the Holy Spirit.

Generally speaking, we can regard charismatic experiences as religious experiences or even mystical religious experiences since the basic characters of the phenomena of a religious experience are the same: ineffability, noetic quality, transiency, and the passivity of the experiencer (James, 1958[1902]: 391). The forms of charismatic experience are very diversified. Charismatic experiences include not only glossolalia, dreams and visions, but also outbursts of uncontrolled laughter and crying, sinking-down, and even vomiting. Although we can say that the new charismatic movement is the continuation of early Pentecostalism, in terms of evangelization, these two movements are different. According to Cox, the early Pentecostals had a strong mission sense because they believed that the 'latter rain' had fallen down upon the faithful in order to equip them to spread the gospel to the world. However, the new trend of charismatic development seems to focus on the experience itself and the aspect of divine healing (Cox, 1995: 106–10). Glossolalia for them is not only a way of speaking to God, but also a delightful experience. Cox states:

> Speaking in tongues was thus detached from the Last Days eschatology. It was understood not primarily as a supernatural tool for world mission but as a deliverance from the iron cage of grammar and a graceful provision to those who did not have the strength or the fluency to pray with their own words. (Cox, 1995: 87)

Moreover, it seems that for charismatics different forms of the baptism of the Spirit such as speaking in tongues, 'being slain in the Spirit', sobering repentance, shaking, laughing, jumping, and many other expressions are kinds of therapeutic experiences devoted to personal health and well-being. They are seen as God's direct intervention in human situations so that human brokenness, through this immediate 'touching' of God, can be made whole again.

Thus the experiential dimension of religious life for charismatics is much emphasized. Although charismatic experiences have challenged traditional theology which puts emphasis on the cognitive and intellectual side of our faith, religious experiences are not the crux of a religious faith. Religious experiences are significant only because they have an effect on our life. Thus how the experiencer is changed or transformed by the experience is much more crucial than how we can attain such an experience. The latter is means, while the former is end. In other words, to experience is not enough, 'what it is' brings us to reflect the meaning of the experience. Our concern then is to investigate how these charismatic experiences transform Christian lives. In order to comprehend how charismatics are transformed by different charismatic experiences, it is necessary to understand the nature of charismatic/religious experience. I will use William James's definition of religion as a framework for discussing the nature and function of religious experience. I then intend to show how James's theory applies to charismatic spirituality. Finally I explain what self-transformation implies in terms of the immanence of God in the Christian community.

## William James's Definition of Religion

William James, one of the founders of modern psychology, is concerned with the power of religious experiences on one's life. For James the essence of religious faith is an individual experience of the divine. He quotes many examples of religious experience that brought people from miserable, ineffective agony to creativity and effectiveness. James' point is that beliefs about the world can have a profound effect on our psychological and physical health. According to William James, religions consist of

> the feelings, acts, and experiences of individual men in their solitude, so far as they apprehend themselves to stand in relation to whatever they may consider the divine. (James, 1958[1902]: 42)

That is to say, the nature of religion is relationship with the divine. This relationship is built upon the degree of immediate luminousness and how the luminousness transforms one's life into morality. James further explains that this human–divine relationship can be built through prayer. James defines prayer as 'every kind of inward communion or conversation with the power recognized as divine' (James, 1958[1902]: 352). Religion for him is prayer communion with the divine.

Therefore James affirms that 'prayer is real religion' (James, 1958 [1902]: 352). As James says,

> Religion is nothing if it be not the vital act by which the entire mind seeks to save itself by clinging to the principle from which it draws

its life. This act is prayer, by which term I understand no vain exercise of words, no mere repetition of certain sacred formulae, but the very movement itself of the soul, putting itself in a personal relation of contact with the mysterious power of which it feels the presence. (James, 1958[1902]: 352)

It is in this concept of prayer that James views religious experience as the root of religion. Through immediate contact with the divine, one's life can be transformed by taking a new way of seeing the world and acting within it. However, we should notice that religious experience for James is played upon by the divine powers beyond human will. It is a gift from the divine (James, 1958[1902]: 388). That is to say, religious experience is divine initiative and humans are the receivers of this grace.

For James the purpose of religion is to experience a more satisfying life. He quotes Professor Leuba's sayings,

'in this way: God is not known, he is not understood; he is used ... Not God, but life, more life, a larger, richer, more satisfying life is, in the last analysis, the end of religion. The love of life, at any and every level of development, is the religious impulse.' (James, 1958[1902]: 382)

In other words, through prayers, our life can be transformed to the extent that we enhance the value of our existence. Thus the divine for James is to be utilized in order for the believer to yearn to be free and to exist in a satisfactory manner. The value of religious experience is to produce the fruits of life for the believer. Religious experience is then functional and pragmatic.

## Applying James's Religious Theory to an Explanation of Pentecostalism

From the above analysis, we can say that James's definition of religion and his explanation of how religious experience plays a functional role in our lives' transformation seem to be well suited to an explanation of charismatic spirituality. What James has shown is also the charismatics' concern.

First of all, as James grants more power to the individual to utilize the divine, charismatics are also concerned with the power of religious experiences on the believer's life. Thus they seek visions and dreams for the direction of life, enjoy speaking in tongues for a delightful, comforting experience and ask for faith in order to be healed. Charismatics lay emphasis on different forms of religious experience so as to be empowered to live a good life. With the power of the Holy Spirit, charismatics are infused with spiritual gifts to cope with daily problems such as sicknesses, financial problems, relational conflicts, family problems, business concerns and every imaginable earthly issue. It is done in anticipation of God's direct intervention in human situations. Charismatic experience is not just a noetic phenomenon, but also a way of empowerment living in this world.

Second, as religious experiences for James do not yield any knowledge of God, charismatics are not concerned with the cognitive and intellectual aspect of Christian theology. The core message of charismaticism is human experience of the Spirit. Since religious experience is wider than any bodily sense can encompass, charismatics lay emphasis on the functional power of spiritual gifts which often appear to have little to do with deeper meaning and significance. As Christian doctrines have been set apart, the experiential aspect of Christianity has come to the arena. Charismaticism then to a certain extent is highly subjective, in the sense that a charismatic's strong conviction comes from his/her experience of God's power in the Spirit, not from reasoning and understanding of Christian doctrine. Nevertheless, it is the experiential aspect of the Spirit which makes charismatics who they are. Thus religious experience is the key for self-transformation.

Third, while James is not concerned with morality as the fruit of religious experience, charismatics do not come to consider the spiritual value of moral helpfulness as it reorients the direction of the individual. However, they do have a strong sense of conviction and commitment to their religious experience and earnestly expect God's miracle and healing; charismatics often experience 'signs and wonders' in their mission work. Charismatics might have neglected the negative sides of religious experience if they lose the moral aspect of a religion and character-building in spiritual formation. We cannot neglect the fact that the moral and political justifications for martyrdom, suicide bombing, genocide and nationalist violence are often drawn from spiritually transformative experiences.

As we have mentioned that Confucian self-cultivation awakens one's moral nature, it is to this side of Confucianism that we turn our dialogue.

## A Comparison between Confucian Self-Cultivation and Charismatic Self-Transformation

The traditions of Confucians and charismatic Christians are so apparently diverse that it is difficult to bridge the gap between the two. Although Confucians seem to emphasize the traditional virtues, while charismatics are subjected to modern culture, an interesting comparison can be drawn between Confucian self-cultivation and Christian self-transformation. By interacting with these two traditions, we claim that the self in these two traditions is the primary point of reference for life, and if morality is not the ground on which the self is based, life cannot be embraced but rather disintegrates.

What the perspectives of Confucians and charismatics have in common is an affirmation of the human self. The self for both of them is not static, in the sense that the self is always in the process of development and empowerment. With regard to Confucianism, the self through self-cultivation can be developed into a related self; while for charismatics the self, by the infusion of the Holy Spirit, can be empowered to cope with different difficulties in our daily lives. Through self-cultivation or baptism of the Holy Spirit, personal transformation is possible. Life is always in the process of self-fulfilment. This continued self-development in these two traditions is the focus of their spiritual concern. Although both Confucians and charismatics share a concern for the functional development of the self, their form of functionalism is different. That is to say, they have different notions of living a good life.

## A Critique of Charismatic Christianity from a Confucian perspective

### A Liberated Self Versus a Regulated Self

In terms of the happy life, charismatics seek the liberation of self, which Confucians would deem as a life without control. For charismatics the liberation of the self begins with the infusion of the Holy Spirit which eventually brings self to transformation. Then religious experience, especially with intense and highly emotional feeling, is the crux of self-transformation. Life can be transformed by releasing our spiritual gifts. By means of them, we are able to serve freely in congregational life, and be motivated for evangelism and missions. The lives of charismatics from the Confucian point of view are highly unregulated in the sense that they are so dependent upon the divine initiative experience, to the extent that human ability is deemed to be indistinctive. Charismatics do not need to be self-cultivated in order to be transformed. They act so freely that there is no need for them to be self-consciously aware of what they are doing in so many social contexts. *Li* cannot be acted out since charismatics are not concerned with how we are disposed to act toward others. There are no regulations for life. Consequently, humans are not moral agents, for charismatics.

Nevertheless for Confucians, morality is the basic principle governing all human relationships and without which human lives will be at stake. We can say that liberation is key to charismatics and morality is the norm for Confucians. As we have discussed before, *jen* and *li* are an internal and an external criterion of morality respectively, they are interdependent upon each other (Confucius, 1979: 67). Thus self-cultivation is important for the turn to life in Confucianism. Confucians emphasize self-cultivation in order to bring the self's desires into conformity with *li*, and *jen* can be actualized. We can say that self-cultivation is a ceaseless effort which is an end itself and its primary purpose is self-realization (Tu, 1979: 27f.). As a moral human being in the Confucian tradition, one does not only cultivate oneself with right feeling, but also by expressing these feelings in the proper context (Tu, 1979). Accordingly, *li* has to be understood as a dynamic movement, which involves the act of self-transformation. It is a dynamic movement within the context of the dichotomy of individual self and collective social circumstance. It is manifested concretely in the four developmental stages of human beings, that is, cultivating personal life, regulating familial relations, ordering the affairs of the state, and bringing peace to the world. Thus through self-cultivation, humans can be related: related to self, to others, to the whole universe and to Heaven and Earth. The Confucian self has to be regulated but not liberated.

## A Self-Seeking Religion Versus a Self-Relating Religion

Based on the above-mentioned characteristic of the Confucian self, Confucians would criticize Pentecostalism as a form of self-seeking spirituality. Charismatics base their happiness on self satisfaction in the sense that they always seek personal empowerment to cope with daily problems. Thus they neglect human responsibility. The self is no longer a responsible self but a self seeking its own fulfilment. Since Confucians see humans as moral agents, an individual is always a responsible self. Basically, the Confucian self is essentially a concept of moral relationships. That is to say, the self is always the starting-point for a wider concern for the lives of others. The Confucian self is a responsible self in the sense that it is a relational self. Thus relationality holds the key to understanding the nature of humans' deepest ethical and spiritual values and behaviours as well. Most of who and what a person is, is determined by the others with whom that person interacts. In order to live in harmony, the self should act out *jen*. Since injustice is the basic rupture in the cosmos and in all human relationships, the transformation of self is about a consciousness of *jen* which makes a person just. A just person not only acts justly but also relates to others humanly. However, charismatics seem to be concerned with a psychological journey which Confucians would regard as an individualistic spirituality which does not benefit our society. Hence, Christianity in its charismatic version turns out to be a private religion in a global world.

All in all, by criticizing charismatics from a Confucian perspective, I have tried to bring to light that the same kind of point that was expressed by Confucians, well over two millennia ago, can give insight to the modern religious movement of charismatic Christianity. But my claim is not that the tradition of Confucianism is so much to be appreciated that charismatics should lose their distinctive religious elements so that they can be identified with Confucians. Since its early development, Christianity has always participated in larger cultural systems which Christians bring into their communities. They borrow from these systems and use them in new ways within Christian society. As a result, Christianity becomes a world religion. Viewing Confucianism as a cultural system and Christians as hybrids, my attempt is to bring charismatics to a new horizon of witnessing in the global world.

## Notes

1 For a detailed introduction to Chu Hsi's contributions to Confucianism, see Au, 2002: 3.

2 See Wacker, 2001. According to Wacker, today, almost 525 million people around the world identify themselves as Pentecostals or charismatics.

3 Pentecostalism can be divided into three groups: 'Classical' Pentecostals, those who are members of the standard Pentecostal groups, most of which originated in the first quarter of the twentieth century; the charismatics, or those in other denominations who received the 'baptism of the Holy Spirit', and the so-

called 'neo-charismatics', the groups formed in the last half of the century, most of which are not affiliated with the Pentecostal denominations. The charismatics are present in the majority of the denominations of Christendom, normally having their own associations as part of their denominations.

# 10. Pentecostalism and Normalization

## ANDREW THOMAS

Western Europe in the twentieth century has been the location for two major movements of liberation: the first came during the opening decades, when liberal thinkers and artists attempted to throw off the burden of Victorian values and inhibitions; the second occurred in the sixties, when 'hippies', captured by beauty and disgusted with hierarchy, carved out new ways of life in protest against prevalent bourgeois values.

These developments bear the description 'liberative' because people are inclined to think of them as emerging from a worldview that was oppressive, into an open space that is free from boundaries and claustrophobic limitations. But we are not obliged to accept this description. In retrospect, historians have set question-marks over the description of Victorian culture as an asexual, inhibited discourse with strict guidelines for normal behaviour (cf. especially Foucault, 1990[1976]). It would seem that what we had got used to referring to as liberation may in reality have been a transfer of discourse from one arena to another. What had been described as a release from normalizing factors was really an initiation into new ones. Here the role of psychoanalysis in discourse and forms of life is a deciding factor.

In this essay I intend to look at how the behaviour characteristic of charismatic movements in Great Britain can be seen as liberative, and to what extent they merely represent a transference of the strategies of normalization to new spheres. Although focusing on the gift of tongues, it will also be important to take into account the bizarre actions named 'the manifestations of the Spirit'.

Why is it important to study normalization when talking about globalization? Surely it is a field dominated by studies of Western Europe – at best the North Atlantic – and is certainly irrelevant for a post-colonial world? Is this not the worst kind of Eurocentrism? But let us not fall into the trap of thinking that these globalizing processes are abstract neutral developments in the history of ideas and international relations. The processes of globalization involve import and export. It is not simply a case of more people in the world being able to use the internet; it is about more people in the world buying from Microsoft. We are not simply talking about the increase of the exchange of ideas; globalization involves the increasing exchange of specific, strategic ideas. So sociologists must look into their history to see where the disciplines they export are founded on European institutions; psychologists must be suspicious of their own arena of study as constructing a European society, a Western normality; and theologians must look to what is being exported, and how it reflects the constraints of our own history and worldview. It may well prove that in the processes of globalization, hegemonic powers do not simply gain money, but the power to control normality. And that is a commodity worth a great deal.

## Liberation from Normalization?

British charismaticism – which is the prime focus of this study – holds many of the sources of resistance to society's normalizing forces in common with other variants of Christianity. Just as Jesus broke away from stable Second-Temple Judaic society through new eating rules, resistance to the prevailing economic system and undermining family life (Wright, 1996: 369–442), so charismatics demonstrate their independence through fasting, tithing and family groups, expressing the fatherhood of God and the brotherhood of man. These kinds of resistance are not to be taken lightly in Western psychiatric capitalist society, with its dependence on the market, bias towards the consumer and strict definitions of what is normal and what is perverse. They are not, however, exclusive to the charismatic movement.

One point of resistance to normalization that has, especially recently, been a major facet of this branch of the Church is the provocative behaviour called the manifestation of the Spirit. When the Spirit 'falls' – and here I am thinking particularly of churches associated with the Toronto blessings – the people start acting strangely.

There are a number of different methodologies that could be brought to bear on this phenomenon; many ways of describing what is happening here. In my time at a charismatic church in England, I often wondered what would happen were we to bring psychoanalysts into the room, and how they would interpret what was happening. I would see some people rolling their shoulder as if they were warming up for a tennis match, and others suddenly strain their every muscle to tense themselves in what seemed to me to be a fighting stance. This all in addition to (seemingly) unprovoked screaming, the usual quaking and shaking, with a background of tongue-speaking and hysterical (*note the tempting medical metaphor*) laughter. All of these manifestations could be interpreted in various ways: obviously doctors might call it pathological behaviour, medical anthropologists might put it into the context of systems of healing, and others would perhaps categorize it as normal religious behaviour. I shall be calling it 'strange behaviour'.

The defining aspect of these actions is that they are not normal. This behaviour crosses boundaries and defies inhibitions – hence the charismatic leaders' constant encouragement to 'let go'; to 'not worry about what your neighbour is doing or thinking', and so on. The movement appears to be trying to break out of the control of abnormality that is in place in Western culture. For abnormality has a history, just as inhibitions do – and this is what Foucault was (failing) to analyse in his early historical work.

Foucault's *History of Madness in the Classical Age* (Foucault, 1961; 1973) is a much maligned (Still and Velody, 1992) story of the events that led to the opening of the first asylums at the end of the eighteenth century, at the time of another great liberation, the French Revolution, and the birth of psychiatry. The story takes us from the mediaeval reverie of the ship of fools that travelled from port to port in order to set down and carry off folly throughout European urban culture, through industrial workhouses, poorhouses, and hospitals of folly, to the psychiatric hospitals that impress their categories of mental illness onto 'liberated' patients through confession and discipline. It tracks the transformations that European society went through in moving from monarchical rule to the control of the soul.

What does Foucault mean with this control of the soul? In the history of madness, he draws a line along the experience of madness from the confinement of the mad during the Renaissance to the diagnoses handed out in the modern era. This continuity is evidenced in myth and institution. The image of the benevolent philanthropist releasing the insane from the prison-like enclosures at Bicêtre is deeply engraved in the French imagination, and the asylums that were instituted in those days are still with us. In a fit of liberalism, classical man began a humane treatment of the mad, and so made the transition to modernism.

How did the asylums work? At first, they were not greatly different from the prisons. There were, of course, no more chains, but the threat of violence was by no means erased. Discipline was still the order of the day, and the leaders of the asylums rarely hesitated in confining their patients should the need arise. No more chains: merely the threat of chains. But as the movement prevailed in Europe, the asylums became steadily more often places of study and observation – hence the birth of the category of 'mental illness'. The patients were thera-pied into admitting their status as mentally ill, so that this confession (a key concept – cf. Foucault, 1990[1976]: 65) became the benchmark of their progress in treatment, and their ticket out of the asylum.

Foucault describes the construction of such categories through asymmetrical observation as methods of societal control. When con-cepts such as 'criminal', 'delinquent', 'mentally ill' and so on become common fare in a society, then corresponding descriptions such as 'law-abiding', 'good citizen', and 'healthy' become the norm. And when the former people can be contained and controlled, the latter are normalized.

This happened through the twin movements of forms of knowledge and institution. As strange people were contained, they were studied (usually through panoptic buildings), observed, and sent out into soci-ety as examples of cured delinquents or mental patients. So that now, it is perfectly natural to mention in passing the *hysterical* laugh-ter of charismatics. Psychiatric terminology is disseminated through-out Western discourse, and the implication of these words is that something is wrong – something involving the options of freedom and confinement.[1] Having rejected a suspicion of women's instability through the free-moving womb, it embraces a field of knowledge con-stituted by observation and the confinement of souls.

The application of Foucault's analyses to the manifestations of the Spirit should be fairly clear. While in the mediaeval era, Europeans were inclined to send babbling, staggering, laughing people to the neighbouring town, and in the Renaissance they would be locked up, the modern era in Foucault's history tends to call them mentally ill and send them to a psychiatrist until they confess their condition (for a detailed critique and discussion of this history, cf. Gutting, 1994; Still and Velody, 1992). But when these things happen in charismatic churches, they are given honour, and attributed to the presence of the Holy Spirit. Psychiatric categories are spurned, and God is given the glory.

So the Toronto blessings help to challenge the normalizing powers inherent in the modern Western worldview. We may no longer say that normal people don't run up and hug strangers on the street spontaneously. Neither may we say without justification that shivering is a sign of madness. But charismatics will claim that we should not necessarily say these are signs of mental illness either. They are just manifestations of the Holy Spirit at work in the Church.


## Liberation from Language?

To what extent is speaking in tongues a part of this resistance to normality? What is significant for us about glossolalia, is that it is *not* the language of psychiatry. Indeed, there is no field of knowledge that can be derived from asymmetrical observation and distributed throughout the discourse of tongues. It is not a language shared by a community that describes and excludes 'weirdoes', and neither does it contain any way of categorizing people as off their trolley, so that normalization simply can not happen through normal language while someone is speaking in tongues. Instead, speaking in tongues sets itself up as a private language, free from the confines of public normality and verbal inhibition. Through this practice, charismatics are liberated from the confines of a normalizing discourse.

Language normalizes through forming our worldview, being the way we describe ourselves to each other. We confess, forgive, thank, and desire in the concepts taught us from childhood. We are formed by our language. So does the gift of tongues break out of that?

A short excursion into twentieth-century language philosophy is perhaps called for in order to understand the appeal of a private language. Probably the philosophical tradition to have most felt the problem of a flawed and confining language is the Anglo-American analytic school of philosophy. Here, at the beginning of the last century, as ecstatic fireworks were going off in Azusa Street at the birth of Pentecostalism, great tomes were written to found a language on a pure logical system. These books were half-descriptive, half-prescriptive works on language and how we are to set out arguments, after the revolution started off by Gottlob Frege (Frege, 1980[1884]). In Frege's system there were no terms for madness, no oppressive categories or fields of knowledge, just stipulations and propositions. It was a pure world of analytic thought, where every mistake was obvious, and every proposition self-evident.

The Achilles heel of this movement was the search for something to drive these stipulations – how do words mean, by themselves? The natural answer would be that so long as we all use the same rules together, everyone will know exactly what is going on inside my head when I talk – hence the 'convention' theory of meaning, held by thinkers throughout the ages (Plato's *Cratylus*; Augustine's *On Christian Teaching*).

On the surface of things, this step is itself a reasonable one to take. It is perfectly fair to say that I know what I mean, so that's OK (if we take it for granted that everyone can use rules, and Wittgenstein did, with some reservations). The whole of modern philosophy is based on this kind of step – I know what is going on in my head, and so long as I talk about that, I can not be proved wrong (Descartes). It is at this point that Wittgenstein came (in both his early and later work) to demonstrate the vanity of this way of thinking, by challenging the assumption that our meaning is somehow prior to our speaking.

Wittgenstein's private language argument has come to be a famous turning-point in Anglo-American philosophy. Although the argument stretches throughout his posthumous classic, *Philosophical Investigations*, the crux of it can be shown in the illustration of the beetle in the box which I will give in Wittgenstein's own words, as no one could compose philosophy like him:

> Suppose everyone had a box with something in it: we call it a 'beetle'. No one can look into anyone else's box, and everyone says he knows what a beetle is only by looking at his beetle. – Here it would be quite possible for everyone to have something different in his box. One might even imagine such a thing constantly changing. – But suppose the word 'beetle' had a use in these languages? – If so it would not be used as the name of a thing. The thing in the box has no place in the language-game at all; not even as a something: for the box might even be empty. (Wittgenstein, 2001[1953]: 293)

So that if an attempt is made to justify a use of language (or sounds, or phonemes) through maintaining that they are a reference to something only the speaker is witness to (prior thoughts), then problems will certainly arise in maintaining that this use constitutes a system of communication, because there is no common reference available. But if a word has communicative value, it cannot be that of '*x*' referring to x.

So that private languages do not exist. Merely using the language on its own to describe or express – independently of forms of common life – will not do. Speakers are committed to commonality – to categories and offence, to presumption and grammar.

Speaking in tongues sets itself up as a private language: it is something understood by neither speaker nor hearer, unless it be interpreted, at which point the gift of tongues gives way to the gift of interpretation, according to the Pauline schema of 1 Corinthians 12 and 14. In fact, the only person who does understand is the only one who does not need to hear the truth, namely God. It is primarily for this reason that glossolalia can not be termed a language, and not simply because of any lack of grammar, morphology, etc. (cf. the suggestive discussion of 'speaking with tongues' in Wittgenstein, 2001[1953]: §528) but precisely because of what defines it as speaking in tongues: its incomprehensibility.

Since this is the case, then, speaking in tongues does not give an alternative for self-expression in community. Instead, it distracts that human need, forming the main element of common confession in the Church, but never allowing any form of communication (in any logical sense) whereby subjects may seek and express their truth.

## Private Languages and Solitude

Can we not apply other analyses, though, to this kind of experience? Need we say that glossolalia is a language? Isn't the application of essentially non-theological analyses illicit, disallowing the existence of an individual's unique communication with God? Perhaps a more useful tool might be provided in de Certeau's explanation of ecstatic or foolish utterance as the absence of discourse (Certeau, 1992[1982]: 31–48). The holy fools of late antiquity created a world of loneliness in the community through their bizarre lifestyle, but they did not make sense. The only ones who express themselves are people who claim to speak for them – bewildered, scorched commentators whose lives have brushed against the holy Other. And their witness is one of babble and nonsense:

> Sometimes also he pretended to babble, for he said that of all semblances, this one is most fitting and most useful to those who simulate folly [156] for the sake of Christ. (Leontius, 1996: IV.155f.)

Might not speaking in tongues parallel such behaviour? Might it not be the case that the scandal of holiness is simply offensive to study? This kind of challenge may not be ignored by theologians, so that it is only with caution that we may draw attention to a departure from the holy fools tradition.

De Certeau emphasizes the point about the holy fools that they were not seductive. They did not draw other fools to themselves, or require conversion. Indeed, the earliest fool fled once she was found out (Palladius, 1965: ch. XXIV). Similarly, Symeon the Holy Fool kept his foolery as a closely guarded secret. His withdrawal from discourse was not meant to attract others, but to stand alone. De Certeau comments,

> Eccentric, bare-chested and brazen, jovial and brutal, this provoker wants to 'overturn edification' according to the narrator. He boldly carries transgression into the camp of the self-righteous. He irritates, amuses, wins admiration or blows, but he does not divert language toward that which is without place. He is not seductive. (Certeau, 1992[1982]: 40)

What happens when this kind of discursive lack becomes the entrance point of a community, such as speaking in tongues has become for the Pentecostal movement? In this case, the radical absence of discourse has received a meaning – that of a rite of passage. That which has no meaning is brought into play through constructing an identity. And when that contract is made, the freedom of ecstasy is eliminated. It is then moulded by structures of normalization in the new community.

It is probably for this reason that speaking in tongues bears the marks of socialization processes. Coleman (2000: 130) notes that many in the church he studied actually repeated phrases often heard on the lips of the founder of that particular movement, the 'Word of Life' in Sweden. In Britain, there are charismatic leaders that sensitively help people over the barrier of self-consciousness by telling them of their own first rite with sounds that clearly weren't especially authentic sounding ('yallaballaballaballa'), and started out from there. What we first thought completely free improvisation is shown to be a fairly rigid idiom with its own scale and chord patterns (cf. Cox, 1995: 143–57).

This parting of the ways between the ecstatics of late antiquity and those of late modernity is notable for another reason. To initiate another into a discourse which is radically meaningless and unclear betrays a desire for totalitarianism. As Foucault himself remarked:

> I do not like obscurity because I consider it to be a form of despotism; one must put oneself in danger of making mistakes; one must

be willing to risk coming to say things that, probably, will be difficult to express and which, evidently, can be a bit confused. (Foucault, 1999: 130)

In a similar way, Wittgensteinians such as Stanley Cavell and Fergus Kerr interpret the private language argument as mounting an attack on a deeply seated temptation: that is, the wish

for one's language to be wedded to the world *apart from having to make sense to others* – apart from having to face charges from them of *not making sense*. (Kerr, 1997: 122, commenting on Cavell's interpretation of Wittgenstein)

So Wittgenstein's requirements of making sense are directed towards speakers who are attempting to set up their own private discourse, of which they are the sole reigning monarchs.

While it is all very well to recommend the non-verbal, pre-rational forms of theology and church on the grounds that at the end of the day, we do what we want, not what we think, it is also necessary to bear in mind that however inspiring they may be, it is in the flesh that we negotiate relationships – in our flesh we honour, shame, love – in our flesh we bare our hearts before God in worship. And it is in our flesh that we discover we are wrong.

When a community is constituted by a withdrawal from meaning and judgement, then any act of recommending ourselves – something we must remember St Paul attempted and failed to avoid throughout his time as church leader – becomes a gross act of power over others. Similarly, withdrawing from discourse in obedience makes one a slave to the rulers of that community – and herein lies the kenotic actions of these foolish late antique monks, who submitted to radical obedience. And it is perhaps for this reason that the Corinthian correspondence plays down ecstatic utterance in church, replacing it with love that is patient, and prophecy, so that we 'may be reproved by all and called to account by all' (1 Corinthians 14.24, NRSV).

Just as the 'hippies' of the sixties found themselves entangled in a controlling society and normalizing discourse of sexuality according to Foucault's analysis, so may modern ecstatic Christians find their wildness contained by a discourse that constructs its complex of honour and shame – and thereby its reference to God – through meaningless utterance. However, this does not mean that the value of glossolalia is totally undermined. Through constituting loneliness, ridding themselves of power and resisting seductive discourse, holy fools in late antiquity managed to mock the world and witness to the Other. Late modern mysticism is thus given a choice between integration and resistance to normalizing forces on both sides. Globalized psychoanalytical discourse offers the truth of humanity in its normalizing confessions. But on the other hand, in tongues and dance, in twaddle and foolery, the Pentecostal movements represent a seductive source of resistance to globalizing normality.

*Note*

1  It is important to distinguish between this kind of discourse analysis and the more popular anti-psychiatry movement – evidenced in the work of the British thinkers Laing and Cooper – from which Foucault distanced himself, as an anti-strategist, suspicious of easy solutions and all-encompassing systems.

# 11. Resistance to Domination as a Charism of the Holy Spirit

## HAROLD WELLS

Two powerful spiritual and theological movements coexist within our worldwide Christian family; I refer to the Pentecostalists and the liberationists. Though they often appear to be polar opposites, I propose to offer here a biblical and theological basis for dialogue and possible convergence of Pentecostalist and liberationist pneumatologies. In accordance with the best of these two young traditions, I shall suggest that resistance to domination – especially in recent times, resistance to an idolatrous global empire – has to be seen as a movement of the Holy Spirit. If, by faith, we affirm a divine presence in the world which is at work for justice, peace and wholeness, then those (whether within the churches or outside of them) who strive to resist dominant, oppressive powers must be seen as gifted by the Spirit. In recent decades it has been, of course, the liberationist theologies that have emphasized Christian resistance to oppression, but generally they have not been notable for an emphasis on the Spirit. It has been especially the Pentecostalists who in recent years have prompted us to enquire into the experience and charisms of the Spirit, though this movement has not usually, in most places, emphasized liberation from systemic social evils. However, Pentecostalist and liberationist approaches are far from antithetical; indeed they are potentially very congenial in that both place great emphasis on 'experience' in the life of faith, and both have relevance to circumstances of poverty and oppression. This line of thought suggests a need today for a convergence of the Pentecostalist and liberationist spiritualities and theological perspectives, a move that has already begun to happen in many places.[1]

## Experience: Pentecostalist and Liberationist

As one who speaks out of political/liberationist and pro-feminist perspectives, I am grateful for the impetus that has come from the Pentecostalist movement, directing our attention to the dimension of experience of the Spirit. By 'Pentecostalist' I refer not only to those explicitly named 'Pentecostals' within 'Pentecostal' denominations, but to that wider 'charismatic' movement found within almost all denominations around the world. The remarkable growth of Pentecostalism of various kinds in many places, especially among poor and marginalized people, demands the attention especially of those who identify with the liberationist theologies. Recall the wry comment of a Catholic nun in Brazil, cited by Harvey Cox, who said, 'The Catholic bishops may want to encourage a preferential option for the poor, but the poor seem to have a preference for the pentecostals'. Those of us who live and work out of a liberationist vision tend to be quite 'rational' and socio-analytical, while in the Pentecostalist tradition, intense experience of the Spirit is often extraordinary and wondrous, with its particular emphasis on tongues and miraculous healing. But the American Pentecostal theologian Steven Land rightly suggests that in a postmodern era we may begin to overcome the dichotomy of reason and emotion, and move toward a better integration of 'beliefs, practices and affections' (Land, 1993: 122–3).

In fact liberationists do emphasize experience in various ways. I use the term 'liberationist' broadly to include all the interrelated theologies which operate fundamentally from an option for the poor or for the marginalized or oppressed, including black American and Latin American liberation theologies, South African and West African, Korean Minjung and other regional contextual theologies, as well as the wide spectrum of feminist and womanist theologies, the postcolonial theologies, and more recently in the north and west, gay/lesbian theologies. As different as these are, each from the others, they are all wont to speak of experiences of suffering, or of oppression or marginalization, namely black experience or women's experience or homosexual experience, or of specific colonial or cultural experience – as operative factors in biblical interpretation and Christian practice. 'Experience' here is often a negative term, naming grounds for angry protest and for critical hermenuetics of scripture and tradition.

However, experience in the liberationist streams can also refer positively to new awareness, awakening and empowerment for those on the underside. For example, when a Christian woman is awakened, perhaps through the wider, cultural feminist movement, to her marginalization as female, and feels empowered to assert her equality with men, she may indeed experience this as a holy gift of the Spirit at work – around her, and within her.[2] When African, Asian or North American indigenous people, living in a postcolonial situation and awakened to their longstanding oppression, find old or new wisdom in their own forgotten spiritual traditions, and strength to resist neo-colonial oppression, they too may feel the liberating work of the Spirit.[3] Similarly, when a Christian man of homosexual orientation, encouraged by the wider gay/lesbian liberation movement, finds the courage to affirm his orientation publicly, he too may experience this as an empowerment of the Holy Spirit.[4] We note that, as distinct from experience in the Pentecostalist stream, this liberationist experience of the Spirit of God is usually understood as something occurring within natural, human processes, with the emphasis on rational social analysis. While personal *metanoia* is often part of liberationist discourse, the emphasis is on socio-political, structural transformation. In conversation with Pentecostalists, liberationists may consider whether such profound experiences of empowerment may be seen as a kind of 'baptism in the Holy Spirit'.

Yet Pentecostalism, we may recall, also arose originally under the leadership of the black American William Seymour, out of his experiences of deprivation and racist exclusion. The Pentecostal movement (though its origins are complex and controversial) must be seen as a pneumatic experience of empowerment for resistance and self-affirmation. Seymour, whose vision was a mixture of prophetism and apocalypticism, wanted to overcome American inequalities in a world in which blacks and whites, men and women, would live and work together, and led his Azusa Street revival as a kind of vanguard for the coming of the Kingdom (Althouse, 2003: 22f., 32f.). Linking Adventist eschatology and racial integration, the early Pentecostals believed they could be agents of a social revolution, hastening the coming of the Kingdom by proclaiming Christ and the 'latter rain' of the Spirit to all the world (MacRobert, 1988: 80). The electrifying experience of Spirit baptism and tongues assured them that this was so. We may say that, with Seymour, the desired convergence of liberationist and Pentecostalist visions was already nascently present, and this is a heritage upon which Pentecostalists can build.

To cite a sharply contrasting experience of liberation which is more akin to the liberationist theologies, we may today speak of movements of resistance to neoliberal capitalist globalization, such as the World Social Forum and its local manifestations. This 'plural, diversified, non-confessional, non-governmental and non-party' movement as such is not 'religious' at all, though people of various religions are involved in it along with secular folk. This 'open meeting place', opposed to the use of violence, and opposed to neoliberalism and to domination of the world by capital and any form of imperialism, is committed to 'building a planetary society directed towards fruitful relationships among humankind and between it and the earth'.[5] Here we find a vast network of 'globalization from below' (Cormie, 1999) in which new technological systems of transportation and communication are turned against dominant powers. If, according to Isaiah 45.1, even Babylonian Cyrus could be anointed for the emancipation of Israel, surely then peace- and justice-loving people, religious or secular, may be agents of the Spirit's work in the world. As Christians we may seek to discern in such movements and events the growth of God's life-giving, liberating Reign, as that is disclosed normatively for us in Jesus Christ and scripture. With the eyes of faith we cannot fail to see, I contend, a continuity of the movement of the Creator Spirit as a spirit of resistance, from biblical prophecy, through Jesus and the early Church, in Pentecostalism, in liberationist Christian social activism, and in secular movements for justice and peace. We need, then, a broad inclusive pneumatology, which is pertinent to the whole of our lives and the whole of our experience in the world.

It seems useful to begin by considering biblical prophecy as the root of such a broad vision of the work of the Spirit.

## The *Ruah* of Prophecy: A Spirit of Resistance

Even a cursory perusal of the canonical prophets informs us that the essential character of Hebrew prophecy was resistance to dominant powers as empowered by the Spirit. 'By a prophet the Lord brought Israel out of Egypt,' says Hosea (12.14). The great founding liberative event of the people of Israel was later seen as an event of the Spirit, who inspired Moses for his prophetic resistance to the oppressive Pharaoh and his leadership of the people out of slavery. We are told that the Spirit that was upon Moses for his liberative work was passed on to others (Numbers 11.17). His successors, the 'judges' of Israel, were also gifted by the *ruah* of God. We hear of the Spirit of God at work in their essentially political, and often violent work of establishing Israel as a nation. We have to take note that today Palestinian and neo-colonial voices have been raised in protest against this violent *ruah* of conquest.[6] But less subject to hermeneutical deconstruction, perhaps, is the story in 1 Samuel 11 of Saul in confrontation with Israel's victorious enemy, Nahash the Ammonite. Though Israel had been ready to surrender peacefully, the Ammonite had announced his intention to gouge out everyone's right eye, to put disgrace upon all Israel. 'All the people wept aloud!' But 'the Spirit of God came upon Saul in power when he heard these words, and his anger was greatly kindled' (1 Samuel 11.6). This anger was followed by a cunning political and military strategy of trickery and deception by which Saul resisted and defeated the tyranny of the Ammonites, sparing the people this misery and humiliation. Here, quite ordinary human functions – outrage about cruelty and injustice, and a shrewd strategy of resistance – are seen as gifts of the Spirit to Israel. The people are freed from passivity and paralysis, and the Spirit is experienced as the power that turns the tide.[7]

We should take note that, apart from prophecy as such, many Hebrew texts associate the Spirit with what might be regarded as the ordinary and the natural. In a priestly text of Exodus we hear that God has given this same *ruah elohim* to Bezalel, a spirit of skill, understanding and knowledge manifest in craftsmanship and works of art (Exodus 31.3). This may be seen as a stable gift of 'in-spiration', a kind of divine inhabitation in the creature, or presence of transcendence within the natural. Akin to this, in the first creation story in Genesis, is the presence of the *ruah elohim* brooding over the waters of creation, to bring light out of darkness and order out of chaos (Genesis 1.2). We find similar associations of the Spirit with creation, with natural physical blessings, and with human understanding, in Isaiah (e.g. 32.15), in the Psalms (33.6; 104.30) and especially in the Wisdom literature (e.g. Job 37.8; Wisdom 1.7).

It is significant, however, that the pre-exilic canonical prophets generally avoided Spirit-talk concerning their own inspiration, and were highly critical of the prophets of the royal court. Following in the tradition of Nathan, who spoke out so courageously to King David, Amos, Hosea, Isaiah and Jeremiah, all offer critical socio-ethical, political comment on what is going on in the world around them. The gift of the prophets is to see through lies. Protesting eloquently against idolatry and social injustice, they dissociate themselves from the allegedly Spirit-inspired professional prophets. Hosea declares that 'the prophet is a fool, the man of the Spirit is mad' (Hosea 9.7).

Jeremiah even mocks these prophets as having *become wind*, because the Word is not in them (Jeremiah 5.13). We may say that they found no ethical discernment or political insight in their messages, no challenging words of wisdom for the rulers. One prophet, Micah, is an exception in that he does claim the inspiration of the Spirit: 'I am filled with power, with the Spirit of the Lord . . . to declare to Jacob his crimes and to Israel his sins' (Micah 3.8) Micah condemns the false prophets who, for their own gain, tell the powerful what they want to hear; he himself sets forth a courageous message of outrage and protest, together with hopeful visions of a world of peace (4.3).

Moreover, in the prophetic texts of Messianic hope, the one to come will be empowered by the Spirit for works of justice and peace. The Spirit will rest upon the expected one, because of whom the wolf will dwell with the lamb, and the leopard lie down with the kid (Isaiah 11.2–9) and upon a Servant of God who will bring forth justice to the nations (Isaiah 42.1–4). Isaiah 61 also speaks of one anointed by the Spirit who will bring good news to the oppressed and liberty to captives (61.1–2). One could mention a multitude of such texts associating the Spirit with justice and peace in human relations.

## Spirit-Filled Jesus

The New Testament authors, of course, find these hopes fulfilled in Jesus of Nazareth. According to Matthew (12.18–20) he is the Servant upon whom the Spirit will rest and who will bring justice to victory. According to Luke (4.16) he is the anointed one, who brings good news to the poor, release to captives, sight to the blind, and liberty to the oppressed. He will put down the mighty from their seats and exalt the humble and meek (Luke 1.53). In the synoptic Gospels the Spirit's work in Jesus the Christ is precisely to bring justice, peace and wholeness to this world. They continually associate Jesus with the Spirit, who descends upon him in his baptism (Mark 1.10 and parallels), and drives him into the wilderness to be tempted (Mark 1.12 and parallels). He heals and casts out demons in the power of the Spirit (Matthew 12.28). So intimate is the Spirit with Jesus in his very identity, that he is even said to be conceived of the Spirit in the womb of a virgin (Matthew 1.20; Luke 1.35), and 'filled by the Holy Spirit' before his birth (Luke 1.15). So utterly at one is Jesus with the Spirit, and the Spirit with Jesus, that in a trinitarian theology, the Holy Spirit is called both 'Spirit of God' and the 'Spirit of Christ' (as in Romans

8.9), and Jesus himself might well be called 'the Christ of the Spirit' (Moltmann, 1992: 60–5).

This Spirit-filled Jesus, like the prophets before him, is one who resists dominant oppressive powers. For nearly four decades now, liberationist christologies have emphasized the political character of the life and ministry of Jesus: that he was engaged in political struggle, that he lived and worked, preached and taught, in solidarity with the poor, the sick, the oppressed and marginalized people, that he was executed on a political charge. Recently the 'third wave' of historical Jesus studies, drawing upon new research in Graeco-Roman and Judaic history and archaeology, has been enriching our knowledge of the context in which Jesus of Nazareth lived. Though historical Jesus studies are almost never unanimous and always controversial, some recent studies are quite persuasive, fleshing out the character of Jesus as resistant to dominant powers in a way that corroborates long-existing liberation christologies.

Richard Horsley, just one of the many historical Jesus scholars working today, has set forth an imaginative reconstruction of the historical Jesus as an effective and courageous resistor to the imperial power of Rome in ancient Palestine. Rome was indeed (as Horsley puts it) the sole superpower of 'a new global system of economics, culture and civil administration' (Horsley, 2003: 140–3; Horsley and Silberman, 1997: 10). Jesus cannot be understood apart from this context, in which Rome appointed local client rulers to control local populations, and with the support of Roman military force, extracted resources and tribute, draining wealth from the conquered territories into Rome. Horsley paints a vivid picture of the immediate context of oppression and rebellion which were part of Jesus' own experience. We must imagine a traumatized, paralysed people, terrorized by the Herodian police and tax collectors, frequently beaten or killed at the least sign of resistance. The Gospel stories of Jesus afford glimpses into circumstances of widespread debt, poverty, disease and mental illness (Horsley and Silberman, 1997: chs 2–3).

Jesus and his followers moved about the Galilean villages calling people to live in solidarity, to share generously with one another, to forgive debts, to be loyal to marriages and families, to worship only the God of Israel (Horsley, 2003: 127). Such practices would be the beginning of the Reign of God, of which Jesus spoke so constantly, and which he announced as already present, and yet to come. The compassion and hope that Jesus inspired was accompanied by many healings, especially perhaps of desperate people traumatized by violence, hunger, stress, helplessness and chronic depression. According to Horsley, Jesus' acts of healing should be seen as 'the restoration of creative energy which he shared with others (and which many of his followers believed was divine). They were not aimed solely at individuals but served as a way of transforming wider community life' (Horsley and Silberman, 1997: 50).

Horsley perhaps gives too little emphasis to the divine/pneumatic and apocalyptic element in the ministry of Jesus, but he is surely right that Jesus' healing work should not be understood as separate from his social/emancipatory work. It was seen as a sign of the presence of God's Reign growing among them. 'If it is by the Spirit of God that I cast out demons, then the Kingdom of God has come to you,' says the Matthean Jesus (Matthew 12.28).

There is widespread consensus that it was especially Jesus' cleansing of the temple that led to his crucifixion by the Romans. Again, there existed a long tradition of criticism, or outright resistance to the temple and its sacrificial system, by the canonical prophets. Jesus was accused of having put curses on the temple, or of threatening to destroy it (Mark 14.58; 15.29; Matthew 26.61; John 2.19). His dramatic attack, clearing and controlling the temple court, and echoing the words of Jeremiah that it had become a 'den of robbers' (Jeremiah 7.11; Mark 11.17), again places him firmly in the prophetic anti-temple tradition, and constitutes a clear act of political protest and resistance against the dominant powers. Jesus' action in the temple must be seen not merely as a defence of its religious sanctity, or protest against petty cheating on the part of moneychangers, but against a whole international system of economic exploitation, centred in the temple, which played a major role in the impoverishment of the peasants (Horsley and Silberman, 1997: 73–8). The Romans, their Jewish puppet rulers, and the high-priestly class, needed to be rid of Jesus, who, as leader of a substantial band of followers from Galilee, threatened their authority and wealth.

What followed, of course, was the arrest and tortured death of Jesus by crucifixion. As a resistor to Rome and Rome's collaborators, Spirit-filled Jesus was considered dangerous enough to be publicly crucified as a warning to everyone that opposition to the imperial power and its local agents would be met with savage and brutal reprisals.

Jesus' followers, in the months and years that followed, interpreted his cross as redemptive, and the book of Hebrews ascribed his courage and faithfulness in death to 'the eternal Spirit' (Hebrews 9.14). Paul also associated his resurrection with the Spirit: 'If the Spirit of him who raised Jesus from the dead dwells in you, he who raised Christ from the dead will give life to your mortal bodies also through his Spirit that dwells in you' (Romans 8.11). In the tradition of Daniel, we recall, resurrection was expected as vindication and justice for the victims of oppression. To proclaim that he was raised was precisely to claim that Jesus had been vindicated as a righteous martyr who had died because of his acts of resistance, in faithfulness to God (Daniel 12.2–3).

## Anti-Imperial Church

But did the community of Jesus' followers continue to be one of resistance, in the power of the Spirit? Or did it become merely a new religion of personal salvation? Recent Pauline scholarship helps us to see that the congregations associated with Paul, at least, were indeed communities of resistance to the imperial order. Jesus, the crucified leader and prophet, having been raised up and vindicated by God, was now honoured with all the highest titles of the Jewish faith tradition – Messiah, Servant, Son of Man, Son of God, Good Shepherd, Emmanuel, Wisdom of God, Word of God, and so on, but also, remarkably, the august titles normally assigned to Caesar in the Graeco-Roman world: *kurios*, Lord or Sovereign, one to be unconditionally obeyed; *soter*, Saviour, who brings justice and peace to the world. Since Caesar was *kurios* and *soter*, the early Church had turned the imperial titles of the emperor on their head and, with delicious irony, had assigned them to a crucified man! This was powerful counter-propaganda, which in itself had potential to radically undermine the empire. According to Paul, to confess that Jesus, rather than Caesar, was *kurios*, was itself a charism of the Holy Spirit (1 Corinthians 12.3).

Horsley points out that Paul used the religious/ideological rhetoric of the empire to powerful effect. 'After Octavian's great victory at Actium . . . "peace and security" [had been] imposed on the empire by its saviour and the "good news" [*evangelion*] spread far and wide . . .' (Horsley, 2000: 76). Numerous temples, shrines and statues of the Emperor, rituals extolling him as a god and Son of God, were part of a vast ideological system which held the empire together, often winning over the admiration even of vanquished peoples. But now, for the Christians, the true *evangelion* or good news was no longer that of the military victories of a conqueror, but the resurrection victory of a lowly peasant leader of a resistance movement. The rhetoric of the emperor cult was now subverted by allegiance to this new, rival 'emperor'. According to Luke, in Acts, the Christians were accused of 'turning the world upside down, . . . saying there is another king named Jesus' (Acts 17.6–7). In a global world order based upon the drudgery of slaves, in which Jesus had been executed like a slave, Paul now spoke of Jesus as one who 'was in the form of God' who had willingly 'emptied himself, taking the form of a slave' and had 'humbled himself to the point of death, even death on a cross' (Philippians 2.6–8). His followers should now cease to be 'slaves of sin' and, following Jesus, willingly become 'slaves of righteousness' (Romans 6.18)

The Pauline communities co-opted imperial rhetoric, then, and challenged the steeply hierarchical class societies of the empire, which sharply divided a tiny elite of great wealth and power from a great mass of very poor folk, both slave and free (Horsley, 1998: 26). A highly status-conscious, individualist system of patronage and rank contrasted sharply with Paul's vision of the Church as the 'body of Christ', in which every member's gift of the Spirit is important and indispensable, and where, indeed, 'those members of the body that we think less honourable we clothe with greater honour, and our less respectable members are treated with greater respect . . .' (1 Corinthians 12.23). The very existence of such a community of equals, including even slaves, constituted an affront to a system built upon slave labour, patronage and the cult of the emperor. A community that recognized another *kurios* and *soter*, and redefined 'good news', as well as slavery, has to be seen as a prophetic community of resistance to the imperial rule of Rome (Wright, 2000).

## Charisms of the Spirit in the Pauline Church

In view of these considerations we may ask why resistance to domination has not often been identified in Christian tradition as a charism of the Spirit. It is obvious, I suppose, that historically the churches have too often been identified precisely with these same dominant powers. Already in the New Testament documents we see signs of compromise with the empire, in the Christians' need to minimize conflict with Rome by whitewashing Pontius Pilate, and tending to blame the Jews rather than the Romans for Jesus' death (Crossan, 1995). In our time numerically declining minority churches in secularizing contexts often steer away from clear social and political stances in order to avoid losing the financial contributions of prosperous people. Perhaps a certain ambiguity in the scriptures themselves, as well as institutional self-interest, have disinclined the churches to discern the Spirit's work in social and political resistance.

The Pauline lists of the Spirit's charisms in the New Testament offer us a glimpse of a church that was blessed with both extraordinary and ordinary charisms of the Spirit. In 1 Corinthians 12 we hear of the gifts of the Spirit to the Church: wisdom, knowledge, the gift of faith, of healing, the working of miracles, prophecy, the discernment of gifts, tongues, and the interpretation of tongues. Later in the same chapter we hear of apostles, prophets and teachers. We have a similar but more limited list in Romans 12, where we hear of the *charismata*, first of prophecy and of service; also of the teacher, the exhorter, the giver and the leader. It would be anachronistic to expect to find mention here of 'social activist' or 'political protester'. The Roman Empire of the first century was hardly the time or place for petitions, letter-writing campaigns to government leaders, non-violent demonstrations, or the organization of political parties. Yet Paul does seem to be including natural human gifts of creation, which are also directed and empowered by the Spirit. Those who lead and organize are also seen to be 'pneumatic' in the service of God's Reign.

We may find in the term 'prophecy' something akin to the ministry of those who today give voice to the voiceless, struggle for peace, and protest on behalf of the natural environment. Presumably these terms were used to name persons and ministries in continuity with those of the canonical prophets. Romans 12 places 'prophecy' first among the gifts, and in 1 Corinthians and Ephesians (4.11) prophets are twice mentioned second only to apostles, suggesting their great prominence in those churches. It is difficult to know what Christian prophecy looked like in the Church of Paul's time (Montague, 1976: 323). These prophets are sometimes said to receive direct guidance from the Holy Spirit (Acts 13.1–4), suggesting that prophecy may often have been in some sense ecstatic in character, involving inspired speech, and yet it was certainly communicable speech. Paul places *agape* love above all other gifts, urging the Corinthians to pursue love and the spiritual gifts, and especially 'that you may prophesy' (1 Corinthians 14.1).

In our contexts, then, the leaders and organizers of our social action committees who feel outrage about injustice, who tirelessly strive for justice and equality, should be regarded as gifted with the love, inspiration and energies of the Holy Spirit.

## Convergence?

When we consider the idolatrous imperialisms of the ancient world, of Egypt, Babylon and especially Rome's aspirations for a global world order under its own economic and military hegemony, the parallels with the rule of capital under the auspices of today's superpower are striking.[8] The anonymous, but compulsory neoliberal regime of uncontrolled markets, legitimized by quasi-religious concepts, and enforced when necessary by overwhelming military violence,[9] looks more and more like a new Rome, calling forth new resistors in the spirit of the prophets, of Jesus and of Paul. Since the end of the Cold War, some have seen in capitalist globalization the end of hope for a world of solidarity and justice. Yet finding our identity in the Spirit-filled Jesus, taking him as our critical criterion, we find assurance that no empire will have the last word, since the resisting Jesus is also the risen Christ of the Spirit.[10]

There is every reason, then, for liberationists and Pentecostalists to listen to one another, to grow, and to work together as agents of the Spirit for God's Reign in the world. The liberationists' tendency (with some significant exceptions[11]) to neglect Spirit-talk suggests that they need to be more open to the ecstatic, and to spiritual empowerment from beyond themselves. The underdevelopment of liberationist pneumatology may tempt Pentecostalists and other traditional Christians to dismiss the liberationist socio-political thrust as merely ideological and lacking in biblical foundation and the guidance of the Spirit. It may suggest that liberationists are merely moralists who struggle in their own power against mighty forces. On the other hand, Pentecostal theologians themselves have recently called for more active political discipleship on the part of Pentecostals. The American Hispanic Pentecostal Eldin Villafañe, for example, calls for a more holistic theology of salvation and a spirituality that brings together piety, contemplation, and action for social transformation (Villafañe, 1994: 6; 1993: 165). He affirms that the Holy Spirit has a 'political agenda' in creation to bring about the Reign of God, and calls for a Pentecostal social ethic and a 'pneumatic political discipleship' (Villafañe, 1996: 162).

We need, then, a broad inclusive pneumatology, including openness to the ecstatic, together with acknowledgement of the Spirit's presence in the natural created order. Converging liberationist and Pentecostalist pneumatologies today must include a recognition and celebration of resistance to dominant powers as a charism of the Holy Spirit. Such a charism entails gifts of outrage, courage, compassion, persistence and indeed intelligent strategy, welling up within us, in the service of God's Reign.

## Notes

1 See, for example, Villafañe, 2000, 1993. See Harvey Cox's story of Benedita da Silva, a Brazilian black Pentecostal politician (Cox, 1995: 163–8).

2 We see an example of this in Karen Baker-Fletcher, 'The strength of my life', in Townes, 1997.

3 Donaldson and Kwok, 2002; 'A Brazilian example: "Listening to what the Spirit is saying to the churches": Popular Interpretation of the Bible in Brazil', in Sugirtharajah, 1995.

4 See examples of queer theology, both gay and lesbian, in Cleaver, 1995; Stone, 2001.

5 The World Social Forum met at Mumbai, India, in 2004. For its statement of purpose, quoted here, see 'World Social Forum' on the internet: www.forumsocialmundial.org.br/main.asp?id_menu=4&cd_language=2, accessed 10 September 2004.

6 See Naim S. Ateek, 'A Palestinian perspective: biblical perspectives on the Land'; also Robert Allan Warrior, 'A Native American perspective: Canaanites, cowboys and Indians', in Sugirtharajah, 1995.

7 See discussion of this in Welker, 1994.

8 Consider the rule of such 'client' figures as Sukarno of Indonesia, Saddam Hussein of Iraq; note American operations over the years in Guatemala, Chile, Philippines, Iran, Sudan, Iraq, and so on. See analysis in Mitchell and Schoeffel, 2002; Chomsky, 2002.

9 See helpful discussions of this in Freitas, 2001; Schreiter, 2001.

10 See discussion in Stålsett, 2003.

11 A significant exception is the volume of José Comblin (Comblin, 1989).

# 12. Revisioning Pneumatology in Transcultural Spaces

### SIGURD BERGMANN

## 'The Spirit Dwells Among Us'

In his Homily on the Holy Spirit, which was probably prepared for the Ecumenical Council in Constantinople, in 381, Gregory of Nazianz summarizes the challenge to theology: 'Now the Spirit himself dwells among us, and supplies . . . a clearer demonstration of Himself.'[1] The same challenge is still valid today.

The Spirit has taken his/her dwelling among us ($\epsilon\mu\pi o\lambda\iota\tau\epsilon\nu\epsilon\tau\alpha\iota$). The creation now exists in the time of the Spirit. The Spirit reveals him/herself and acts. S/he creates liberating life. The text of the Creed called her 'the Giver of Life', and the one who gives the 'life of the coming world'. Gregory claims that this now happens 'clearer' and that humans now are able to rationally understand and to bodily experience and interpret the work of the Spirit.

With regard to the fact that Gregory's theology has been so influential on the nature of the whole early Church that the Spirit has been accepted as the third divine person in the Trinity in the image of God in East and West; and with regard to the consensus of the Council that the Spirit is 'Lord', which in itself is a solution to the conflict about the belief that the Spirit and the Son are of the same essence ($\acute{o}\mu oo\upsilon\sigma\iota o\nu$) (Kelly, 1977[1958]: 258ff.); it is incredible how many times in the history of Christianity pneumatology has been reduced and marginalized. The task of interpreting life in the light of the belief in the Holy Spirit has consequently been relegated to the shadows. Therefore it seems to be an ongoing task to keep in mind the central significance which pneumatology has had for the cultural and theological development of Christianity and to recover again its voluminous linguistic and metaphoric richness for the interpretation of our experiences with 'the God of the Here and Now'.

I will in this contribution seek for answers to one single question: why, in what context, and how to revision Christian pneumatology today. First, I ask why we should revision pneumatology today. Second, I will sketch two main characteristics of the ongoing globalization process with great relevance for the interpretation of God. The third, final step investigates how such an alternative development could take place. With the help of the notion of 'atmosphere' I offer a draft for an 'aesth/ethical' pneumatology in transcultural spaces.

## Fire from Heaven, Bushfires on Earth – Why Revision Pneumatology?

A well-known thesis claims that the intensification of pneumatology in the history of Christianity takes place in different kinds of crises. The German patristic scholar Wolfgang Hauschild has proposed to interpret the development of pneumatological doctrine in connection with crisis phenomena, which it 'signals, interprets and tries to overcome productively' (Hauschild, 1984: 196).

Without doubt, the rise and fall of pneumatology is embedded in cultural and historical processes, but it seems unconvincing to relate it only to what one believes to be a critical state. First, the understanding and agreement about what characterizes a critical state could vary highly depending on different actors in a church community of interpretation. Second, one can ask why pneumatology in certain critical times has *not* developed its constructive potential, for example in the Reformation, in the German church struggle or in liberation theology.[2]

It would seem more fruitful to weaken the thesis a bit and suppose that pneumatology intensifies in contexts where the believers feel that a spatial limiting, a cultural unfreedom and a threat to personal religious integrity threatens to reduce the 'Fire from heaven'. Obviously God-talk in expressions of pneumatology is able to widen the metaphorics beyond the human and so can create wideness and freedom in the open spaces of theological imagination. It does not seem impossible to suppose a connection between the experience of a violently reduced life space and the experience of being able to break out of this with the help of pneumatology and to transform the places of captivity into open plains of freedom. The challenge to revise and renew pneumatology emerges therefore as an answer to situations in local and global states at the same time as it emerges as an ever newly actualized demand from the inner systematics of Christian theology.

Alluding to the Cappadocian doctrine of wisdom: without a reflection on God in the Spirit dwelling on earth one cannot reflect on the incarnation of God in the Son, our brother. Without a reflection on the life-giving Spirit one cannot interpret the cosmic and local christologies of the New Testament. Without an imagination of the invisible but experiential acting of God beyond human metaphorics one cannot make it evident that it is the Christ of the gospel who has risen today. Pneumatology is the necessary condition of christology.[3]

The second systematic reason is soteriological. It represents a continuation of the former reason for pneumatology as the condition of christology, which leads us to the thesis that soteriology after the return of the earthly and historical Son to the Father necessarily needs to be developed as pneumatology. The following question is at the centre of this task: How does the Spirit give life among us and to all that moves, lives and exists? How is the Spirit acting in, with and for all who are longing for liberation in a creation which 'groans and suffers together until now' (Romans 8.22) in its struggle to give birth to new life?

A third reason can be developed from the doctrine of creation. It departs from several strong traditions in the Jewish religion, which are reflected in the Old Testament's constituting a tight relation between spirit and life.[4] Not only incarnation theology and soteriology but also the belief in God as the Lord of the earth and the Creator of everything between earth and heaven makes it necessary to express the dynamic and creative experiences with this God and his/her *logoi*, *vestigia* and transfigurations in the shape of a reflection on the Spirit who gives life, preserves life and fulfils the whole creation.

A fourth reason should be mentioned. A Christian reflection on the future in accordance with classical eschatology needs, as well as the doctrine of salvation, to be developed as a reflection on the Spirit who, according to the Nicene Creed of Constantinople (NC), creates the life of the world to come: ζωην του μελλοντος αιωνος. In continuity with the ecumenical council one should also today reflect on the Spirit as the agent of the design of the future from where God comes to meet us. Pneumatology should develop how this adventic experience is to be expressed, that life is a gift to us, which comes both from the past behind us and from the future in front of us. The Spirit who moves through the borders of time and space is at the focus of eschatological theology. Where is the Spirit's life of the coming world emerging?

With regard to the external context I hypothetically depart from the claim that globalization and its predecessors modernization and secularization together with the present de-secularization and re-sacralization sharpens and deepens the challenge even more. The emergence of Pentecostalism and its spread represents therefore not only a phenomenon of interest for sociologists but also something highly significant for pastoral and academic theology.

What is it in globalization that works as a catalyst for a revisioning and renewal of pneumatology? In a shallow perspective one could understand globalization itself as a materialized and applied doctrine of the Spirit, where the economically tamed power blows over the world as it likes. Globalization, understood as an expansion, despatialization and disembeddedness, could simply be interpreted as a secularized version of the codes of early Christian pneumatology: 'The wind blows wherever it pleases. You hear its sound, but you cannot tell where it comes from or where it is going. So it is with everyone born of the Spirit' (John 3.8). The process of globalization gives life (even if only for a few), it transforms (makes some rich and others poor), sets free and blows cosmically, even if it blows totally without any goal with the exception of the accumulation of finance capital representing the utilitarian highest and intrinsic value of life.

Could one even regard the Christian faith in the Spirit and his/her invisible power to transform the whole world and all people as a historical and ideological key element for the man-made economics and cultural globalization and its autonomous processes, which are started by man but cannot any longer be tamed or managed by him? Did the Empire of mammonism maybe derive its codes for unlimited and transforming power from spiritual belief, which was neglected by the established religions but which has survived in the substreams of European history?

I will no longer follow this speculative trace. All too many sources in the history of ideas and society tell us that there was no direct transfer taking place from Christian pneumatology's fall and economic development, even if deeper underlying cultural codes of thinking and acting could steer us more than we perceive. The 'power of history', as Georg Picht has called it, often reveals itself especially in the unsolved problems of society. If there were any truth in the thought that pneumatology represents a necessary but neglected task in the internal dynamic of our history of civilization it would be obvious why other social powers regard it as their mission to take care of the need and to stage the power of thinking and acting, which sets the whole world on spiritual fire. Pentecostalism has never regarded its own mission as limited to the local but always understood it as global.[5]

Joining the sharp controversies between the Roman Empire and the believers' reign in the book of Revelation one could also today polarize: it is not 'fire from heaven' but the fire from the dark inside of humanity that runs the development. 'Herrenlose Gewalten' (the powers without masters) Karl Barth called the powers which were ruling over man and which he identified in technology, science and the idolatries of politics. Georg Simmel was already analysing the sociology of money more than a hundred years ago, and he came to a similar conclusion that the money-managed exchange actions radically change the sociocultural relations of human beings and their self-understandings (on Barth, see Plonz, 1995; Simmel, 1977[1900]). Could a renewed reflection on God's invisible but embodied liberative acting in the world contribute to the creation of a cultural countervailing power, which would be able to balance the untamed and culturally goalless economic life destroying processes of globalization? Could the 'fire from heaven' transform the destructive flames of economic globalization? Could the vision of the authors of *Empire*, where 'the Multitude' constructs the countervailing power to idolatry, converge with a biblical apocalyptic like Revelation's vision of the multitude praising the reign of God?

> Then I heard what sounded like a great multitude, like the roar of rushing waters and like loud peals of thunder, shouting: Hallelujah! For our Lord God Almighty reigns. (Revelation 19.6)

Just as the theologians of the twentieth century regarded secularization as the central challenge to emancipate from institutional and dogmatical straitjackets and to transform theology, today globalization represents the central challenge to theology as pneumatology, especially in a situation when secularization is turned into de-secularization and re-sacralization where a new courage shapes creative religious life-interpretations, religious rituals and ethical systems of acting, which are nurtured neither from science nor from established religious traditions but sooner provoke them. The internal systematics of Christianity, the economic accumulation of idolatry in praxis and theory in globalization, the cultural dynamics of globalization and the at present increasing re-sacralization create together an unavoidable challenge to reconstruct the best from the early Church's and later times' spiritualities and pneumatologies at the same time as they challenge to seek new creative inventions of experiential and experimental expressions of the life-giving Holy Spirit.

Ulrich Beck's very significant evidence for the fact that modernization and its inheritor globalization represent a catalyst for reflexivization should also be regarded as highly valid for religion and theology (Beck, 1993: ch. 3). Globalization processes create the need for a critical self-reflection of the identity of the believers and their community. Globalization challenges us to reconstruct and creatively reinvent in rational forms how and where the Spirit dwells among us here and now and how s/he demonstrates this more and more clearly in an Empire of globalization still increasing its power.

## Translocal and Transcultural Passages

What is it, on closer review, that offers central points of connection for a pneumatologic revisioning? In the following I will choose two phenomena, which have been characterized as central and significant in the discourse about globalization, namely the dynamics of de- and respatialization and the transformation of cultural encounters in the understanding of 'culture'.

### The Dynamics of De- and Respatialization

The problem of de- and respatialization represents a central field of problems in the discourse about globalization. The process of globalization and its capacity to change and dissolve local, geographical and physical interconnectednesses has been summarized in notions like 'disembeddedness' (Giddens), 'the colonialization of the life-worlds through the system' (Habermas), and 'de-spatialization' (Appadurai).

Arjun Appadurai's reflections on the production of locality offer a significant contribution to the understanding of the new spaces of globalization. Appadurai uses the notion of neighbourhood in order to describe the context in which humans produce 'locality'. Locality represents for him 'a structure of feeling' and 'a property of social life'. It is produced in a neighbourhood, which is 'a multiplex interpretive site' (Appadurai, 2001[1995]: 105). Man/woman is located in a social space, which is meaningfully structured. Such spaces are produced in neighbourhoods.

Appadurai develops further the notion of 'ethnoscape' in order to describe the de-territorialization, generalization and contextualization of neighbourhood. The local community becomes in this way a general and pluralistic task on a larger scale. Ethnoscapes are not necessarily physical spaces but they represent a kind of active land-scape of acting where one construes locality in close alliances and communities.

This perspective also models in an excellent way the processes of mobilization among the indigenous people both in general and in par-ticular in Northern Scandinavian Sápmi, which also include persons far away from the traditional land. The UN forum for indigenous people tries with varying degrees of success to visualize this process in the global discourse, where the expression of religion and arts plays an increasingly significant role. The question of how religious traditions, processes and identifications contribute to the construction of locality represents a neglected field, which could create many exciting per-spectives. Hypothetically I assume that the reconstruction of pre-Christian religious traditions as they appear in the aboriginal arts in many world regions today contributes to the production of locality in Appadurai's sense. Religious imaginations, practices and rituals create in this context a significant and strong cultural power.

It is of course true that globalization speeds up the dissolution of relationships that individuals and groups have to specific places and spaces, but one cannot ignore the fact that the contemporary de-spatialization also triggers countering forces in the form of relocaliz-ing movements which take many different forms. Without doubt the experience of humanity's loss of a spatial connection with the life world and the longing for a relocation triggered by the global decon-textualization dynamics are among the most powerful driving forces in ecological spirituality. The environmental movement's vision of an alternative society and, most importantly, of an alternative earth space, which is no longer ruled by large-scale forces which in the service of money accumulation destroy relationships between organ-isms and their surroundings, stands out as a critique of civilization of unexpectedly large proportions.

With regard to religion Peter Beyer has argued that this has devel-oped in a kind of anti-systemic production, and with regard to the phenomenon of despatialization one must ask how religious processes even imply a critique of and an alternative to despatialization. Could religion, in a similar way to art, contribute to a radical organization of respatialization on both global and local scales? If yes, what would that mean for the revisioning of pneumatology?

## Transculturation

A second characteristic of globalization is found in the change of cultural encounters, a fact which makes it necessary to create a new theory of culture. The late modern[6] world system of economic globalization, particularization and cultural exchanges challenges our conventional concepts of culture and religion. The inner differentiation of culture, its external networking and the hybridization of individual and collective identities makes it necessary to look for new concepts of 'culture' and religious correlations of tradition and situation. Religious traditions are regarded as cultural elements in a dialectics of both renewal and continuity.

The German philosopher Wolfgang Welsch has presented a concept of culture which is contrasted to conventional and at present influential concepts (Welsch, 2001). Welsch promotes an understanding of 'transculturality', which is modelled to replace the traditional concept of culture as a single entity and the concept of multiculturality. The old concept of *single cultures* is characterized by social homogenization. Culture is here understood as that which gives meaning to the whole of life for a limited population. Culture is meant to be the culture of one people, which could be clearly differentiated from other cultures. Modern differentiated societies cannot be understood by this concept. They are not any longer characterized by uniformity. Gender distinctions, generation distinctions, different working contexts are some of the aspects that make life meaningful in a lot of different ways for people in the same area and population. The concept of a single culture does not highlight the aspect of intermingling and cultural exchange. Cultural racism is the most consequent application of this concept. It has to be regarded more as a political ideology for the sake of one group's power over others than as a scientific theory for cultural studies. Cultures and societies are always, already in the Stone Age, characterized by both identity and communication and exchange, by both continuity and change.

The classical concept of culture is not only analytically wrong but it is also politically dangerous. Unfortunately it is still used in many contexts as a tool for power construction. Samuel Huntington's famous and influential but nevertheless controversial and untrue claim of a 'clash of civilizations' is founded on the idea of clearly identifiable civilizations. The idea of single cultures as a conceptual tool of contemporary world politics is obviously not in accordance with the processes of global migration, cultural hybridization and economic unlimited flows, which characterize globalization in late modernity. With regard to religion, Huntington's thesis has no empirical evidence at all, and it has been faulted with reference to the same kind of political processes going on in fundamentalist approaches in different religious and cultural traditions as Hinduism, Islam and Christianity as well as in different political ideologies.[7]

Two other concepts are often used in debates. The concept of *interculturality* focuses on the conflict between cultures. Modern pluralism brings cultures in communication which each other and the term of interculturality is modelled to understand what is happening in the encounter between different cultures. Some argue for a strict separation of them, each into a kind of ethnic ghetto, while others argue for tolerance and humanistic modes of respecting each other and living together. Also this concept is highly problematic because of its dependency on the classical concept of single cultures. Cultures are not clearly delimited islands or spheres, which could be separated from each other. A solution of intercultural problems cannot be gained from the perspective of cultures as islands.

Another concept is centred on the term *multiculturality*. This vision of one society that is built up by several different cultures is perhaps the only concept that is applied in the political ideologies of the European nation states today. But this concept also presupposes the idea of a single pure culture as an isolated island with clear characteristics. Even if the values and intentions of promoting this concept are rooted in humanistic traditions for the best of all it necessarily leads to ghettoization and cultural fundamentalism.

All these three concepts of culture are analytically incorrect and normatively deceptive. Cultures do not any longer have the forms of homogeneity and distinct identities.[8] Present cultures are passing through the classical cultural boundaries. They are characterized by mixtures, fusions, synergies and exchange processes.[9] That is why we need a concept of transculturality.

Cultures today are much more externally connected than the single culture concept shows. The modern society is complex and highly differentiated, also in the economic silent zones of the world. Migration processes do not any longer make you belong to a single territory. Mobility makes people more or less global or regional. Cultures are in late modernity characterized by hybridization.[10]

With regard to religion we need to observe the scaling between macro- and microlevels as a highly significant phenomenon for a revisioned pneumatology. Experiences with the Holy Sprit cannot be reduced to subjective individual spheres but might also be understood as experiences with regional and global processes, a fact strongly emphasized by Harvey Cox in his focus on spirituality, Pentecostalism and the urban context: How is the Spirit at work in different spatial and cultural levels in the city?

Another point is that our understanding of culture also influences our cultural life and action. If we remain in the old concept of single cultures we will not be able to meet the needs of a modern social situation with its implicit problems. Ideological rhetoric of multiculturalism does not solve any problems if individuals no longer understand themselves as belonging to one pure and clear tribe. Multiculturalism also furthers the violent social organization of tribes fighting each other even if this is not its intention. Pentecostalism also seems to me to radically challenge the single- and multi-culture narratives.

An understanding of transculturality does not encourage the capacity to become different and exclusive in a hierarchical power system, but the ability to relate to each other, to communicate and to exchange ideas and action patterns and to undergo transition.

Religious traditions have in the same way as cultural traditions always been constructed in a communicative process of both exchange and identity preservation. Tradition has always emerged and been developed in a dialectic of preservation and change. Continuity needs change and transformation needs some stability. The challenge for religious studies in this perspective is quite similar to that in cultural studies – even if cultural studies are not able to interpret the cultural 'surplus' of 'religion' – and it can be formulated in a central question. How are the patterns of encounters and exchanges between the multiplicity of worldview and ethos developed in late modernity?[11] How could a concept of transculturality be related to a concept of transreligiosity? Could the rise of Pentecostalism be interpreted as a reshaping of religion in a reciprocal interaction with transculturality?

## The Spirit-in-between – Atmospheres of Inhabitation

My last section will propose two central notions for a revisioned pneumatology in transcultural spaces and places. The first notion is developed directly in continuity with biblical and Eastern patristic models for interpreting what the 'fire from heaven' does on earth. The second is developed from phenomenology and ecological aesthetics.

My proposal is to construct a revised pneumatology around the themes of the Spirit's inhabitation and atmospheres.

The notion of 'inhabitation' from the traditions offers a potential to develop pneumatology in a new key. The experience of God's indwelling among us humans represents a foundational characteristic of Jewish and Christian faith. The spatial question moves into focus: *Where* does God dwell here and now?

In the encounter with Moses on Mount Sinai God expressed clearly his/her wish to be with his/her people: 'Let them make for me a sanctuary, that I may live among them' (Exodus 25.8). After the fulfilment of the artistic 'Tent of Meeting' (Exodus 27.21) God could meet his/her people in it. The story took its beginning at the place where the people of Israel in the community of the covenant with a Liberator, who was present at that place, sought their way out of captivity in order to live as a 'contrasting society' (cf. Duchrow and Hinkelammert, 2004: 22ff.) to the imperial reigns of the world.

When God later became flesh the evangelists interpreted God in the light of this handed-over experience. St John summarized the mystery of incarnation: 'Now the Word became flesh and took up residence among us' (John 1.14). Gregory of Nazianz developed in the fourth century his – and through the ecumenical council in 381 the whole Church's ecumenical – trinitarian theology of the history of salvation with the help of the idea of the Spirit's ongoing revelation. The *Incarnation* of the Son of God continues after Ascension Day through the *Inhabitation* of the Holy Spirit.

While the Jewish belief in creation images the birthplace of the world with God's Spirit 'moving over the surface of the chaos waters' (Genesis 1.2), the wisdom literature establishes a necessary relation between the breathing of God, *ruach*, and the emergence and preservation of the living: 'When you send your life-giving breath, they are created, and you replenish the surface of the ground' (Psalm 104.30).

The relationship of the Spirit and life and between the Spirit and the earth continues to be a main element in the Jewish-Christian religion and it is summarized in the ecumenical creed about the Spirit as the Life-Giver and the Life of the world to come.[12] Inhabitation does not mean that the world *is* God. God dwells in the world but s/he is not the world, which Sallie McFague and to some extent also Jürgen Moltmann have claimed with emphasis (McFague, 2001; Moltmann, 2002). Quite the opposite, God continues to be a God who dwells in the darkness. Inhabitation is an ongoing dynamic process where God goes into and beyond the world and transfigures it from within. The

Creator remains a sovereign God who fulfils in love what s/he has begun.

Joining the Jewish architect Peter Eisenman one could say that God is 'scaling'. 'Scaling' means a sliding motion between different spatial scales (Bergmann, 2005b: 48). God is changing between all scales of the universe, from the smallest units, atoms, microbes, souls, bodies and society to the largest units, world history, universe, atmosphere and interplanetary space.

Further notion study will help us in a new pneumatology to overcome conventional limits, such as for example the sharp distinction of subject and object in identity philosophy. Joining the German philosopher Gernot Böhme I will depart from the notion of 'atmosphere' in order to reflect on the perceptions and interpretations of the Spirit dwelling and acting among us, moving through the different interspaces and scales of creation. Böhme develops aesthetics as a reflection on human perceptions of the living 'Gefüge', which surrounds her. He develops his ecological aesthetics of nature (Böhme, 1995; 1989) with the help of the notion of atmosphere.

Atmosphere works as a central term in the new aesthetics, which investigates the qualities of the surroundings and human well-being (Böhme, 1995). The atmosphere emerges in the interspace between outer human surrounding and inner bodily–soul–spiritual being. It is not at all diffuse and uncertain, shallow or subjective but it offers a notion which in an exciting way thematizes the interrelatedness of the outer and inner, the bodily and spiritual, the surrounding and the internalized. In co-operation with related terms such as aura, chord and charisma, atmosphere is suitable as a central notion for an aesthetically enlightened theology of the Holy Spirit in space and place.

With regard to the relationship between Spirit and space, nature aesthetics leads us to the question of how the Spirit meets us in the human and in its surroundings. How does the Spirit meet us in the surroundings and in natural spaces between the human and other beings? How is the Holy Spirit at work between us and between nature and culture? This formulation of the problem represents both a classical theological question and a challenge to other scientific disciplines such as architecture.

The notion of 'atmosphere' could help us to focus or view more clearly the modes of the revelation of the Spirit. If we with a very fruitful definition (Lessing, 1985) understand the 'Spirit' as 'the being of the one at or with the other', the spatial dimension of pneumatology becomes a central one: Where and how is the Spirit at work with regard to the other? Where and how does the Spirit give life? Who are 'the others' with which s/he acts? The insight in the 'metaphysics of the prepositions' (H. Doerrie) is in this case of great significance. The question in the driving force of the Christian classical tradition is not whether the Spirit dwells *in* us or not, whether the Spirit liberates only *in* the Church or even *outside*. What is important is to ask how and where the Spirit is at work, who blows wherever s/he wants to and who liberates through the truth (John 14.16f.; 8.32; 2 Corinthians 3.17; cf. Galatians 5.1).

The point of the Christian doctrine of the Spirit is that God's Holy Spirit can work *in*, *with* and *through* all places, spaces and scales of creation. Humans cannot put limits on God's work. The opposite of inner and outer does not represent any border for the Creator. All natural and human borders are always open for the transcending Spirit. We can meet the Life-Giver in the most unexpected places.

The character of an atmosphere is that it does not emerge as a causal consequence of human actions. An atmosphere surrounds something. It shines from a living creature, a thing, a place or an artefact. We can experience atmospheres both intuitively and reflexively. Atmospheres emerge, they can endure and they can disappear in the spaces *between* us and something. Obviously humans cannot create atmospheres, but they can create artefacts, which in themselves are capable of producing and mediating atmospheres.

Atmospheres are characterized through their being both human and physical, both subjective and objective. There is no longer any distinction between subject and object but the encounter of both in a common phenomenon, which is at the focus of reflection. Men and women perceive themselves in the mirror of their natural surrounding and their artistically and technically designed surroundings.

The Spirit enters the stage and leaves it, moves between the places. God's Holy Spirit scales between the personal inner and the cosmic life spaces. 'Synergism' in the Eastern Church's salvational theology means that the Spirit, the human being and the four elements of nature are co-operating for the sake of the whole creation's liberation.

With the help of the experiences and the notion of atmosphere we can focus on the spatial dimension of this active communication of the human and the divine. According to the Ecumenical Creed the Spirit gives life and makes the life of the world to come. The created beings can perceive and experience the atmospheres of the actions of the Spirit, even if not everywhere and at the same time in all places. The Spirit is neither a machine nor a building nor an impersonal energy. It is not a rationalized truth either, which can be bound together into an agglomeration of signs in a book.

We can not dwell in the Spirit, but the Spirit dwells in us, in others and in the spaces-in-between them and us. The Spirit is 'The Go-Between God' (Taylor, 1972). Atmospheres are offering us guides, traces, links, which are connecting us to the Spirit. Atmospheres are the *vestigia Dei* (God's traces on earth). God's Spirit leaves these blueprints behind and lures us to follow them. With the help of these spherical traces in the spaces-between we can navigate in God's horizon; negotiate on the centre and periphery of the globalized world in a new way. We can follow the Spirit into a transfigured creation. Maybe the 'lost ecumenical vision' (Hollenweger, 1999b: 186ff.) of Pentecostalism could be recovered in this way.

## Notes

1 Gregory of Nazianz, *Oratio* 31.26 (cf. Bergmann, 2005a; 1995).

2 Pneumatology seems to be of marginal interst in Latin American liberation theology. Comblin's approach for a liberation theology of the Spirit represents one of the few reflections (Bergmann, 1995: 353; Comblin, 1989). In spite of this, concepts from liberation theology are integrated in an exciting way into contemporary Pentecostalism and base community life in Latin America. (For various insights from the inside see Bergunder, 2003.)

3 Aagård, 1975: 24. On the relation of Christology and pneumatology with regard to resistance, cf. also Harold Wells's contribution to this volume.

4 Cf. Lars Thunberg's essay, 'Ande och liv hos kyrkofäderna' (in Thunberg, 1988: 25–36).

5 Pentecostalism in itself must from the start be understood as a global event, even if it took its beginning in North America (cf. Bergunder, 2003: 203).

6 I prefer the concept of 'late modernity' as it has been developed by Beck and others instead of 'postmodernism', which suggests a state of having-left-modernity-behind. 'Late modernity' makes it possible to investigate the complex relations of continuity and change in different forms and periods of modernity itself. Late modernity in this sense is neither modernity nor postmodernity (cf. Beck, 1988: 15; Klotz, 1994: 159). Beck offers the notion of 'the second modernity'. The end of modernity did not take place but turned the former into a revised modernity: the second modernity.

7 Meyer (1997: 45–60) criticizes, among many others, Huntington's postulate with the empirical evidence of an 'identity-mania' and fundamentalism in *all* world religions as well as in both right- and left-wing political ideologies.

8 Cultural studies offer many kinds of evidence for this crucial insight. Appudarai (2001[1995]: 109) locates his studies of the global production of locality in a world 'that has become deterritorialized (Guattari and Deleuze, 1987), diasporic, and transnational'. For Beyer (1994: introduction), the phenomenon of heterogenization represents the main challenge for a sociological analysis of the

religious practices where people are using the many particular possibilities to resist the powerful forces of homogenization. Berger (Berger, Berger and Kellner, 1973) was among the first in the 1970s who recognized the crucial challenge to understand the emergence of what nowadays often is described as 'multiple identities', while Hannerz (1996) uses the notions of 'cosmopolitanism' and 'hybridization' in order to characterize late modernity.

9 The processes of hybridization, localization and 'glo-c-alization' are obvious in the so-called 'World Arts', and they are developed in an exciting key in the visual arts of the indigenous and aboriginal people in different regions of the planet. Cf. my ongoing research project 'World arts and religion in the margin', including the contemporary arts of Sápmi, Australia and Peru (cf. Bergmann, 1998a, 1998b, 2003b, 1999).

10 Cf. Hannerz, 1996: 111.

11 If we use a pragmatic definition of 'religion' as the interrelatedness of worldview and ethos, religion is located *between* ideas and actions. Religion should not be understood only as an ideological system, as a net of ideas and beliefs in metaphysical realities. It should neither be reduced to social action with regard to liturgy, community and institutions. Religion could – in harmony with Clifford Geertz's ethnology – be regarded as something constituted by both ideas and actions. It consists of worldviews and sociocultural communicative actions with regard to others and to nature. (Cf. Geertz's essay 'Religion as a cultural system', in Bergmann, 2003a; Geertz, 1973; Bergmann, 2005c).

12 On the significance of the concept of 'Life' for a Christian pneumatology and ethics in an Asian globalized context cf. Wai Man Yuen's contribution in this book and Bock, 2004.

# 13. Offering On-Time Deliverance:
## The Pathos of Neo-Pentecostalism and the Spirits of Globalization

### STURLA J. STÅLSETT

## 'Agora!'

'Right now!'

We are shouting, all of us, on command. We are in the Cathedral of Faith, in Porto Alegre, Brazil, a cold Friday evening in May 2004. This is one of the huge temples of the Igreja Universal Reino de Deus (IURD), the most successful Neo-Pentecostal church in Brazil (cf. the contributions by Furre and Esperandio above).[1] We are not that many gathered this evening, only a few hundred in a church built for at least six thousand. The low turnout could be due to the low temperature. Besides, this is after all the sixth meeting here today.

But inside, the temperature is soon rising. The *bispo* on the huge stage has just vividly read – or rather re-enacted – the Gospel from Matthew 8:

> When he came down from the mountainside, large crowds followed him. A man with leprosy came and knelt before him and said, 'Lord, if you are willing, you can make me clean.' Jesus reached out his hand and touched the man. 'I am willing,' he said. 'Be clean!' Immediately he was cured of his leprosy. Then Jesus said to him, 'See that you don't tell anyone. But go, show yourself to the priest and offer the gift Moses commanded, as a testimony to them.' (vv. 1-4, NIV)

'When was the man with leprosy healed?' The *bispo* shouts into the wireless microphone. 'Was it five minutes later?'

We respond, one voice: 'No!'

'Was it the morning after?'

'No!'

'Was it a week later?'

'No!'

'It was immediately! It was at once!! It was right now!'

'*Agora!*'

'Surely, you have come here for a reason,' the *bispo* continues. 'If you are here tonight, it is because you suffer; you have a problem. So come to the podium, right now, and be released in the name of Jesus.'

We all come. And in the following half hour or so, we witness a powerful presentation in words and deeds of what must be something close to the IURD Neo-Pentecostal theology in a nutshell. It moves from corporeal need and desire, expressed in loud prayers in faith that are responded to by acts of exorcism and immediate healing, and ends up in the act of sacrifice (here: offering money).

## Neo-Pentecostal Pathos and Neoliberal Spirit

The aim of my chapter here is to address the main theme of this book, the interrelationship between globalization and Pentecostal and other experiential spiritualities. Taking into account insights from several of the preceding chapters, and reflecting on the version of the Gospel presented in the Cathedral of Faith of the IURD that Friday night in Porto Alegre, I will explore the interconnection between these two mega-trends by focusing on two main characteristics that they seem to have in common: first, an emphasis on immediate satisfaction of desire, and second, a search for 'victory' through sacrifice. In my view, these two points are central in the 'selective affinity' between neoliberalism and Neo-Pentecostalism which may contribute to understanding why and in what ways they seem to mutually reinforce one another.

One hundred years after Max Weber (1976[1904–5]) wrote his trail-blazing essay on 'The Protestant Ethic and the Spirit of Capitalism', I think the contributions in the present volume have shown that his question about the interconnection between religious worldviews and practices and transformations in society is still pertinent. As Harvey Cox writes in his opening chapter, Peter Berger has enthusiastically used Weber's thesis to present the Pentecostal growth as a 'new Protestant internationale [that] will produce results similar to those of the preceding one – to wit, the emergence of a solid bourgeoisie, with virtues conducive to the development of a democratic capitalism' (Martin, 1993: ix). Berger also gave a lecture at the University of Oslo some years ago entitled 'Max Weber is alive and well, living in Guatemala.' One need not share Berger's enthusiasm to agree with him that Weber's approach, in spite of its many critics, may still be useful. Our contemporary theme however requires some modifications of the terms used in Weber's classic title.

First, we define 'Protestant' as 'Pentecostal', and even more precisely as 'Neo-Pentecostal'. I think, in other words, that it is justified and helpful to distinguish between classical or traditional Pentecostalism and Neo-Pentecostalism. Berge Furre gives some good reasons for this when he distinguishes IURD from other Pentecostals in his chapter (pp. 39–51, above). The Neo-Pentecostal churches put their primary emphasis on spiritual warfare, exorcisms, immediate healings and personal prosperity here and now. This has notably replaced traditional Pentecostalism's emphasis on *glossolalia* (speaking in tongues); on strict, pietistic morals; on Jesus' second coming, and on eternal salvation in heaven above.

There are of course no clear-cut differences here. The new is never totally new. For that reason many scholars argue that the distinction Pentecostalism/Neo-Pentecostalism is 'superficial'.[2] Whether one prefers to give priority to continuity or difference, however, significant changes have undoubtedly taken place within Protestantism over the last century. In this process we have seen a shift of emphasis from rationality to experience, from making sense of faith to sensing the faith, from arguments to sentiments and emotions (cf. Esperandio's chapter, pp. 52–64) or, as I suggest, from 'ethic' to 'pathos'.

Capitalism has obviously undergone profound changes during the last hundred years, too. In the focus on the unilateral 'victory' of market capitalism after the end of the Cold War, it is often forgotten what a multifaceted phenomenon capitalism is. There are obviously many different forms and 'cultures of capitalism' that are related to religious traditions and practices in different ways (cf. Graf, 2002). The kind of capitalism most prevalent in the globalized age is strongly marked by neoliberal economic theory and ideology. The interesting 'selective affinity' that we should pay particular attention to is therefore the one between neo-Pentecostalism and *neoliberal* globalization. The most striking common traits of these two are in my view the emphasis on the immediate, the present moment, and the sacrificial logic underpinning their respective ideology/theology and practices.

## Immediate Satisfaction of Desire

### Rule of the Present

In his suggestive essay on globalization as the 'end of geography' from 1997, Paul Virilio claimed that there is a new sense of global time, an 'acceleration of reality itself, in which instantaneity makes the significance of distance disappear' (Virilio, 1997).[3] Everything is here, right now; made present and accessible by way of the omnipresent 24-hour media coverage. This over-emphasis on the present moment, the instantaneous, which the geographer Alex Harvey called 'compression of time' (and space) in the globalized age, has also been presented as the 'terror' or 'tyranny' of the present moment. As Zygmunt Bauman has shown, this 'terror of the present' has at least three dimensions. One is directly related to digital revolution (Bauman, 1998: 14ff.; cf. Stålsett, 2003). This is the on-line reality in which both the past and the future are swallowed into an everlasting, fleeting, mediated presence.

Another aspect has to do with the character of the consumer culture. Production today, says Bauman, is not primarily about satisfying human needs. It is not even first about satisfying human desire. Production today is primarily production of desires, desires that – in an instant – can be satisfied. Or rather, *almost* satisfied. For the consumption does not quench desire completely, but creates a thirst for more. 'Desire does not desire the satisfaction of desire. Desire desires desire,' Bauman quotes Mark C. Taylor and Esa Saarinen. Thus the consumer is always on the move, reaching out for something else, something more.

Third, the 'terror' of the everlasting moment, the rule of *l'instantanéité* in Virilio's word, can be seen in the dramatic transformations in the organization of labour under globalization (Bauman, 1998: 10ff.). The euphemistically called 'flexibilization of work' means short-term contracts, short-term investments and commitments, under-employment and the rise of informal economy. This, in turn, leads to widespread uncertainty and fear among employees, and the exclusion of many more from the access to safe and dignified work. The late Pierre Bourdieu sees this 'absolute reign of flexibility' as a 'structural violence' which to him belongs to the essence of neoliberalism, the hegemonic ideology and driving force in present-day globalization (Bourdieu, 1998; cf. Bourdieu, 1999).

Neoliberal globalization is thus characterized by an intensified focus on the instantaneous: it is 'real time' economy, on-line reality, and permanent live coverage. The demands of the eternal moment are on-time and on-the-spot delivery and the immediate satisfaction of desire. It creates a competitive culture – Bourdieu calls it Darwinian (Bourdieu, 1998) – in which the winner takes it all and the loser has no one to blame but him or herself. In the words of the Brazilian theologian Jung Mo Sung, it is '*uma economia sem coração*', a heartless economy (Mo Sung, 1992). How can Neo-Pentecostalism be seen as a response to these demands of the moment and this widespread feeling of uncertainty and fear that they create?

## Religion of the Present

Not the following day, not next week – '*agora!*' In IURD preaching, '*O reino dos céus é hoje*' – 'The kingdom of heaven is today.'[4] Neo-Pentecostalism is offering on-time deliverance – deliverance from evil, from suffering, and poverty. '*Pare sofrer!*' ('stop suffering') is the principal IURD slogan.

In this emphasis on immediate results, Neo-Pentecostalism also shifts focus away from both the past and the future. In his book on religious tradition, transmission and emotions in contemporary Latin American Protestantism, Paulo Barrera points to what he sees as a fundamental difference between Protestantism and Pentecostalism: the capacity of Pentecostalism to dispense with its own tradition in the process of constructing its legitimacy (Barrera Rivera, 2001: 17).[5] Traditional Protestantism always founded its legitimacy – the truth of its preaching and the validity of its sacraments and liturgies – on correspondence with the historical-biblical sources. This rootedness in history and in the scriptures required a well-developed system of education of the church members, which, in turn, required long-term strategies, loyalty to the confessional tradition and community, discipline and rationality. Pentecostalism today, by contrast, does not need this rootedness in history and rationality. Religious transmission today is gradually becoming less articulated around the reproduction of the founding tradition, turning more into a matter of transmission of emotions, says Barrera. There is a move from ratio and ethos to pathos. In this way, Pentecostal religions are 'religions of the present' (Barrera Rivera, 2001: 52). There is a compression of time and space: The founding event has come near through the experience of the presence of the Holy Spirit in the Church. It can and should always be repeated, and replaced, by new experiences in the cult (Barrera Rivera, 2001: 227).

It is surprising – taking into account classical Pentecostalism's emphasis on the Second Coming – to observe that this also leads to a certain disinterest in the future (Barrera Rivera, 2001: 232). Salvation, satisfaction, victory is within reach, here and now. Faith is expected to give concrete results, it should 'produce'.

In his doctoral thesis on IURD theology and in particular its ecclesiology, the Swedish theologian Anders Ruuth concludes that IURD is a church aimed at satisfying needs, needs that have to be dealt with right away. This church is characterized by an *imediatismo* according to Ruuth (1995: 257). While IURD certainly is oriented towards satisfying needs, the central object of their *imediatismo* is even more the *desires* of people. In the consumerist society desire is the driving force. In mainstream Christian tradition human desire holds a central although ambivalent place. In the Augustinian and Lutheran strands, desire has been closely associated with sin and rebellion against God. By contrast, IURD Neo-Pentecostalism seems to give desire a more affirmative role. It certainly does not hide it; it does not at all seem to be ashamed of it. Desire is rather re-established as a legitimate and constructive force that should find fulfilment, when it is expressed in faith. The loud prayers in any IURD meeting leave no doubt about this centrality of desire: 'Oh Lord, I do not accept this misery! I want to have success! I want victory, in the name of Jesus!' (see above, Esperandio, pp. 60–2).

Ricardo Bitum sees this as one of the distinguishing marks of Neo-Pentecostalism:

> the new Pentecostal wave called Neo-Pentecostalism approaches this world desiring from it everything that it can offer. Financial prosperity, health, happiness, goods, wealth, in a word, the best of this earth rightfully belongs to the believer. This right is acquired after a brief relationship with God. To know God, for the Neo-Pentecostal, is to be allowed to make use of all that which s/he ever desired, but never could have. (Bitum, 1996: 133)

In this way, the immediate production and satisfaction of desire in neoliberal market ideology finds its religious parallel and response in the '*imediatismo*' and restitution of (consumptionist) desire in Neo-Pentecostal preaching and practice.

## Victory through Sacrifice

### Sacrificial Religion

'*Sai! Sai! Sssssai!*' (Get out!) Back in the Cathedral of Faith, the *bispo* and his pastors and assistants pray to God and command and curse the devils and demons in and around us with voices that could make heavy metal singers envious, and with a speed that could compete with many rappers. And although what we experience now is not fully a rave party, it is not totally different either; this is the 'plunging into chaos', with the purpose of conquering it, that Cox – very rightly I think – observed in his opening chapter (see p. 17).

Then it all calms down. Now the *bispo* gradually enters the second part of his text interpretation. This is the time for sacrifice, for offering our gift to the Lord: 'Then Jesus said to him, "See that you don't tell anyone. But go, show yourself to the priest and offer the gift Moses commanded, as a testimony to them." '

The *bispo* launches a preventive attack on his possible and actual critics. He refers to the many charges against the IURD, for being nothing but a money machine, always after the money of the faithful: 'You have heard all of this, haven't you.' People nodding. 'Are they right? Are you buying religious services from the church?' 'No.' People shaking their heads, smiling. 'What happens is, you see, that these people don't know their Bible; they don't know Jesus. What does Jesus say? "Go to the priest and offer the gift Moses commanded . . .".' And the *bispo* explains how Jesus came to fulfil the good Law of Moses – 'he was God, wasn't he? . . . and the commandments and the Law were from God, weren't they?' – not to subvert it or break it. And then, he moves to direct application: 'So, do I have the right to ask for your offerings to the Church, for the sake of the testimony of the gospel, or do I not?' 'You do.'

Consequently, the *bispo* now invites us up to the altar on the podium to offer money, first those willing to give more than 50 *reais*, thereafter everyone else. Altogether three times in this meeting (as the IURD prefers to call their religious gatherings) we are invited to offer money to the church.

Sacrificial theology is at the heart of Neo-Pentecostalism. Faith is expected to produce results – concrete and immediate results. But this can only happen through sacrifice, which is the individual's demonstration of faith. According to the founder and supreme leader of IURD, *bispo* Edir Macedo, 'the offering is the instrument by which the human being can approach God' (Macedo, 2001: 15). Since Jesus is the perfect offering, all other offerings must be perfect, too, he argues. If it is not perfect, it will not be accepted, and it will not produce the results that they should.

What to offer? Many things, according to Macedo, but primarily money: 'Money is the blood of the Church, I tend to say. Because it carries with it parts of the person's life (time, sweat, intelligence and effort) . . .' (Macedo, 2001: 19ff.). All Christians are permanently obliged to be offering to God spiritual sacrifices (Macedo, 2001: 21). And this will, when it is according to the will of God, and is carried out in faith, produce fruits. Surely:

> It is impossible for the offering person not to have spiritual and financial return when the offering is according to the will of God. I believe that the Christians in their majority live a life on the border of poverty and misery because their offerings have demonstrated the lack of love, fear and respect for God. (Macedo, 2001: 33)

In summing up his study of Edir Macedo's theology, Paulo Ayres Mattos (2002) underlines this centrality of the sacrifice in two major belief affirmations: First,

> Macedo believes that sacrifice, as the highest expression of people's faith in and obedience to God's word implies always a kind of exchange covenant, trade contract, or transaction between partners, in which mutual duties, rights and privileges are rightfully established. (Mattos, 2002: 95)

And second,

> Macedo believes that sacrifice, as the shortest distance between desire and accomplishment, implies always in the experience of conversion the person's deliverance from Satan's dominion, by means of exorcism, breaking the chains of the demonic sickness, and restoring his or her rights to spiritual-emotional well-being and physical-material possessions. (Mattos, 2002: 97)

This centrality of sacrificial theology is not limited to the Brazilian IURD, but can be seen to be a common trait in Neo-Pentecostal spirituality – although in various forms and degrees (particularly regarding the centrality of money). This is where I see a second major affinity with neoliberal globalization. What, then, would be the link between neoliberalism and sacrifices?

### Sacrificial Economy

Neoliberalism is actually not that new. In fact, its birth year, if any, would be 1938 at the Walter Lippmann colloquium in Paris, in which the Austrian economists Ludwig von Mises (1881–1973) and Friedrich A. von Hayek (1899–1992) participated, perhaps the two most influential thinkers and economists (followed by e.g. Milton Friedman and Karl Popper) of the neoliberal 'school' (Dixon, 1998: 6; Ferraro, 1997: 36f.). Although the neoliberal programme has primarily been presented in pamphlets, business strategies and political economical programmes, one of its founding texts is Hayek's classic *The Road to Serfdom* from 1944.

Neoliberalism did not 'come to power', however, until the 1970s. First under General Augusto Pinochet in Chile from 1973, later under the governments of Margaret Thatcher (British Prime Minister, 1979–90) and the late Ronald Reagan (US President 1980–8). Both publicly stated their admiration for Hayek and *The Road to Serfdom*.[6] With these governments the road is prepared for the unprecedented hegemony of neoliberal doctrine in economic policies, through the adaptation of it by the IMF and World Bank and the subsequent worldwide 'naturalization' of these policies of highly contested and contestable economic 'truths'. The neoliberal utopia of the single, self-regulating market was successfully presented as anti-utopian, an-ideological and as the only rational alternative (the so-called 'TINA': 'There Is No Alternative', attributed to Thatcher) at the 'end of history' (Fukuyama). In her *Short History of Neoliberalism*, the well-known economist and globalization critic Susan George writes:

> Starting from a tiny embryo at the University of Chicago with the philosopher-economist Friedrich von Hayek and his students like Milton Friedman at its nucleus, the neo-liberals and their funders have created a huge international network of foundations, institutes, research centers, publications, scholars, writers and public relations hacks to develop, package and push their ideas and doctrine relentlessly. (. . .) They have spent hundreds of millions of dollars, but the result has been worth every penny to them because they have made neo-liberalism seem as if it were the natural and normal condition of humankind. No matter how many disasters of

all kinds the neo-liberal system has visibly created, no matter what financial crises it may engender, no matter how many losers and outcasts it may create, it is still made to seem inevitable, like an act of God, the only possible economic and social order available to us. (George, 1999)

The social exclusion and increased poverty that comes with market liberalism as a result of 'adjustment' policies, economic deregulation, privatization, cut-down on social services, public sector, and so on, are in neoliberal discourse presented as 'necessary' although temporary 'social costs'. But as Cox and others have pointed out, the positive results that were promised to 'trickle down' also to the poor majority have still not come. Instead social polarization and poverty continue to increase worldwide. The results of Thatcher's application of the neoliberal doctrine are revealing: in pre-Thatcher Britain, about one person in ten was classed as living below the poverty line. In the mid-1990s one person in four was officially poor. Ronald Reagan's policies also led to a drastic increase in social exclusion and polarization: in 1977, the top 1 per cent of American families had average incomes 65 times as great as those of the bottom 10 per cent. A decade later, the top 1 per cent was 115 times as well off as the bottom decile (George, 1999).

'Inevitable, like an act of God'. It is noteworthy, in our context, the way in which the economist Susan George resorts to a 'theological' language in order to describe the way neoliberalism works. This corresponds well with the way liberation theologians in Latin America since the 1980s have criticized what they see as the 'sacrificial core' of neoliberalism.[7] These theologians see this globalized economic model as characterized by a logic that is deeply theological or, rather, idolatrous. In their view, neoliberalism should be seen as involving an implicit 'resacralization' in disguise, that is, a resacralization/idolatrization of Money, and of the Market. When neoliberal economic policy more or less explicitly advocates that the social 'costs' resulting from structural 'adjustments', debt payments, and so on are 'necessary' in order to reach economic balance, growth, prosperity, it resembles sacrificial religions' claim that sacrifices to the gods are necessary to obtain deliverance. 'The people is sacrificed for the demands of the market', the theologian Julio Santa Ana writes, commenting on the debt crises in Latin America in the early 1980s (Santa Ana, 1986). This is a sacrificial violence, he claims. The poor sectors in Latin America are made into scapegoats in order to safeguard the well-being of the minorities living in opulence. This sacrificial violence is aimed at 'purifying society', removing all the possible impediments for a full participation in the 'free' market. Since the 'necessity' of these sacrifices is attributed to the supra-human laws of the Market, it takes on a transcendental dimension. It becomes something that both 'fascinates' and 'terrifies', says Santa Ana, thus referring to Rudolf Otto's classic definition of the sacred as *'tremendum et fascinosum'*.

## Justifying Victimization and Supporting the Victims?

Now, we ask again, does the explicit re-sacralization of culture seen in the Neo-Pentecostal revival correspond to this implicit re-sacralization of the Market in political economy?

According to René Girard the role of religion is typically to legitimize and make invisible (by 'rationalizing' or 'naturalizing') the victimization of scapegoats (Girard, 1977; Girard, Oughourlian and Lefort, 1987). Religion can convince people that sacrificing the lives and well-being of human persons to the secular gods of globalization is necessary, and even good. By its sacrificial emphasis (and particularly taking into account the centrality of money in the sacrificial logic demonstrated above), Neo-Pentecostal theology and practice can be seen as reinforcing the neoliberal worldview of market globalization. It can be seen as – willingly or not – providing a religious justification for globalized social exclusion. In all, Neo-Pentecostal churches do not appear to be questioning the sacrificial logic inherent in present-day market fundamentalism, but rather subscribe to it through promoting a similar logic in their religious cult and worldview. Where neoliberalism sacralizes money and preaches the Gospel of the Free, Messianic Market, Neo-Pentecostalism comes close to seeing humans' relationship with God as an economic transaction: 'What you give is what you'll get.'

Yet this is not the whole picture. The interconnection between the two phenomena we are studying is more complex than simply the one justifying the other. Among the hard questions that need to be posed is the following: If Neo-Pentecostalism implicitly or explicitly serves as a religious blessing of violent political and economic processes of marginalization, why does it then continue to grow, and even grow particularly among people themselves excluded by this 'sacrificial' economic system?

The answer may be that Neo-Pentecostalism also offers consolation, support and strategies for not just survival but even upward mobilization in neoliberal market societies. If we do not hold that all those attending regularly to IURD meetings are simply being fooled, and completely unconscious or confused about their own needs and interests, they must experience something in these meetings that makes them come back, week by week, day by day, even bringing their friends and families along. In the worship with its exorcisms (even when never totally getting rid of those demons) and offerings (even when there is no immediate return) they must experience a kind of relief, and sense a measure of empowerment.

From Weber to the recent literature, many skills and positive qualities offered by Protestantism and Pentecostalism in a capitalist society have been pointed out. The conversion experience generally leads to moral improvement and increased work discipline, which in its turn engenders confidence, betterment in family relations, and formation of strong mutual networks of support and services, also including financial favours and job/business opportunities. Most of this of course also applies to Neo-Pentecostalism. In addition, with regard to the two points particularly addressed in this chapter, it is possible that they too may be interpreted as in some sense having a positive effect for the believer affected by the pressures of globalization.

First, the affirmation of desire in theology and preaching and the establishment of a 'free', cultic space for letting both frustrated and fulfilled desires come to open expression may have a therapeutic function at the individual level. It also has its 'permissive' side, reducing a certain internal pressure in the believer: he or she is 'set free' and can more readily and without timidity or shame enter into the general flow of aspirations and desires for economic success and bodily healing and well-being.

And second, as shown by Esperandio's analysis above, there may actually in and through the sacrificial practices in Neo-Pentecostal worship be taking place a certain strengthening of the Self. In confronting anonymous and overwhelming economic forces, the believer is offered a way out of any general sense of impotence: Something can (and should) be done. You can join the Church; you can receive exorcism; you can show your faith (and hence personal worth and dignity) through offering your money.

This is the paradoxical picture emerging, then: Neo-Pentecostal religion may be seen as lending religious justification to victimizing economic processes, at the same time as it renders spiritual and practical support to the victims of these processes.

## The Theological Challenge: Towards a Non-Sacrificial Pneumatology of the Cross

The rise of experiential spiritualites and (Neo-)Pentocostalism in a globalized age is a complex phenomenon. As we have seen, any attempt at identifying a single causal logic in the nexus between the two will necessarily be simplistic. I have identified two main points of convergence which nonetheless seem to be of crucial importance both in terms of an adequate interpretation of the nature, direction and possible consequences of the Pentecostalism/globalization coincidence, and in terms of theological reflection and praxis in relation to this situation.

The significance of this convergence needs to be critically tested and developed further. A case could be made, for example, that there is actually nothing (theologically) wrong with immediacy, impatience, the longing for seeing fruits, results, progress, transformation of human beings and of the world, emerging from faith in God. Indeed, one could point to the fact that this is also a central concern in liberation theology – generally thought to be the opposite of Neo-Pentecostal theology (but see also Wells in this volume). Would not that be an aspect of the *kairos*, the biblical concept that gave name to the most radical theological critique of apartheid formulated by South African churches?

Furthermore, there could also be good reason to welcome rather than criticize a certain theological restitution of the value of human desire (if this is really what is happening in the Neo-Pentecostal religiosity) – as a force for good, for fellowship, even for intimacy and expression of bodily love. In all, that would appear to be a step forward from a still widespread tendency in mainstream Christianity to demonize corporeal desire *en bloc*.

In line with this one could claim that even within and beyond the spiritualizing tendency of all Pentecostal renewal, there also takes place a certain recovery of the body in Neo-Pentecostal religion and worship (Campos, 1997: 331–6). This would then be something that should be applauded, particularly in the age of ever more body-less and secretly body-despising processes of globalization.

As to the sacrificial logic, one could critically ask: Does not this after all belong to the core of the Christian message of salvation in the cross? Could there in the Neo-Pentecostal understanding of sacrifice – widely shared throughout Christianity in content, although in differing forms – even be a sound 'spiritualizing' of a drive deeply imbedded in human 'nature' to present offerings to the Giver of Life; a channelling away of the potential violence inherent in all sacrificial structures (Girard, Oughourlian and Lefort, 1987)?

In any case, there are, as can be appreciated in the contributions in this volume, indeed important resources and potential for both resistance and critically needed theological renewal implicit in the phenomena that we are studying. It is due time to overcome the arrogant neglect and marginalization of the Pentecostal mode of Christian spirituality in academic theology. The racist and androcentric overtones of this neglect have been only too evident.

On the other hand, particularly because of the 'immediatist' and sacrificial nature of (Neo-)Pentecostalism and the way in which these characteristics interact with the politico-economic ideology of neoliberalism, I maintain that a critical approach is called for. Pathos without ethos and ratio is as dangerous (cf. Knutby) as ethos and ratio without pathos is dry, boring – and even dangerous too, opening the possibility for cruelty and cynicism (cf. Sigurd Bergmann's aesth/ethics.

I therefore see a need for renewed theological reflection in this field – a critical, liberating theology in the perspective of the victims challenged by the rise of the charismatic and experiential spiritualities (cf. above, Salomonsen, Wells). There is a need for counterbalancing the pragmatic, 'immediatist' and experiential side of Christian spirituality with the understanding of Christian life in the Spirit as a 'walk', a 'way', a process, a 'learning to learn' (Segundo, 1976), a slowly growing to become what one already is in God. There is a need to stress the 'invisible', the apparently non-transformative (the '*simul* iustus et peccator' in the Lutheran formulation), ever in this life uncompleted nature of Christian salvation. There is a need to reaffirm the value of human vulnerability, not as a fault to be overcome, or a threat that calls for security measures, but as a God-willed constitutive dimension of what it means to be human; a vulnerability that in the incarnation of Christ and the inhabitation of the Spirit is a vulnerability even shared by Godself; a vulnerability that also is the precondition for ethical behaviour, and a permanent feature of the good life since it is the condition and character of love itself (cf. Stålsett et al., 2002; Stålsett, 2004).

And there is, not least, a need to oppose any legitimization of human sacrifices, implicit or explicit, corporeal or 'spiritual'. There is a need for a non-sacrificial theology – a need that goes far beyond the

Pentecostal strands of Christianity. God the Spirit speaks – or rather sighs, whispers and screams – in our world through the voices of victims. In the Knutbys, the *favelas*, the Gazas, the Aids hospitals and the prison camps of this world the Spirit is the indwelling presence of the co-suffering and co-resisting God. The Spirit as God's strength in vulnerability, God's victory in failure, God's solidarity with the ones not healed that night in the Cathedral of Faith in Porto Alegre, would be central points in a pneumatological theology of the cross highly called for in the presence of the spirits of globalization.

## Notes

1 It should be remembered, though, that IURD is not the biggest Pentecostal church in Brazil.The more traditional *Assembleia de Deus* has according to the statistics about four times as many members, or some 10 million.

2 Barrera prefers to speak of 'Pentecostal religions' in the plural (even non-Christian, in principle) (Barrera Rivera, 2001: 234f.).

3 Cf. Bergmann's discussion of despatialization/respatialization, pp. 188–9, above.

4 Paulo De Velasco, pastor da IURD, Isto É Senhor, 22.11.89 (quoted by Mariano, 1995: 145).

5 This and all other translations in this chapter are mine.

6 See http://www.hayekcenter.org/friedrichhayek/hayekfftrts.html

7 Assmann and Hinkelammert, 1989; Assmann, 1991; Hinkelammert, 1981; Richard, 1980; Santa Ana, 1986; cf. Stålsett, 2001.

# Further Reading

Aagård, A. M. (1975), 'Gottes Geist und Geschichte', *Lutherische Monatshefte* 14, pp. 22–4

Ahlberg, N. (1990), *New Challenges, Old Strategies: Themes of Variation and Conflict among Pakistani Muslims in Norway*, Helsinki: Finnish Anthropological Society

Ahlstrand, K. (2003), 'Softening in inter-faith discourse', http://emmausnett.no/ressurser/ahlstrand_softening.shtml

Althouse, P. (2003), *Spirit of the Last Days: Pentecostal Eschatology in Conversation with Jürgen Moltmann*, Journal of Pentecostal Theology. Supplement Series 25, London and New York: Sheffield Academic Press

Alvarez, C., ed. (1992), *Pentecostalismo y liberación. Una experiencia latinoamericana*, San José: Departamento Ecuménico de Investigaciones

Ames, R. T., Dissanayake, W. and Kasulis, T. P., eds (1994), *Self as Person in Asian Theory and Practice*, Albany: State University of New York Press

Anderson, A. (1992), *Bazalwane: African Pentecostals in South Africa*, Manualia didactica 19, Pretoria: University of South Africa

Appadurai, A. (2001), 'The production of locality', *Religion im Prozeß der Globalisierung*, Würzburg: Ergon, pp. 99–123

Assmann, H., ed. (1991), *Sobre ídolos y sacrificios. René Girard con teólogos de la liberación*, San José: Departamento Ecuménico de Investigaciones

Assmann, H. and Hinkelammert, F. J. (1989), *Idolatria do mercado*, Petrópolis: Vozes

Au, K. M. (2002), *Paul Tillich and Chu Hsi: A Comparison of their Views of Human Condition*, New York: Peter Lang

Barrera Rivera, P. (2001), *Tradição, transmissão e emoção religiosa. Sociologia do protestantismo contemporâneo na América Latina*, São Paulo: Olho d'Água

Bauman, Z. (1998), *Globalization: The Human Consequences*, Cambridge: Polity Press

Beck, U. (1988), *Gegengifte: die organisierte Unverantwortlichkeit*, Frankfurt am Main: Suhrkamp

Beck, U. (1993), *Die Erfindung des Politischen: zu einer Theorie reflexiver*, Edition Suhrkamp, Frankfurt am Main: Suhrkamp

Berger, P. L. (1999), *The Desecularization of the World: Resurgent Religion and World Politics*, Washington, DC: Ethics and Public Policy Center

Berger, P. L., Berger, B. and Kellner, H. (1973), *The Homeless Mind: Modernization and Consciousness*, New York: Random House

Berger, P. L. and Hsiao, H.-h., eds (1988), *In Search of an East Asian Development Model*, New Brunswick, NJ: Transaction Books

Berger, P. L. and Luckmann, T. (1966), *The Social Construction of Reality: A Treatise in the Sociology of Knowledge*, Garden City, NY: Doubleday

Bergmann, S. (1995), *Geist, der Natur befreit: Die trinitarische Kosmologie Gregors von Nazianz im Horizont einer ökologischen Theologie der Befreiung*, Mainz: Matthias-Grünewald-Verlag

Bergmann, S. (1998a), '"Cold cradle of stone, warm soft arms" – Cultural landscape in Sápmi', in S. Anderzén and R. E. Kristiansen, eds, *Ecology of Spirit: Cultural Plurality and Religious Identity in the Barents Region*, Alphabeta Varia, Album Religionum Umense 6, Umeå: University of Umeå, pp 100–9

Bergmann, S. (1998b), 'Das Fremde wahrnehmen: Die öko- und ethnologische Herausforderung der Bildkunst und Theologie', in *Kunst-Positionen: Kunst als gegenwärtiges Thema evangelischer und katholischer Theologie*, Stuttgart: Kohlhammer Verlag, pp. 96–120

Bergmann, S. (1999), ' "Ich bin hier mit ihnen, und dort" – Eine Verflechtung der samischen Bildwelt Ulrika Tapios mit der Reflexion der Ritualisierung, Hybridisierung und interkulturellen Kunsttheologie', in *Menschwerden im Kulturwandel: Kontexte kultureller Identität als Wegmarken interkultureller Kompetenz/Initiationen und ihre Inkulturationsprozesse*, Luzern: Edition Exodus, pp. 474–512

Bergmann, S. (2003a), *God in Context: A Survey of Contextual Theology*, Aldershot: Ashgate

Bergmann, S. (2003b), *I begynnelsen är bilden: en befriande bild–konst–kultur-teologi*, Stockholm: Proprius

Bergmann, S. (2005a), *Creation Set Free: The Spirit as Liberator of Nature*, Grand Rapids: Eerdmans

Bergmann, S. (2005b), 'Space and Spirit: Towards a Theology of Inhabitation', in *Architecture, Aesth/Ethics and Religion*, Frankfurt am Main: Verlag für interkulturelle Kommunikation (IKO), pp. 45–103

Bergmann, S. (2005c), 'Religion, Culture and God's Here and Now: Contextual Theology in Dialogue with Social Anthropology', *Svensk Teologisk Kvartalsskrift* 81, pp. 67–76

Bergunder, M. (2003), 'Mission und Pfingstbewegung', in *Leitfaden Ökumenische Missionstheologie*, Gütersloh: Kaiser/Gütersloher Verlagshaus, pp. 200–19

Beyer, P. (1994), *Religion and Globalization*, London and Thousand Oaks, CA: Sage

Bitum, R. (1996), 'O Neopentecostalismo e sua Inserção no Mercado Moderno', Masters thesis, Universidade Metodista de São Paulo, São Bernardo do Campo

Bjartvik, G. O. (2002), 'Islamsk-kristen allianse påvirker FN', *Vårt Land*, 20 June

Bobsin, O. (1995), 'Teologia da Prosperidade ou estratégia de sobrevivência', *Estudos Teológicos* 35: 1

Bock, K. Y. (2004), 'Power and life in the context of globalisation: a biblical and theological perspective', *Madang: Journal of Contextual Theology in East Asia* 1, pp. 5–24

Böhme, G. (1989), *Für eine ökologische Naturästhetik*, Frankfurt am Main: Suhrkamp

Böhme, G. (1995), *Atmosphäre: Essays zur neuen Ästhetik*, Frankfurt am Main: Suhrkamp

Borg, M. (2003), *The Heart of Christianity: Rediscovering a Life of Faith*, San Francisco: HarperSanFrancisco

Bottomore, T. B., ed. (1964), *Karl Marx: Early Writings*, trans. T. B. Bottomore, New York: McGraw-Hill

Boudewijnse, B. e. a., ed. (1991), *Algo más que ópio. Una lectura antropológica del pentecostalismo latinoamericano y caribeño*, San José: Departamento Ecuménico de Investigaciones

Bourdieu, P. (1998), 'The essence of neoliberalism', *Le Monde Diplomatique*, December

Bourdieu, P. (1999), *Moteld. Texter mot nyliberalismens utbredning*, trans. B. Gustavsson, Stockholm/Stehag: Brutus Östlings Bokförlag Symposium

Brain, J. B. (1983), *Christian Indians in Natal 1860–1911: An Historical and Statistical Study*, Cape Town: Oxford University Press

Brekke, T. (2002), *Gud i norsk politikk: religion og politisk makt*, Oslo: Pax

Campos, L. S. (1997), *Teatro, templo e mercado: organização e marketing de um empreendimento neopentecostal*, Petropolis, São Paulo, São Bernardo do Campo: Editora Vozes; Simposio Editora UMESP

Certeau, M. d. (1992)[1982], *The Mystic Fable*, trans. M. B. Smith, Religion and Postmodernism, Chicago: University of Chicago Press

Chan, W.-t. (1963), *A Source Book in Chinese Philosophy*, Princeton, NJ: Princeton University Press

Chan, W.-t. (1969), *Neo-Confucianism, etc.: Essays*, Hanover, NH: Oriental Society

Chappell, P. G. (1989), 'Kenneth Hagin, sr.', in *Twentieth-Century Shapers of American Popular Religion*, New York: Greenwood Press, pp. 186–93

Chomsky, N. (2002), 9–11, An Open Media Book, New York: Seven Stories Press

Chung, D. (1959), *Religious Syncretism in Korean Society*, Yale University Press

Clammer, J. (1984), 'Secularization and religious change in contemporary Asia', *Southeast Asian Journal of Social Science* 12, p. 1

Clark, C. A. (1961), *Religions of Old Korea*, Seoul: Christian Literature Society of Korea

Cleaver, R. (1995), *Know My Name: A Gay Liberation Theology*, Louisville, KY: Westminster John Knox Press

Clothier, N. (1987), *Black Valour: The South African Native Labour Contingent, 1916–1918, and the Sinking of the Mendi*, Pietermaritzburg: University of Natal Press

Coleman, S. (2000), *The Globalisation of Charismatic Christianity: Spreading the Gospel of Prosperity*, Cambridge Studies in Ideology and Religion 12, Cambridge and New York: Cambridge University Press

Comaroff, J. and Comaroff, J. L. (1991), *Of Revelation and Revolution*, Chicago: University of Chicago Press

Comblin, J. (1989), *The Holy Spirit and Liberation*, trans. P. Burns, Theology and Liberation Series, Maryknoll, NY: Orbis Books

Confucius (1979), *The Analects of Confucius*, trans. D. C. Lau, The Penguin Classics, Harmondsworth: Penguin Books

Cormie, L. (1999), 'Genesis of a new world: globalization from above vs globalization from below', in *Twentieth Century*, Maryknoll, NY: Orbis, pp. 118–31

Cox, H. G. (1995), *Fire from Heaven: The Rise of Pentecostal Spirituality and the*

*Reshaping of Religion in the Twenty-First Century*, Reading, MA: Addison-Wesley.

Cox, H. G. (1999), 'Foreword', in *Pentecostals After a Century: Global Perspectives on a Movement in Transition*, Journal of Pentecostal Theology Supplement Series 15, Sheffield: Sheffield Academic Press, pp. 7–12

Crossan, J. D. (1995), *Who Killed Jesus? Exposing the Roots of Anti-Semitism in the Gospel Story of the Death of Jesus*, San Francisco: HarperSanFrancisco

Cua, A. S. (1978), *Dimensions of Moral Creativity: Paradigms, Principles and Ideals*, University Park and London: Pennsylvania State University Press

Davenport, T. R. H. (1991), *South Africa: A Modern History*, London: Macmillan

Delaney, C. L. (1998), *Abraham on Trial: The Social Legacy of Biblical Myth*, Princeton, NJ: Princeton University Press

Dixon, K. (1998), *Les évangélistes du marché. Les intellectuels britanniques et le néo-libéralisme*, Paris: Raisons d'Agir Éditions

Doerrie, H. (1969), 'Präpositionen und Metaphysik: Wechselwirkung zweier Prinzipienreihen', *MH* 26, pp. 217–28

Donaldson, L. E. and Kwok, P.-l., eds (2002), *Postcolonialism, Feminism, and Religious Discourse*, New York: Routledge

Draper, J. A. (2002a), 'The marriage of the Lamb and the Isigodlo in iBandla labancwele of the Zulu Prophet George Khambule', paper delivered at *The Power of Oral History, Memory, Healing, and Development*, Pietermaritzburg, South Africa, 24–7 June

Draper, J. A. (2002b), 'Worshipping with angels in the New Jerusalem: George Khambule and *Ibandla Labancwele*', paper delivered at *Orality, Literacy and the World of the Spirit*, Free University of Brussels

Draper, J. A. (2003a), 'The closed text and the heavenly telephone: the role of the bricoleur in oral mediation of sacred text in the case of George Khambule and the Gospel of John', in *Orality, Literacy, and Colonialism in Southern Africa*, Atlanta: Society of Biblical Literature, pp. 57–89

Draper, J. A. (2003b), 'The ritualization of memory: the interface of written and oral tradition in Ibandla Labancwele of George Khambule', paper delivered at *Orality, Literacy and Memory*, Rice University, 10–12 October

Draper, J. A. (2004), 'George Khambule and the Book of Revelation: Prophet of the Open Heaven', *Neotestamentica* 38: 2, pp. 101–24

Draper, J. A. (2005) 'The Bricoleur from Oral Performance to Written Text: Early Christian Prophets and African Prophets', in R. A. Horsley, J. A. Draper and J. Miles Foley, *Performing the Gospel: Mark, Orality and Memory*, Minneapolis: Augsburg

Duchrow, U. and Hinkelammert, F. J. (2004), *Property for People, Not for Profit: Alternatives to the Global Tyranny*, London: Zed

Edvardsen, A. (1997), 'Jesus og Isa – Gud og Allah', *Vårt Land*, 2 June, p. 25

Edvardsen, A. (1999a), 'Meg har Gud vist', *Troens Bevis* 39: June, pp. 24–9

Edvardsen, A. (1999b), *State Leader Promo*, Kvinesdal: International Mass-Communication Service Sarons Dal

Edvardsen, A. (2000), *Miracle: Pakistan Oct. 2002*, Kvinesdal: International Mass-Communication Service Sarons Dal

Edvardsen, A. (2001a), 'Jeg har sett lysene fra titusener av uevangeliserte byer der Jesu lys aldri har nådd', *Troens Bevis*, 41: January, pp. 4–5

Edvardsen, A. (2001b), 'Mirakelbabyen som ble oppvakt fra de døde', *Troens Bevis* 41: June, pp. 6–7

Edvardsen, A. (2001c), 'Mitt livs største vennskapskorstog', *Troens Bevis* 41: January, pp. 6–12

Edvardsen, A. (2002a), 'Et historisk mirakelkorstog i islamske Pakistan', *Troens Bevis* 42: November, pp. 6–13

Edvardsen, A. (2002b), 'Fra Aril Edvardsens dagbok i Pakistan', *Troens Bevis* 42: November, pp. 24–41

Edvardsen, A. (2003), 'Evangeliet til muslimverdenen: Koranen – muslimenes bro til Jesus', *Troens Bevis* 43: February, pp. 24–39

Edvardsen, A. (2004a), 'Borgere av 2 riker i kamp mot fundamentalisme', *Troens Bevis* 44: April, pp. 4–5

Edvardsen, A. (2004b), 'Historien om Sudans Mahdi og møtet med hans barnebarn Sadiq al Mahdi, *Troens Bevis* 44: April, pp. 14–19

Edvardsen, A. (2004c), 'Møtet med Sudans mest innflytelsesrike religiøse og politiske leder', *Troens Bevis* 44: September, pp. 26–32

Edvardsen, A. (2005), 'Jeg så Sudan strekke sine hender mot Gud', *Troens Bevis* 45: April, pp. 4–18

Eliade, M. (1972), *Shamanism: Archaic Techniques of Ecstasy*, trans. W. Trask, Bollingen Series 76, Princeton, NJ: Princeton University Press

Elliott, C. (1989), *Sword & Spirit*, London: BBC Books

EWISA (1987), *Evangelical Witness in South Africa: A Critique of Evangelical Theology and Practice by South African Evangelicals Themselves*, London: Evangelical Alliance

Ferraro, A. R. (1997), 'O movimento neoliberal: Gênese, natureza e trajetória', *Sociedade em Debate* 3: 4, pp 33–58

Fida, M. (2001), 'Jeg trodde jeg hadde hørt Aril preke', *Troens Bevis* 41: January, pp. 24–5

Fida, M. (2002), 'Aril Edvardsen på nært hold i Pakistan', *Troens Bevis* 42: November, pp. 14–23

Finke, R. and Stark, R. (1988), 'Religious economies and sacred canopies: religious mobilization in American cities, 1906', *American Sociological Review* 53, pp. 41–9

Foucault, M. (1961), *Folie et déraison; histoire de la folie à l'âge classique*, Civilisations d'hier et d'aujourd'hui, Paris: Plon

Foucault, M. (1973), *Madness and Civilization: A History of Insanity in the Age of Reason*, trans. R. Howard, New York: Vintage Books

Foucault, M. (1990)[1976], *The Will to Knowledge*, trans. R. Hurley, History of Sexuality, London: Penguin

Foucault, M. (1999), *Religion and Culture*, ed. Jeremy Carrette, New York: Routledge

Frege, G. (1980)[1884], *The Foundations of Arithmetic: A Logico-Mathematical Enquiry into the Concept of Number*, trans. J. L. Austin, Evanston, IL: Northwestern University Press

Freitas, M.-C.-d. (2001), 'The mission of religious men and women in Latin America today: a liberating mission in a neoliberal world', in *Mission in the Third Millennium*, Maryknoll, NY: Orbis, pp. 88–116

Garrard-Burnett, V. and Stoll, D. (1993), *Rethinking Protestantism in Latin*

*America*, Philadelphia: Temple University Press

Geertz, C. (1973), *The Interpretation of Cultures: Selected Essays*, New York: Basic Books

George, S. (1999), *A Short History of Neoliberalism*, http://www.globalpolicy.org

Getter, L. (2002), 'Showing faith in discretion', *The Los Angeles Times*, 27 September

Gilbert, A. D. (1976), *Religion and Society in Industrial England: Church, Chapel, and Social Change, 1740–1914*, London and New York: Longman

Girard, R. (1977), *Violence and the Sacred*, Baltimore: Johns Hopkins University Press

Girard, R., Oughourlian, J.-M. and Lefort, G. (1987), *Things Hidden since the Foundation of the World*, Stanford, CA: Stanford University Press

Gjerstad, T. (2004), 'Lukkede Jesus-møter på Tinget', *Dagbladet*, pp. 6–7

Gjerstad, T. and Ellingsen, P. (2004), 'Bondeviks mektige brorskap', *Dagbladet Magasinet* 4: December, pp. 16–25

Gleeson, I. (1994), *The Unknown Force: Black, Indian and Coloured Soldiers through Two World Wars*, Rivonia: Ashanti

Graf, F. W. (2002), 'Religion and globalization', in *For All People: Global Theologies in Context*, Grand Rapids, MI and Cambridge: William B. Eerdmans, pp. 63–72

Grayson, J.-H. (1995), 'Elements of Protestant accommodation to Korean religious culture: a personal ethnographic perspective', *Missiology* 23, pp. 43–59

Guattari, F. and Deleuze, G. (1987), *A Thousand Plateaus: Capitalism and Schizophrenia*, Minneapolis: University of Minnesota Press

Gutting, G. (1994), 'Foucault and the history of madness', in *The Cambridge Companion to Foucault*, Cambridge: Cambridge University Press, pp. 47–70

Halévy, E. (1949), *A History of the English People in the Nineteenth Century*, London: E. Benn

Hannerz, U. (1996), *Transnational Connections: Culture, People, Places*, Comedia, London and New York: Routledge

Hatch, N. O. and Hamilton, M. S. (1992), 'Can evangelism survive its success?', *Christianity Today*, 5 October

Hauschild, W.-D. (1984), 'Geist IV. Dogmengeschichtlich', in *Theologische Realenzyklopädie*, Berlin and New York: W. de Gruyter, pp. 196–218

Held, D. and McGrew, A. (2000), *Global Transformations: Politics, Economics and Culture*, Cambridge: Polity Press

Hinkelammert, F. J. (1981), *Las Armas Ideológicas de la Muerte*, San José: Departamento Ecuménico de Investigaciones

Holbek, J. E. (2003), 'Aril Edvardsen ut mot "ondsinnet sladder"', *Vårt Land*, 13 November, pp. 12–13

Hollenweger, W. J. (1999a), 'The Black roots of Pentecostalism', in *Pentecostals After a Century: Global Perspectives on a Movement in Transition*, Journal of Pentecostal Theology Supplement Series 15, Sheffield: Sheffield Academic Press, pp. 33–44

Hollenweger, W. J. (1999b), 'Crucial issues for Pentecostals', in *Pentecostals After a Century: Global Perspectives on a Movement in Transition*, Sheffield: Sheffield Academic Press, pp. 176–96

Horsley, R. A. (1998), *1 Corinthians*, Abingdon New Testament Commentaries, Nashville: Abingdon Press

Horsley, R. A. (2000), 'Rhetoric and empire – and 1 Corinthians', in *Paul and Politics*, Harrisburg, PA: Trinity Press International, pp. 72–102

Horsley, R. A. (2003), *Jesus and Empire: The Kingdom of God and the New World Disorder*, Minneapolis, MN: Fortress Press

Horsley, R. A. and Silberman, N. A. (1997), *The Message and the Kingdom: How Jesus and Paul Ignited a Revolution and Transformed the Ancient World*, New York: Grossett/Putnam

James, W. (1958)[1902], *The Varieties of Religious Experience: A Study in Human Nature*, New York: New American Library

Johnston, D. (2003), *Faith-Based Diplomacy: Trumping Realpolitik*, Oxford and New York: Oxford University Press

Johnston, D. and Sampson, C., eds (1994), *Religion: The Missing Dimension of Statecraft*, New York: Oxford University Press

Kelly, J. N. D. (1977)[1958], *Early Christian Doctrines*, London: A. & C. Black

Kerr, F. (1997), *Immortal Longings: Versions of Transcending Humanity*, Notre Dame, IN: University of Notre Dame Press

Khambule, G. M. (1925–49), 'Diaries 1–4; Liturgies 1–3; Hymnbooks 1–2', unpublished manuscript, Uppsala

Kim, A.-E. (2000), 'Korean religious culture and its affinity to Christianity: the rise of Protestant Christianity in South Korea', *Sociology of Religion* 61: 2, pp. 117–33

Kirkpatrick, E. M. and Schwarz, C. eds (1983), *Chambers 20th Century Dictionary*, Edinburgh: Chambers

Klotz, H. (1994), *Kunst im 20. Jahrhundert: Moderne – Postmoderne – Zweite Moderne*, Munich: Beck

Kohut, H. (1988), *Psicologia do Self e a cultura humana*, Porto Alegre: Artes Médicas

Kyung-Dong, K. (1988), 'The distinctive features of South Korea's development', in *In Search of an East Asian Development Model*, New Brunswick, NJ: Transaction Books, pp. 197–219

Lacan, J. (1996), *O Seminário. Livro 1: os escritos técnicos de Freud*, Rio de Janeiro: Zahar

Land, S. J. (1993), *Pentecostal Spirituality: A Passion for the Kingdom*, Journal of Pentecostal Theology Supplement Series 1, Sheffield: Sheffield Academic Press

Leed, E. J. (1979), *No Man's Land: Combat and Identity in World War I*, Cambridge and New York: Cambridge University Press

Leer-Salvesen, T. (2003), 'Guds løve', *Klassekampen*, 20 September, pp. 30–1

Leirvik, O. (1999), *Images of Jesus Christ in Islam: Introduction, Survey of Research, Issues of Dialogue*, Studia Missionalia Upsaliensia, Uppsala: Swedish Institute of Missionary Research

Leirvik, O. (2001)[1996], *Religionsdialog på norsk*, Oslo: Pax Forlag

Leirvik, O. (2004), 'Liberal and conservative responses to globalisation: the case of Norwegian Pentecostal missionary Aril Edvardsen', in *The Power of Faiths in Global Politics*, Oslo: Novus, pp. 129–42

Leontius (1996), 'Vita S. Symeonis Sali', in *Symeon the Holy Fool: Leontius's Life and the Late Antique City*, ed. and trans. D. Krueger, Berkeley: University of California Press, appendix

Lessing, E. (1985), 'Geist V. Dogmatisch und ethisch', in *Theologische Realenzyklopädie*, Berlin and New York: W. de Gruyter, pp. 218–37

Lønning, P. (1997), *Fundamentalisme. Ord til fordømmelse – ord til fordummelse? En begrepshistorisk undersøkelse*, Bergen: Ariadne

Lovett, L. (1975), 'Black origins of the Pentecostal movement', in *Aspects of Pentecostal-Charismatic Origins*, Society for Pentecostal Studies, Plainfield, NJ: Logos International, pp. 123–41

Lovett, L. (1988), 'Black holiness – Pentecostalism', in *Dictionary of Pentecostal and Charismatic Movements*, Grand Rapids, MI: Regency Reference Library

Luhmann, N. (1982), *The Differentiation of Society*, trans. S. Holmes and C. Larmore, European Perspectives, New York: Columbia University Press

Ma, W. (2000), 'The Korean Pentecostal movement: retrospect and prospect for the new century', paper delivered at *Challenges and Opportunities for Asian Pentecostals*, Asian Seminary of Christian Ministries, Makati, Philippines, 25 August

Macedo, E. (2001), *O Perfeito Sacrifício: o significado espiritual dos dízimos e ofertas*, Rio de Janeiro: Universal

MacRobert, I. (1988), *The Black Roots and White Racism of Early Pentecostalism in the USA*, New York: St. Martin's Press

Mariano, R. (1995), *Neopentecostalismo: os pentecostais estão mudando*, Universidade de São Paulo

Martin, D. (1993), *Tongues of Fire: The Explosion of Protestantism in Latin America*, Oxford: Blackwell

Martin, D. (2001), *Pentecostalism: The World Their Parish*, Religion and Modernity, Oxford and Malden, MA: Blackwell

Mattos, P. A. (2002), *An Introduction to the Theology of Bishop Edir Macedo: A Theological Case Study of a New Brazilian Pentecostal Church*, Indianapolis, IN: Christian Theological Seminary

McFague, S. (2001), *Life Abundant: Rethinking Theology and Economy for a Planet in Peril*, Minneapolis: Fortress Press

McGuire, M. B. (1997), *Religion: The Social Context*, Belmont, CA: Wadsworth

Meinhold, P. (1972), 'Christianity in the light of modern research', in *Marxism, Communism, and Western Society: A Comparative Encyclopedia*, New York: Herder & Herder

Meyer, T. (1997), *Identitäts-Wahn: die Politisierung des kulturellen Unterschieds*, Aufbau Thema 8516, Berlin: Aufbau

Mhlungu, P. (1941), 'Report in Zulul on various independent churches at Ethelezini', uunpublished manuscript, Uppsala

Mitchell, P. R. and Schoeffel, J., eds (2002), *Understanding Power: The Indispensable Chomsky*, New York: New Press

Mo Sung, J. (1992), *Deus numa economia sem coração. Pobreza e neoliberalismo: un desafio à evangelização*, São Paulo: Edicoes Paulinas

Moltmann, J. (1992), *The Spirit of Life: A Universal Affirmation*, trans. M. Kohl, Minneapolis: Fortress Press

Moltmann, J. (2002), *Wissenschaft und Weisheit: zum Gespräch zwischen Naturwissenschaft und Theologie*, Gütersloh: Chr. Kaiser

Montague, G. T. (1976), *The Holy Spirit: Growth of a Biblical Tradition*, New York: Paulist Press

Mydland, H. (1999), 'Mirakler skjedde i muslimske Pakistan', *Troens Bevis* 39: June, pp. 6–22

Mydland, H. (2000), 'Fredskonferanse som gav gjenklang', *Troens Bevis* 40: January, pp. 30–41

Oommen, G. (2000), 'The emerging Dalit theology: a historical appraisal', *Indian Church History Review* 34: 1, pp. 19–37

Palladius (1965), *Palladius: The Lausiac History*, trans. R. T. Meyer, Ancient Christian Writers, Westminster, MD: Newman Press

Palmer, S. J. (1967), *Korea and Christianity: The Problem of Identification with Tradition*, Seoul: Hollym

Pampallis, J. (1991), *Foundations of the New South Africa*, London: Zed

Pillay, G. J. (1994), *Religion at the Limits? Pentecostalism among Indian South Africans*, Studia Originalia 19, Pretoria: University of South Africa Institute for Theological Research

Plonz, S. (1995), *Die herrenlosen Gewalten: eine Relektüre Karl Barths in befreiungstheologischer Perspektive*, Mainz: Matthias-Grünewald-Verlag

Rem, H. (2004), *Aril Edvardsen. En selvopplevd biografi*, Oslo: Cappelen

Reynalds, J. (2000), 'Shamanistic influences in Korean Pentecostal Christianity: an analysis', www.rickross.com/reference/yoidoyonggi/yoido1.html

RFCC (1991), *The Apostolic Concerned Christians Faith Mission Church: A Challenge to Action by the RFCC*, Braamfontein: Institute for Contextual Theology

Richard, P. (1980), *La lucha de los dioses. Los ídolos de la opresión y la búsqueda del Dios liberador*, San José and Managua: Departamento Ecuménico de Investigaciones and Centro Antonio Valdivieso

Romero, P. (1993), *Super Crentes. O Evangelho segundo Kenneth Hagin, Valnice Milhomens e os Profetas da Prosperidade*, São Paulo: Mundo Cristão

Ruuth, A. (1995), *Igreja Universal Reino de Deus. Gudsrikets Universella Kyrka – en brasiliansk kyrkobildning*, Bibliotheca theologiae practicae, Kyrkovetenskapelige studier, Stockholm: Almquist & Wicksell International

Salomonsen, J. (2002), *Enchanted Feminism: Ritual, Gender and Divinity among the Reclaiming Witches of San Francisco*, Religion and Gender, London and New York: Routledge

Santa Ana, J. d. (1986), 'Costo social y sacrificio a los ídolos', *Pasos* 2, 6

Schreiter, R.-J. (2001), 'Globalization and reconciliation: challenges to mission', in *Mission in the Third Millennium*, Maryknoll, NY: Orbis, pp. 121–43

Scott, J. C. (1990), *Domination and the Arts of Resistance: Hidden Transcripts*, New Haven: Yale University Press

Segundo, J. L. (1976), *Liberation of Theology*, Maryknoll, NY: Orbis

Semmel, B. (1973), *The Methodist Revolution*, New York: Basic Books

Sharlet, J. (2003), 'Jesus plus nothing. Undercover among America's secret theocrats', *Harper's Magazine*, March

Simmel, G. (1977)[1900], *Philosophie des Geldes*, Berlin: Duncker & Humblot

Sjørup, L. (1995), *Fundamentalisme eller fattigdomsbekæmpelse? Pentekostalismen i Latinamerika*, Copenhagen: Center for Udviklingsforskning

Spittler, R.-P. (1988), 'Implicit values in Pentecostal missions', *Missiology* 16, pp. 409–24

Stålsett, S. (1995), 'Når de fattige blir pinsevenner. Frigjøringsteologien og protestantismens vekst i Latin-Amerika', *Norsk Teologisk Tidsskrift* 95: 4, pp. 223–40

Stålsett, S. J. (2001), 'Det messianske marked. Frigjøringsteologisk kritikk av nyliberalismen', *Kirke og kultur* 106: 1, pp. 12–26

Stålsett, S. J. (2003), 'Discovering Jesus in a globalised world', in *Discovering Jesus in Our Place: Contextual Christologies in a Globalised World*, Delhi: ISPCK, pp. 1–23

Stålsett, S. J. (2004), 'Vulnerabilidad, dignidad y justicia: valores éticos fundamentales en un mundo globalizado', *Pasos* 3, pp., 13–19

Stålsett, S. and Leirvik, O., eds (2004), *The Power of Faith in Global Politics*, Oslo: Novus

Stålsett, S. J., Rolfsen, R., Dokken, K., and Haugen, H. M. (2002), *Vulnerability and Security: Current Challenges in Security Policy from an Ethical and Theological Perspective*, expanded version of the Norwegian 'Sårbarhet og sikkerhet' (2000), ed. Church of Norway Council on Ecumenical and International Relations, Oslo

Still, A. and Velody, I. eds (1992), *Rewriting the History of Madness: Studies in Foucault's Histoire de la folie*, London and New York: Routledge

Stoll, D. (1990), *Is Latin America Turning Protestant? The Politics of Evangelical Growth*, Berkeley, Los Angeles: University of California Press

Stone, K. (2001), *Queer Commentary and the Hebrew Bible*, Journal for the Study of the Old Testament Supplement Series 334, Cleveland, OH: Pilgrim Press

Sugirtharajah, R. S., ed. (1995), *Voices from the Margin: Interpreting the Bible in the Third World*, Maryknoll, NY, and London: Orbis and SPCK

Sundkler, B. (1976), *Zulu Zion and some Swazi Zionists*, Oxford Studies in African Affairs, London and New York: Oxford University Press

Synan, V. (1988), 'Seymour, William Joseph', in *Dictionary of Pentecostal and Charismatic Movements*, Grand Rapids, MI: Regency Reference Library

Synan, V. (1992), *The Spirit Said 'Grow'*, Innovations in Mission 4, Monrovia, CA: MARC

Taylor, J. V. (1972), *The Go-Between God: The Holy Spirit and the Christian Mission*, London: SCM Press

Taylor, R. L. (1990), *The Religious Dimensions of Confucianism*, SUNY Series in Religion, Albany: State University of New York Press

Thompson, K. (1986), *Beliefs and Ideology*, Key Ideas, Chichester: Ellis Horwood

Thunberg, L., ed. (1988), *På Åndens betingelser: essays om sprog og spiritualitet: Lars Thunberg på 60–års dagen*, Århus: Anis

Todd, E. (1985), *The Explanation of Ideology: Family Structures and Social Systems*, Family, Sexuality, and Social Relations in Past Times, Oxford and New York: Blackwell

Townes, E. M., ed. (1997), *Embracing the Spirit: Womanist Perspectives on Hope, Salvation, and Transformation*, Bishop Henry McNeal Turner/ Sojourner Truth Series in Black Religion, Maryknoll, NY: Orbis Books

Tu, W.-m. (1979), *Humanity and Self-Cultivation: Essays in Confucian Thought*, Berkeley: Asian Humanities Press

Tu, W.-m. (1994), 'Embodying the universe: a note on Confucian self-realization', in *Self As Person in Asian Theory and Practice*, Albany: State University of New York Press

Turner, V. W. (1969), *The Ritual Process: Structure and Anti-Structure*, The Lewis Henry Morgan Lectures, 1966, London: Routledge & Kegan Paul

ul-Qadri, M. T. (1987), *Islam and Christianity*, Lahore: Idara Minhaj ul-Quran

Villafañe, E. (1993), *The Liberating Spirit: Toward an Hispanic American Pentecostal Social Ethic*, Grand Rapids, MI: W. B. Eerdmans

Villafañe, E. (1994), 'The contours of a Pentecostal social ethic: a North American Hispanic perspective', *Transformation* 11, pp. 6–10

Villafañe, E. (1996), 'The politics of the spirit: reflections on a theology of social transformation for the twenty-first century', *Pneuma* 18, pp. 161–70

Villafañe, E. (2000), 'Latino religion in the United States', in *Major Problems in American Religious History: Documents and Essays*, Major Problems in American History, Boston: Houghton Mifflin, pp. 448–52

Virilio, P. (1997), 'Fin de l'histoire, ou fin de la géographie? Un monde surexposé', *Le Monde Diplomatique*, August, pp. 17

Wacker, G. (2001), *Heaven Below: Early Pentecostals and American Culture*, Cambridge, MA: Harvard University Press

Weber, M. (1963)[1922], *The Sociology of Religion*, trans. E. Fischoff, Boston: Beacon Press

Weber, M. (1976)[1904–5], *The Protestant Ethic and the Spirit of Capitalism*, trans. T. Parsons, London: Allen & Unwin

Welker, M. (1994), *God the Spirit*, trans. J. F. Hoffmeyer, Minneapolis: Fortress Press

Welsch, W. (2001), 'Transculturality: the changing form of cultures today', *Filozofski Vestnik* 22: 2, pp. 59–86

Welsh, D. J. (1971), *The Roots of Segregation: Native Policy in Colonial Natal, 1845–1910*, Cape Town and New York: Oxford University Press

West, G. (1999), 'Contextual bible study: creating sacred and safe place for social transformation', *Grace and Truth* 2, pp. 51–63

West, G. (2001), 'Contextual Bible study in South Africa: a resource for reclaiming and regaining land, dignity and identity', in *Towards an Agenda for Contextual Theology: Essays in Honour of Albert Nolan*, Pietermaritzburg: Cluster, pp. 169–84

Willems, E. (1967), *Followers of the New Faith: Culture Change and the Rise of Protestantism in Brazil and Chile*, Nashville: Vanderbilt University Press

*Witness* (1988), *A Relevant Pentecostal Witness*, Chatsglen

Wittgenstein, L. (2001)[1953], *Philosophical Investigations*, trans. G. E. M. Anscombe, New York: Macmillan

Woodhead, L. (2002), 'Christianity', in *Religions in the Modern World: Traditions and Transformations*, London and New York: Routledge, ch. 7

*World Christian Encyclopedia* (2000), 2nd edn, 2 vols, ed. David Barrett, George Kurian and Todd Johnson, New York: Oxford University Press

Wright, N. T. (1996), *Jesus and the Victory of God*, Christian Origins and the Question of God 2, London: SPCK

Wright, N. T. (2000), 'Paul's gospel and Caesar's empire', in *Paul and Politics*, Harrisburg, PA: Trinity Press International, pp. 160–83

Young, Frances M. (1979), *The Use of Sacrificial Ideas in Greek Christian Writers from the New Testament to John Chrysostom*, Patristic Monograph Series 5, Cambridge, MA: Philadelphia Patristic Foundation

Zhu, X., Lèu, Z. and Chan, W.-t., eds (1967), *Reflections on Things at Hand: The Neo-Confucian Anthology*, trans. W.-t. Chan, UNESCO Collection of Representative Works: Chinese series, New York: Columbia University Press

# Index of Names and Subjects

Alienation 63, 79, 83, 94
Assemblies of God 33, 51, 69, 74, 89, 212
Assmann, H. 212
Azusa Street 18, 40, 66, 68, 88, 164, 172

Baptism 32, 109, 151, 152, 156, 158, 172, 175
Barrera, P. 10, 202, 203, 212
Bauman, Z. 201
Beck, U. 188, 196
Berger, P. 14, 23, 24, 36, 99, 197, 199, 200
Bergmann, S. 9, 194, 196, 197, 211, 212
Beyer, P. 25, 189, 196
Bible, the 6, 18–20, 27, 31–3, 45, 57, 67, 69, 70, 73–89, 98, 102, 111, 118, 120, 125, 131, 140, 142, 171, 173, 175, 179, 180, 182, 185, 202, 204
Bourdieu, P. 201, 202
Buddhism 12, 23, 27

Capitalism 2–5, 10, 12, 14, 15, 20–6, 33–41, 47, 49, 53, 59, 60, 62, 119, 161, 173, 181, 186, 199, 200, 209
Catholic Church, the 3, 5, 12, 13, 16–19, 28, 40, 58, 87, 111, 132, 133, 171
Certeau, M. de 166, 167
Charisms 9, 170, 178–82
Colonialism 5, 6, 40, 65–7, 70, 83, 84, 88, 91–3, 96, 105, 106, 160, 171, 172, 174
Comaroff, J. and Comaroff, J. L. 74
Confucianism 8, 23, 27, 36, 145, 146–51, 155–8
Consumerism 20–2, 37, 48, 59, 161, 201, 203
Control 9–11, 26, 28, 35, 71, 76, 81, 117, 122, 125, 156, 161–3, 168, 176, 177
Cox, H. 1, 3, 5, 21, 29, 31, 33, 40, 41, 52, 65, 71, 84, 109, 129, 151, 152, 167, 171, 182, 192, 199, 204, 207
Culture 5, 6, 8, 9, 13–15, 19–24, 26, 28, 30, 31, 33, 38, 40, 48, 49, 52, 63, 65, 66, 71–82, 85, 94, 95, 97, 100, 106, 109, 119, 124, 126, 139, 156, 158, 160, 162, 171, 172, 176, 183–92, 194, 196, 197, 200–2, 208
Culture, Transculturation 8, 9, 183, 184, 188, 190, 192

Debt 12, 42–4, 58, 62, 176, 207

Demons 27, 29, 31, 32, 42, 44, 49, 51, 53–5, 62, 82, 83, 109, 110, 112–14, 116, 129, 175, 177, 180, 204, 205, 209, 210

Desire 10, 25, 30, 59, 62, 64, 127, 157, 164, 167, 172, 199, 201, 203, 209, 210

Discipline 9, 25, 26, 34, 57, 161–3, 194, 202, 209

Draper, J. A. 6, 8, 19, 90, 91, 97–100, 102, 104, 105

Ecstasy 15, 16, 20, 27, 50, 109, 129, 151, 164, 166–8, 180, 181

Edvardsen, A. 7, 131–43

Emotions 1, 20, 29, 52, 53, 61, 67, 156, 171, 200, 202, 205

Foucault, M. 160, 162, 163, 167–9

Fundamentalism 15, 16, 18–20, 22, 35, 36, 66, 72, 84, 131, 142, 143, 191, 196, 208

Gender 73, 75, 77, 78, 81, 118, 119, 124, 125, 128, 190

George, S. 206, 207

Girard, R. 208, 211

Gregory of Nazianz 9, 183, 193, 196

Hayek, F.A von 206

Hegemony 10, 72, 74, 75, 79, 81–3, 161, 181, 201, 206

Hinduism 20, 70, 71, 76, 82, 88, 191

Hinkelammert, F. J. 193, 212

HIV/AIDS 58, 73, 75, 77, 79–81

Hollenweger, W. J. 68, 84, 196

Holy Spirit, the 3, 8–10, 17, 32, 33, 35, 41, 43, 45, 63, 114, 118, 127, 151, 152, 156, 158, 163, 164, 170, 172, 173, 175, 178, 180–7, 189, 191–7, 202, 210, 212

Hong Kong, China 8, 24

Horsley, R. A. 176–9

Ideology 3, 25, 26, 37, 65, 69, 70, 73–5, 79–84, 88, 95, 117, 178, 181, 186, 190–2, 196, 197, 200, 201, 203, 211

Indentured labour 5, 6, 10, 65–7, 83, 84, 88

Interpretation 6, 8, 27, 54, 61, 77, 79, 81, 102, 106, 107, 117, 118, 122, 125, 126, 128, 130, 151, 161, 162, 166, 168, 171, 174, 177, 180, 182–6, 192, 193, 204, 209, 210

Interreligious dialogue 7, 131–9, 142, 145, 147, 149, 151, 153, 155, 157, 159, 170

Jesus 4, 9, 31, 32, 42, 44, 46, 47, 50, 53–6, 75, 76, 78, 80, 87, 98, 99, 102, 107, 109–11, 113, 114, 118, 120, 122–6, 134–6, 138–40, 142, 143, 161, 166, 172, 173, 175–9, 181, 185, 196, 198–200, 203–5, 211

Johnston, D. 7, 133–5, 139, 143

Khambule, G. M. 6, 8, 90–3, 97–106
Knutby, Sweden 6, 107, 108, 116, 118–20, 122–6, 130, 211
Korea 3, 4, 13, 16, 17, 23, 24, 26–38, 171

Latin America 12, 16, 19, 32, 33, 35, 38–40, 196, 207
Leadership 7, 19, 22, 23, 25, 30, 37, 39, 41–50, 53–6, 59, 62, 67, 69–73, 76, 77, 79–82, 84–6, 88, 89, 105, 107, 113–22, 126, 128, 135, 137, 138, 141, 142, 168, 171–3, 177–80, 198, 199, 204, 212
Legitimacy 5, 107, 108, 109, 113, 114, 116, 124, 129, 139, 181, 202, 203, 208, 211
Leirvik, O. 3, 7, 131, 136, 137, 139
Liberation 9, 14, 15, 22, 30, 42, 53, 83, 156, 157, 160–2, 164, 170–3, 176, 183–5, 187, 193, 195, 196, 207, 210, 211
Liberation theology 9, 14, 22, 170–3, 176, 181, 184, 196
Lovett, L. 66, 88
Luhmann, N. 24

Macedo, E. 39, 41, 45, 47, 48, 204, 205
Madness 105, 130, 162, 164, 174
Magic 7, 27, 34, 50, 60, 104, 109, 114, 122, 124, 126, 127

Martin, D. 10, 31–3, 35
Materialism 4, 36, 37
Mattos, P. A. 205
Migration 10, 49, 51, 67, 190, 191
Miracles 7, 8, 18, 19, 32, 43, 72, 79, 80, 98, 105, 127, 131, 132, 135–40, 143, 155, 171, 180
Mission 2, 7, 13, 21, 27, 28, 33, 34, 40, 45, 50, 65–72, 74, 76, 77, 81, 82, 84, 88, 89, 92, 113, 131, 132, 134–6, 138–42, 152, 155, 157, 186
Moltmann, J. 176, 193
Money 5, 42–6, 56, 57, 60, 61, 92, 114, 161, 187, 189, 199, 204, 205, 207–9
Mysticism 16, 18, 71, 103, 109, 152, 169

Narcissistic Structures 5, 60–3
Neo-liberalism 3, 10–12, 14, 15, 17, 19–22, 39, 48, 63, 161, 200, 203, 206–9
New Age Movements 34, 59, 109
Normalization 8, 9, 160, 161, 163–5, 167–9
North America 4, 6, 7, 12, 17, 18, 27, 33, 35, 36, 41, 46, 55, 56, 59, 66, 67, 69, 72, 76, 82–4, 88, 131–4, 164, 165, 171, 196, 206, 207

Offering 5, 35, 43, 46, 49, 55, 56, 58, 60–2, 113, 114, 196, 198, 199, 202, 204, 205, 209, 211
On-line reality 201

Orality  19, 51, 92, 104, 129,
    157

Party  19, 204
Pathos  10, 198–200, 202, 211
Pentecostal churches
    Charismaticism  1–3, 5–10,
        12, 14, 18, 22, 30, 34, 35,
        40, 45, 46, 64, 66, 72, 87,
        90, 111, 118, 119, 131,
        132, 135–7, 142, 145,
        151–64, 167, 171, 211
    growth of  1, 3, 4, 13–16, 21,
        23, 24, 28, 31–3, 37, 39, 49,
        59, 151, 171, 186, 199
    Neo-Pentecostalism  4, 10, 34,
        39, 66, 72, 88, 109, 130,
        151, 198–200, 202–5,
        208–10
Philosophy  28, 37, 71, 145,
    151, 164, 165, 190, 194,
    206
Pneumatology  8–10, 170, 173,
    181, 183–9, 191–4, 196,
    197, 210, 212
Politics  1–8, 11, 25, 26, 35, 37,
    38, 47, 50, 51, 65–7, 69, 70,
    73, 83, 84, 88, 95, 125,
    130–5, 138, 139, 141–3,
    150, 155, 171–7, 179–82,
    187, 190, 191, 196, 206,
    208, 211
Porto Alegre, Brazil  53, 198,
    199, 212
Postmodernity  3, 12, 22–25, 31,
    37, 49, 50, 52, 63, 84, 167,
    169, 171, 185, 188, 190–2,
    196, 197
Power  3, 5, 6, 8–10, 16–18, 21,
    25, 31, 32, 34, 40, 45, 52–5,
    59–62, 66, 68, 74, 75,

79–82, 88, 90, 95, 98, 99,
    101–5, 107–109, 112, 116,
    119, 121, 122, 127, 130,
    134, 136, 139, 140, 142,
    150–157, 161, 163, 168–
    82, 186–90, 192, 206, 209
    empowerment  5, 6, 8, 45, 61,
        107, 150, 151, 155–7,
        171–3, 175, 180, 181, 209
Preaching  5, 16, 17, 19, 21, 24,
    31, 43, 45, 46, 56, 57, 64,
    70, 76, 88, 97, 111, 125,
    127, 132, 135, 136, 140,
    142, 176, 202, 203, 208,
    209
Primal Belief  3, 8, 21
Prophecy  6, 8, 9, 19, 20, 73, 90,
    97, 98, 102, 103, 108, 109,
    118, 120, 134, 139, 140,
    151, 168, 172–81
Prosperity Gospel  4, 11, 17, 29,
    34, 36, 41–5, 50, 56, 57, 59,
    60, 62, 63, 72, 73, 107,
    200, 203, 207
Psychology  5, 16, 36, 42, 52,
    53, 57, 58, 60, 61, 63, 67,
    71, 73, 84, 99, 108, 110,
    111, 113, 114, 121–3, 127,
    152, 153, 158, 160–4, 169,
    176, 209

Race  5, 6, 49, 50, 65, 67–70,
    72, 76, 83, 88, 91, 93, 94,
    96, 104, 172, 190, 210, 211
Religious experience  1, 45,
    152–5
    experiential spiritualities  1–3,
        6, 8, 10, 11, 19, 21, 39, 40,
        41, 52, 57, 72, 109, 152,
        155, 185, 187, 199, 210,
        211

Resistance 2, 3, 6, 8, 9, 14, 44, 49, 61, 68, 80, 83, 90, 123, 127, 132, 141, 161, 164, 169, 170, 172–4, 176–82, 196, 211, 212

Revelation, book of 6, 90, 97, 99, 105, 106, 187

Rites of passage 94, 167

Ritual 3, 78, 94, 98–104, 109, 116, 125, 126, 129, 147, 178, 187, 189

Sacrifice 5, 7, 10, 44, 60–2, 107, 108, 110–14, 120–3, 125, 126, 129, 177, 199, 200, 204–11

Santa Ana, Julio de 207, 208, 212

Second Coming 4, 200, 203

Seymour, William Joseph 66, 68, 172

Shamanism 4, 16, 17, 23, 26–31, 33, 35, 36, 109

Speaking in tongues 4, 8, 16, 20, 41, 109, 120, 151, 152, 155, 160, 164, 166–9, 171, 172, 180, 200

Stålsett, S. J. 3, 7, 10, 20, 131, 182, 201, 211, 212

Syncretism 16, 36, 38, 63

The Baptist Church 16, 32, 35

Theology 1–4, 7–10, 14, 17, 22, 28, 30, 32, 34, 37, 38, 45, 63, 65–70, 72, 76, 80–4, 89, 107, 109, 113, 116, 117, 120, 122–33, 139, 140, 142, 152, 155, 161, 166, 168, 170–2, 175, 181–8, 193–6, 199, 200, 202–5, 207–12

Transfers 2, 9, 42, 59, 92, 93, 160, 186

Transformation 1, 2, 8–10, 35, 39, 61, 63, 75, 84, 89, 96, 98, 100, 145, 149–58, 162, 172, 177, 181, 184, 186–8, 192, 199, 201, 210, 211
self-transformation 8, 61, 145, 149, 151, 153–8

Universal Church of the Kingdom of God 4, 5, 39–54, 57–64, 114, 115, 130, 198–200, 202–205, 209, 212

Urbanization 19, 23, 24, 32, 39, 50, 104, 162, 192

*Vestigia Dei* 9, 185, 196

Victory 10, 31, 32, 53, 57, 61, 99, 105, 106, 174, 175, 178, 199, 200, 203, 204, 212

Villafañe, E. 181, 182

Violence 6, 7, 26, 76, 81, 82, 95, 131, 155, 163, 173, 174, 180, 181, 192, 201, 207, 208, 211

Virilio, P. 201

War 4, 6, 7, 10, 13, 24, 33, 35, 38, 45, 50, 88, 90–7, 100–2, 104–6, 109, 114, 119, 122, 124, 127, 133, 138, 181, 182, 200

Weber, M. 2, 3, 10, 13, 25, 35, 199, 200, 209

West, G. 73, 77, 83, 89

Wright, N. T. 161, 179